W9-BUA-901

Ambient Intelligence Perspectives

Selected Papers from the First International
Ambient Intelligence Forum 2008

Edited by

Peter Mikulecký

Tereza Lišková

Pavel Čech

and

Vladimír Bureš

Department of Information Technologies,
Faculty of Informatics and Management,
University of Hradec Králové,
Czech Republic

Press

Amsterdam • Berlin • Oxford • Tokyo • Washington, DC

ISBN 978-1-58603-946-2
Library of Congress Control Number: 2008940896

Publisher
IOS Press
Nieuwe Hemweg 6B
1013 BG Amsterdam
The Netherlands
fax: +31 20 687 0019
e-mail: order@iospress.nl

Distributor in the UK and Ireland
Gazelle Books Services Ltd.
White Cross Mills
Hightown
Lancaster LA1 4XS
United Kingdom
fax: +44 1524 63232
e-mail: sales@gazellebooks.co.uk

Distributor in the USA and Canada
IOS Press, Inc.
4502 Rachael Manor Drive
Fairfax, VA 22032
USA
fax: +1 703 323 3668
e-mail: iosbooks@iospress.com

LEGAL NOTICE
The publisher is not responsible for the use which might be made of the following information.

PRINTED IN THE NETHERLANDS

Ambient Intelligence Perspectives
P. Mikulecký et al. (Eds.)
IOS Press, 2009

Foreword

This book contains selected papers from the first international meeting *Ambient Intelligence Forum – AmIF 2008* in Hradec Králové, Czech Republic. The forum is intended as the beginning of a series of rather broadly oriented discussion opportunities for discussing interdisciplinary, if not transdisciplinary aspects of rapidly evolving areas of Ambient Intelligence. This year's conference aims to review and discuss recent advances and promising research trends in AmI technology, intelligent environments, methods, middleware development, as well as applications in areas such as healthcare, product lifecycle, as well as transport services, among others.

The intention to provide an opportunity of a very broad interaction among a wide rank of authors coming from different surroundings means a great enrichment to all participants and gives ground to the success of the conference. Finally it led towards an interesting choice of three invited and twenty five contributed papers, that are published in this book. All papers were carefully reviewed by the international programme committee. Participants from twelve countries contributed to the scientific programme and established a fruitful discussion atmosphere with a number of interesting outcomes.

We wish to express our deep gratitude to all who contributed to the success of the conference and enabled the publication of this book. We wish to thank all the participants, in particular the invited lecturers Prof. Yang Cai (Carnegie – Mellon University), Prof. José Bravo Rodriguez (Castilla – La Mancha University), as well as Prof. Tomáš Sabol (Technical University of Košice), who accepted our invitation. We also thank all contributors and conference participants for creating a very pleasant and fruitful conference atmosphere. Of course, our special thanks go to the members of programme committee.

We further acknowledge the work of all partners who helped organising the conference as well as the generous financial support provided by our sponsors: University of Hradec Králové, Technical University of Košice, Hradec Králové Regional Authority, AITPL European Cluster, FLUID-WIN European Project, the Czech Scientific Foundation Project No. 402/06/1325 AmIMaDeS, and also the firms Poly PLASTY Jaroměř and Unicorn, a.s. Prague.

Last but not least, we wish to thank IOS Press BV, Amsterdam, for a very good collaboration and helpful assistance in preparing this book for press, and of course, for publishing the book. Special thanks go to Dr. Juan Carlos Augusto and Maarten Fröhlich.

In Hradec Králové, October 16th, 2008

Peter Mikulecký, Programme Committee Chair
Pavel Čech, Organizing Committee Chair

Organizers

Partners

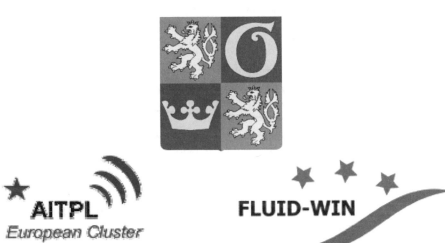

Sponsors

Committees

Program Committee

Chair: Peter Mikulecký

- Xavier Alaman – Autonomous University of Madrid
- Francisco J. Ballesteros – Rey Juan Carlos University
- Mária Bieliková – Slovak Institute of Technology
- Vladimír Bureš – University of Hradec Kralove
- Yang Cai – Carnegie Mellon University
- Pavel Čech – University of Hradec Kralove
- Radoslav Delina – Technical University of Kosice
- Carlos Garcia – University of Carlos III
- Diego Lopez de Ipina – Deusto University
- Peter Mihók – Technical University of Kosice
- Karel Mls – University of Hradec Kralove
- Kamila Olševičová – University of Hradec Kralove
- Daniela Ponce – University of Hradec Kralove
- Carlos Ramos – University of Minho

Organizing Committee

Chair: Pavel Čech

- Tereza Lišková
- Vladimír Bureš
- Kamila Olševičová
- Daniela Ponce
- Karel Mls

Contents

Ambient Intelligence Perspectives
P. Mikulecký et al. (Eds.)
IOS Press, 2009
© *2009 The authors and IOS Press. All rights reserved.*
doi:10.3233/978-1-58603-946-2-1

Invited speakers

Yang Cai

Yang Cai is Director of the Ambient Intelligence Lab and Senior Systems Scientist of Cylab and Institute of Complex Engineered Systems, Carnegie Mellon University, USA. He is an architect of conceptual systems of Instinctive Computing, Empathic Computing and Ambient Diagnostics. He edited the books Ambient Intelligence for Scientific Discovery, Ambient Intelligence for Everyday Life, and Digital Humans, published by Springer. Cai also edited the special issues on Ambient Intelligence for International Journal of Human-Computer Studies and Journal of Information Visualization. His interests include Visual Computing, Instinctive Computing and Rock Art.

Tomas Sabol

Professional background of Tomas Sabol is in information and communication technologies. His research interests are in artificial intelligence, knowledge management, knowledge systems, semantic technologies, ontology-based knowledge modelling, project management, Information society and Knowledge economy development. Working for the Technical University of Kosice, Faculty of Economics and Faculty of Electrical Engineering and Informatics. Tomas has extensive experience in participation and management of international R&D (FP7, FP6, FP5 etc.) projects: FP7-IST-217098 SPIKE, FP6-2004-027020 Access-eGov (coordinator of the project), FP6-2004-027128 SAKE, IST-2005-034891 HYDRA, FP6-IST-27219 DEMO_net, IST-1999-20364 WEBOCRACY (coordinator of the project), IST-1999-29088 PRISMA, IST-2000-26224 BEEP, HPSE-CT-2001-00065 ProductivityGap, Esprit 29015 ENRICH, Esprit 29065 KnowWeb, COPERNICUS CIPA CT94 0149 ENCODE etc.

As an expert in ICT Tomas cooperates with the European Commission and other international institutions, e.g. serving as an evaluator and rapporteur of European eGovernment Award programme (2003, 2005, 2007), evaluator of FP6 IST projects, reviewer of FP5 projects, evaluator of eParticipation projects, etc. In 2003-2005 Tomas was a member of the eEurope Advisory Group (Expert Chamber). He is a member of boards of several national and international conferences, journals, and organisations.

Jose Bravo Rodriguez

Jose Bravo is director of the Modelling Ambient Intelligence (MAmI) research lab of the Castilla-La Mancha University. He is interested in Ubiquitous Computing, Ambient Intelligent, Context Awareness and Identification Technologies applied to Education and Healthcare. Jose Bravo promotes the Symposiun of Ubiquitous Computing and Ambient Intelligence (UCAmI) and is the editor of the books of proceedings and two special issues in the Journal of Universal Computer Science and Intenational Journal of Ad Hoc and Ubiquitous Computing. Additionally, he is organizing the First Iberian Conference on Ubiquitous Computing and Ambient Intelligence (ICUCAmI)

Invited Lectures

Ambient Intelligence Perspectives
P. Mikulecký et al. (Eds.)
IOS Press, 2009
© 2009 The authors and IOS Press. All rights reserved.
doi:10.3233/978-1-58603-946-2-5

Towards Tagging Context

José BRAVO

MAmI Research Lab – Castilla-La Mancha University, Spain

jose.bravo@uclm.es

Ubiquitous Computing paradigm and, most recently, Ambient Intelligence (AmI), are the visions in which technology becomes invisible, embedded, present whenever we need it, enabled by simple interactions, attuned to all our senses and adaptive to users and contexts. A further definition of AmI is as "an exciting new paradigm of information technology, in which people are empowered through a digital environment that is aware of their presence and context sensitive, adaptive and responsive to their needs, habits, gestures and emotions."

These visions promote the goals of: 1) embedding technology into everyday objects, 2) attaining effortless and closer interaction and finally 3) supporting a means for getting needed information anywhere and at anytime. This is our particular idea about Ubiquitous Computing, Natural Interfaces and Ubiquitous Communication. With them, the idea of creating intelligent environments requires unobtrusive hardware, wireless communications, massively distributed devices, natural interfaces and security. To attain this vision it is fundamental to analyze some definitions of the context. A. Dey defines this concept as "any information that can be used to characterize the situation of an entity. An entity is a person, place, or object that is considered relevant to the interaction between a user and an application, including the user and application themselves.". Also, this author defines context awareness as the "context to provide relevant information and/or services to the user, where relevancy depends on the user's task".

In order to design context aware applications it is necessary to observe certain types of context-aware information as being more relevant than others. The user profile and situation, that is, the identity-awareness (IAw), are essential. The relative location of people is location-awareness (LAw). Time-awareness (TAw) is another main type of context-awareness that should be taken into account. The task which the user carries out and everything he wants to do is transformed into Activity-awareness (AAw). Finally, Objective-Awareness (OAw) looks at why the user wants to carry out a task in a certain place. All these types of awareness answer the five basic questions ("Who", "Where", "What", "When" and "Why") which provide the guidelines for context modeling. This kind of information allows us to adapt or build the needed technology to disperse throughout the environment and to model the human behavioral support.

Once the context and its important features are defined, it is time to study new interaction forms proposing the approach to the user by means of more natural interfaces. On this point, Albrecht Schmidt proposes the Implicit Human Computer Interaction (iHCI) concept. He defines it as "the interaction of a human with the environment and with artifacts, which is aimed to accomplish a goal. Within this process the system acquires implicit input from the user and may present implicit output to the user". Schmidt defines implicit input as user perceptions interacting with the physical environment, allowing the system to anticipate the user by offering implicit outputs. In this sense the user can concentrate on the task, not on the tool as Ubiquitous Computing Paradigm proposes. As a next step this author defines Embedded Interaction in two terms: Embedding technologies into artifacts, devices and environments and embedding interactions in the user activities (task or actions).

With the ideas of context and their mentioned characteristics, we have considered some awareness features through two different technologies. We propose these approaches by the identification process. It is a specialized input to by means of identification process. This means that we have the knowledge about the user profile, the context information and the task.

To create context-aware applications it is necessary to adapt sensorial capabilities to provide implicit inputs to the system in order to achieve natural interfaces closer to the users. With this the proactive aspect of the system is guaranteed.

In RFID systems there are basically two elements: tags or transponders, which consist of a microchip that stores data, and an antenna (coupling element) and readers or interrogators have one or more antennas, which emit radio waves and receive signals back from the tag. The "interrogation" signal activates all the tags that are within its reach.

Embedding technology into daily objects and embedding interaction into daily actions, we perceive the context-awareness by the "who", "when" and "where" aspect obtaining "what". So, the identification by RFID is a very good implicit input to the computer. The simple action of walking near the antenna allows the system to read and write information such as an Id. Number, profile and other very useful items of information which may vary depending on the context where the users find themselves. However, it is obvious that we need a fixed and expensive infrastructure placing a great variety of devices (readers and antennas) in the environment around us. Given that fact, new short-range wireless connectivity technology called "Near Field Communications" (NFC), has come into being. Philips and Sony developed this technology, a combination of RFID and interconnection technologies, in 2002. NFC uses a high frequency band of up to 13.56 MHz, with a data transmission speed of 424 Kbits/s and a reach of 10 cm. NFC systems consist of two elements: the initiator, which controls the information exchange and the target, which responds to the requirement of the initiator. This technology, NFC, changes the interaction mode with a simple touch combining the RFID technology with the support of mobile phones; it means process, storage and communications capabilities. In this case, the users decide when they want to perform an activity. This aspect makes the context awareness capabilities more flexible and leads to simpler and more feasible applications. In this model the "when" aspect is not needed, meaning that some responsibilities move to the user, who will take part in the process by means of touch, a fact which allows this model to be more flexible. In addition, the "who" and "what" aspects are combined in the mobile phone.

Ambient Intelligence Perspectives
P. Mikulecký et al. (Eds.)
IOS Press, 2009
© *2009 The authors and IOS Press. All rights reserved.*
doi:10.3233/978-1-58603-946-2-7

Visual Thinking for Ambient Intelligence

Yang CAI,
Carnegie Mellon University, USA
ycai@cmu.edu

The broadband Internet enables users to access more and more images and videos. There has been increasing concerns about the security and privacy of the visual contents coming in or going out of their phones, computers and network servers. We have so much visual information but not enough eyes. Image and video collections grow at a rate that exceeds the capacities of human attention and networks combined.

Visual Thinking Agents (VTAs) aim to reduce the overflow of visual information for both humans and networks.They are embeddable software tools for visual intelligence. Ambient Intelligence Lab (www.cmu.edu/vis) has developed a few concept-proofing prototypes of Visual Thinking Agents, including Visual Digest Network, Visual Privacy and Pattern Detection.

The 'Visual Digest Network' is to send the visual information *on-demand*. It aims to reduce the network bandwidth by orders of magnitude. We have investigated the conceptual design of Visual Digest Network at gaze and object levels. Our goal is to minimize the media footprint during visual communication while sustaining essential semantic data. The Attentive Video Network is designed to detect the operator's gaze and adjust the video resolution at the sensor side across the network. The results show significant improvement of the network bandwidth.

The Object Video Network (http://www.cmu.edu/vis/project3.html) is designed for mobile video and vehicle surveillance applications, where faces and cars are detected. The multi-resolution profiles are configured for the media according to the network footprint. The video is sent across the network with multiple resolutions and metadata, controlled by the bandwidth regulator. The results show that the video is able to be transmitted in many worse conditions.

Visual Privacy is to make *visible* to be *invisible*. Visual privacy is a sensitive case because it literally deals with human private parts. It presents a bold challenge to the field of Computer Science. We are building a virtual human model for designing and evaluating visual privacy technologies before a security system is built. This forward-thinking approach intends to transform the development of visual privacy technologies from being device-specific and proprietary to being device-independent and open source-oriented. It will also transform privacy research into a systematic design process, enabling multidisciplinary innovations in digital human modeling, computer vision, information visualization, and computational aesthetics. The result of this project would benefit the privacy-aware imaging systems in airports and medical systems.

Pattern Detection is to make *invisible* to be *visible*. It aims to detect interesting patterns or anomalous events. We have developed a series of demonstrative models that can reveal hidden visual patterns, including network traffic anomalous events, mobility of wireless user positions, harmful algal blooms in satellite images, and words on the eroded stone surfaces. For more information: http://news.bbc.co.uk/2/hi/technology/7024672.stm

Ambient Intelligence Perspectives
P. Mikulecký et al. (Eds.)
IOS Press, 2009
doi:10.3233/978-1-58603-946-2-8

8

Applications of Semantic Technologies in AmI

Peter KOSTELNIK, Tomas SABOL, Marian MACH
Technical University of Košice, Faculty of Economics, Slovakia
peter.kostelnik@tuke.sk

Abstract. Building and running AmI applications suffers from inflexible and/or difficult to achieve interoperability of basic technological elements. Semantic technologies represent a promising approach how to enable a flexible architectures providing wide range of interoperability (e.g. service-service, service-device, service-goal, etc.). The focus of the presented paper is on incorporating these technologies into the model driven architecture approach to designing and running AmI applications. Employment of semantics is illustrated for design-time as well as run-time. Transition from physical to semantic devices enables developers to work on a higher level when designing applications. Enabling semantics in run-time provides possibility for flexible discovering and resolving.

Keywords. Ambient intelligence, Semantic technologies, Ontology, Semantic middleware, HYDRA project.

1. Introduction

Ambient Intelligence (AmI) represents a vision that technology will become invisible, embedded in our natural surroundings, present whenever we need it, enabled by simple and effortless interactions, attuned to all our senses, adaptive to users and context and autonomously acting [HYDRA D2.2, 2007]. In order to fulfil all these expectations, AmI must amalgamate results from several research areas, for example ubiquitous or pervasive computing (networking of numerous portable low cost devices), intelligent systems (learnable autonomous intelligence), human computer interfaces (multimodal ambient communication with humans), context awareness (reacting according to situational context), etc.

This vision can be realised only through a number of technologies applying modern hardware and software solutions. In particular, an AmI system requires the use of distributed devices and services (e.g. sensors and actuators) to create a pervasive technological layer, able to interact transparently with a user. A key factor for successful deployment of this technological layer is to ensure interoperability of all its elements. The interoperability is important both during runtime as well as at the design phase and affects end users as well as developers of AmI applications.

AmI aims at providing transparent and intelligent electronic services. Generally, these services can be numerous, diverse, and distributed in users' environment. In order to provide services appropriately, several issues have to be solved, for instance the discovery of services (goal and context oriented), invocation of services (context based parametrisation and data transformation), creating, composition and orchestration of services (mediation of their functional as well as non-functional characteristics), etc. Moreover, providing a service depends on devices which can be used to enable the service. It is prone to similar issues on a lower level – discovery, employment and composition of devices.

The problem can be illustrated on service discovery. Most of the existing service discovery mechanisms retrieve services based on whether their descriptions contain particular keywords. In the majority of the cases this leads to low recall and low precision of the retrieved results. The reason of the low recall is that query keywords might be semantically similar but syntactically different from the terms in service descriptions, e.g. 'buy' and 'purchase' (synonyms). The reason for the low precision is that the query keywords might be syntactically equivalent but semantically different from the terms in the service description, e.g. 'order' in the sense of a proper arrangement and 'order' in the sense of a commercial document used to request supply of something (homonyms). Another problem with keyword-based service discovery approaches is that they do not consider the existing relations among keywords – they are not able to perform 'approximate' search in addition to 'exact' search.

The reason is that keyword-based methods can completely capture neither the semantics of user's query nor characteristics (functional as well as quality-based) of services. One possible solution for this problem is to use an ontology-based retrieval. In this approach, semantic ontological models are used for modelling characteristics of services and classification of the services based on their properties. This enables incorporate semantic relations among terms used to describe service properties. Considering the semantics in the query-service matching process can improve the quality of the retrieved results.

In this paper we summarise research on the employment of semantic technologies in AmI applications and present our experiences with these technologies within the Hydra project ("Networked Embedded System middleware for heterogeneous physical devices in a distributed architecture") funded under the 6th Framework Programme of the EU.

2.   European R&D Projects in Ambient Intelligence

Before providing more detailed information on the R&D project HYDRA, on the solution of which the authors of this paper participate, this section provides an overview of European research and development projects related to ambient intelligence [HYDRA D13.9, 2008]. The aim of this project overview is to illustrate main research issues and ambient intelligence application areas.

2.1   Smart Networks

Ambient Networks Phase 2
Website: http://www.ambient-networks.org

Duration: 2006 - 2007 (24 months)

Funding: FP6, IST
The project addresses vision of the future wireless world, which will be filled by a multitude of user devices, and wireless technologies with simple-to-use, anytime-anywhere network access affordable for everyone. The Ambient Networks project addressed these challenges by developing innovative mobile network solutions for increased competition and cooperation in an environment with a multitude of access technologies, network operators and business actors. It offers a complete, coherent wireless network solution based on dynamic composition of networks that provide access to any network through the instant establishment of inter-network agreements. The technical objectives of the project are: to define and validate a complete and coherent solution for ambient networking, based on a range of different scenarios and business cases; to set new standards based on the Ambient Networks solution for future context-aware; multi-domain mobile networks; to ensure the commercial viability by identifying business roles and interfaces as well as deployment concepts and to consider business scenarios that allow different size and types of players to compete and cooperate.

Smart Embedded Network of Sensing Entities (SENSE)
Website: http://www.sense-ist.org/

Duration: 2006 - 2009

Funding: FP6, IST
The SENSE project will develop methods, tools and a test platform for the design, implementation and operation of smart adaptive wireless networks of embedded sensing components. The network is an ambient intelligent system, which adapts to its environment, creates ad-hoc networks of heterogeneous components, and delivers reliable information to its component sensors and the user. The sensors cooperate to build and maintain a coherent global view from local information. Newly added nodes automatically calibrate themselves to the environment, and share knowledge with neighbours. The network is scalable due to local information processing and sharing, and self-organizes based on the physical placement of nodes

2.2   Intelligent Home Environment

Ambient intelligence for the networked home environment (AMIGO)
Website:http://www.hitech-projects.com/euprojects/amigo/index.htm

Duration: 2004-2008

Funding: FP6, IST

The AMIGO project aims at development of open, standardized, interoperable middleware and attractive user services, thus improving end-user usability and attractiveness. The project will show the end-user usability and attractiveness of such a home system by creating and demonstrating prototype applications improving everyday life, addressing all vital user aspects: home care and safety, home information and entertainment, and extension of the home environment by means of ambience sharing for advanced personal communication. The project will further support interoperability between equipment and services within the networked home environment by using standard technology when possible and by making the basic middleware (components and infrastructure) and basic user services available as open source software together with architectural rules for everyone to use. Context-awareness concepts and principles are at the heart of the AMIGO project.

2.3   Ambient Assisted Living

Complete Ambient Assisted Living Experiment (CAALYX)
Website:http://caalyx.eu

Duration: 2007-2009 (24 months)

Funding: FP6, IST

Ambient Assisted Living (AAL), as a specific user-oriented type of "Ambient Intelligence", aims to prolong the time people can live in a decent more independent way by increasing their autonomy and self-confidence, by allowing them to discharge normal everyday activities, by improved monitoring and care of the elderly or ill person, by enhancing their security while ultimately saving resources. CALALYX's main objective is to develop a wearable light device able to measure specific vital signs of the older person, to detect falls and to communicate automatically in real time with his/her caregiver in case of an emergency, wherever the older person happens to be, at home or outside.

Old people's e-services at home (OLDES)
Website:http://www.oldes.eu

Duration: 2007-2010

Funding: FP6, IST

The OLDES project will offer new technological solutions to improve the quality of life of older people. OLDES aims at developing a very low cost and easy to use entertainment and health care platform designed to ease the life of older people in their homes. In order to achieve this, new concepts developed in Information Technologies will be integrated and adapted. OLDES will provide: user entertainment services, through easy-to-access thematic channels and special interest forums supported by animators; and health care facilities based on established Internet and tele-care communication standards. The system will include wireless ambient and medical sensors linked via a contact centre to social services and health care providers. OLDES will also cover the definition, implementation and evaluation of a Knowledge

Management (KM) program, an advanced user profiling system that will enhance the communication between all the stakeholders of the system. The system will be tested at two different locations: Italy over a group of 100 elderly (including 10 suffering with cardio disease) and Czech Republic over a group of 10 diabetic patients. OLDES puts older people at the centre and makes their needs the main priority in all developments.

Other R&D projects on ambient assisted living:
• Perceptive Spaces Promoting Independent Ageing (PERSONA), http://www.aal-persona.org/
• Mainstreaming on ambient intelligence (MonAMI), http://www.monami.info/
• An intelligent interactive services environment for assisted living at home (INHOME), http://www.ist-inhome.eu/

2.4   Security and Privacy

Privacy in an Ambient World (PAW)
Website:http://www.cs.ru.nl/paw

Duration: 2003-2007

Funding: Dutch Ministry of Economic Affairs, IOP GenCom programme
The objective of the PAW project was to develop a privacy protecting architecture that can provide full privacy of the user in an ambient world. A two-tier approach was applied to prevent unwanted collection of data about a user and his actions. Techniques from secure computing were extended to provide private computing. To control the authorised dissemination of data about a user, licensing techniques similar to those used in digital rights management were studied. Since ambient systems are characterised by their low resources and capabilities, PAW's key challenge was to develop an efficient architecture. An advantage of the architecture proposed is decentralization, where no central authority for controlling is necessary. But unfortunately an agent can use data in an un-authorised way and can be held responsible only after the misuse of the data (which is not an ideal solution for real world scenarios).

Security Expert INITiative (SEINIT)
Website:
         http://www.isoc.org/seinit/portal/index.php?option=com_content&task=view&id=53&Itemid=28

Duration: 2003-2006

Funding: FP6, IST
The overall objective of the Security Expert INITiative (SEINIT) project is to ensure a trusted and dependable information security framework, ubiquitous, working across multiple devices, heterogeneous networks, being organisation independent (inter-operable) and centred around an end-user. SEINIT was exploring new information

security models and building the architecture and components to address our nomadic, pervasive, multi-player communicating world. This new solution uses information gathered by ambient intelligence and then deals with the new threats this entails.

2.5   Non-technical Issues of Ambient Intelligence

Safeguards in a World of Ambient Intelligence (SWAMI)

Website: http://www.ist-world.org/ProjectDetails.aspx?ProjectId=212f8a94875941f88cfa0dc321 d60a8f&SourceDatabaseId=7cff9226e582440894200b751bab883f

Duration: 2005-2006

Funding: FP6, IST
The main objective of the SWAMI project is (based also on the review of existing AmI projects, studies, scenarios and roadmaps) to identify the social, legal, organizational and ethical implications related to issues such as privacy, anonymity, security and identity in the context of AmI. This has been achieved through the elaboration of 'dark scenarios' as a centre piece of the SWAMI project methodology. The 'dark scenarios' depict a realistic future that could emerge from the application of new AmI technologies, but focus on the likely adverse effects which often are overlooked by technology developers and policymakers. The first objective of the dark scenario exercise thus consisted of the identification of potential threats and vulnerabilities that need to be mitigated if AmI is to become a future success story.

Development of Long-term Shared Vision on AmI Technologies for a Networked Agro-Food Sector (AMI@NetFood)

Website: http://www.ami-netfood.com/

Duration: 2005-2006

Funding: FP6, IST
The objective of AMI@Netfood project is to support the implementation of the IST Research Priority and Framework Programme, providing a long-term vision on future trends on scientific and technology research oriented to the development and application of Ambient Intelligence technologies in the agro-food domain.

3.   HYDRA Project

The HYDRA project ("Networked Embedded System Middleware for Heterogeneous Physical Devices in a Distributed Architecture"), contract No. 034891, is an Integrated Project (IP) funded by the EC within FP6, Information Society Technologies (IST) Programme. The project started on July 1st, 2006 and its expected duration is 52 months. The project consortium consists of 13 partners from Sweden, Denmark, Germany, Spain, the United Kingdom, Italy, and Slovakia (2 large companies, 5 SMEs, 6 universities and research institutes).

The HYDRA project is addressing the problem, which is frequently faced by producers of devices and components – the need for networking (which is actually becoming a trend) the products available on the market in order to provide higher value-added solutions for their customers. This requirement is implied by citizen centred demands requiring intelligent solutions, where the complexity is hidden behind user-friendly interfaces. It is expected that HYDRA will contribute to the vision of the ambient intelligence world as described in the introductory section.

Overall HYDRA project objectives can be summarised as follows:
1. Development of a middleware based on a Service-oriented Architecture, to which the underlying communication layer is transparent, and consists of:
   - Support for distributed as well as centralised ambient intelligent architectures;
   - Support for reflective (i.e. self-*) properties of components of the middleware;
   - Support for security and trust enabling components.
2. Design of a generic semantic model-based architecture supporting model-driven development of applications.
3. Development of a toolkit for developers to develop applications on the middleware.
4. Design of a business modelling framework for analysing the business sustainability of the developed applications.

From scientific point of view the project is carrying out research as well as application and system integration within the following research areas:
   - Embedded and mobile service-oriented architectures for ubiquitous networked devices;
   - Semantic Model-Driven Architecture for Ambient Intelligence implementation;
   - Ontology-based knowledge modelling;
   - Wireless devices and networks with self-* properties (self-diagnosis, self-configuring, self-healing, etc.);
   - Distributed security and privacy.

The implemented HYDRA middleware and toolkit is validated in real end-user scenarios in three different user domains: a) Facility management (home automation), b) Healthcare, c) Agriculture.

3.1 HYDRA approach to Semantic Model-Driven Architecture

One of the main goals of HYDRA project is to provide the middleware solution for creating applications interconnecting various heterogeneous devices with different services and capabilities. HYDRA aims to develop middleware based on a Service-oriented Architecture (SOA) providing the interoperable access to data, information and knowledge across heterogeneous platforms, including web services, and support true ambient intelligence for ubiquitous networked devices. The SOA and its related standards provide interoperability at syntactic level. However, HYDRA aims at providing interoperability at semantic level as well. One of the objectives is to extend this syntactic interoperability to the application level, i.e. in the terms of semantic interoperability. This is done by combining the use of ontologies with semantic web services. HYDRA introduces the Semantic Model Driven Architecture (MDA), which aims to facilitate application development and to promote semantic interoperability for services and devices. The semantic MDA of HYDRA includes a set of models (ontologies) and describes how these can be used both in design-time and in run-time.

The basic idea behind the HYDRA Semantic MDA is to differentiate between the physical (real) devices and the application's view of the device. This approach leads to introduction of the concept of Semantic Devices [Kostelnik, 2008]. In the easiest case the semantic device represents a model of a real device and serves as logical unit, which can be semantically discovered and provide information about device capabilities, services. But from these simple semantic devices one can construct more complex semantic devices consisting from several "logical units" (other semantic devices) plus defining a "logics" between these semantic devices. Thus semantic devices can be viewed as logical aggregates of devices and their services.

The services offered by the physical devices are designed independently of particular applications in which the device might be used. A semantic device on the other hand represents what the particular application would like to have. For instance, when designing a lighting system for a building it would be more appropriate to model the application as working with a "logical lighting system" that provides services like "working light", "presentation light", and "comfort light" rather than working with a set of independent lamps that can be turned on/off. These semantic devices may in fact consist of aggregates of physical devices, and use different devices to deliver the service depending on the situation. The service "Working light" might be achieved during daytime by pulling up the blind (if it is down) and during evening by turning on a lamp (blind and lamp being HYDRA devices).

Semantic devices should be seen as a programming concept. The application programmer designs and programs his/her application using semantic devices. The semantic device "Heating System" consist of three physical devices: a pump that circulates the water, a thermometer that delivers the temperature and a light that flashes when something is wrong. The developer will only have to use the services offered by the semantic device "Heating System", for instances "Keep temperature: 20 degrees of Celsius" and "Set warning level: 17 degrees of Celsius", and does not need to know the underlying implementation of this particular heating system. The Semantic Device concept is flexible and will support both static mappings as well as dynamic mappings to physical devices.

Static mappings can be both one-to-one (mapping of a semantic device to a physical device) or mappings that allow composition. An example of a one-to-one mapping would be a "semantic pump" that is exposed with all its services to the programmer. An example of a composed mapping is a semantic heating system that is mapped to three different underlying devices – a pump, a thermometer, and a digital lamp.

Static mappings will require knowledge, which devices exist in the runtime environment, for instance the heating system mentioned above will require the existence of the three underlying devices – pump, thermometer and lamp – in for instance a building.

Dynamic mapping will allow semantic devices to be instantiated at runtime. Consider the heating system above. We might define it as consisting of the following devices/services:
- a device that can circulate the water and increase its temperature;
- a device that can measure and deliver temperature;
- a device that can generate an alarm/alert signal if temperature is out of range.

When such a device is entered into the runtime environment it will use service discovery to instantiate itself and it will query the physical devices it discovers, as to which can provide the services/functions the semantic device requires. In this example the semantic device most probably starts by finding a circulation pump. Having done that, it might find two different thermometers, which both claim that they can measure temperature. The semantic device could then query, which of the thermometers can deliver the temperature in Celsius, with what resolution and how often. In this case it might be only one of the thermometers that meets these requirements. Finally, the semantic device could search the network if there is a physical device that can be used to generate an alarm if the temperature drops below a threshold or increases too much. By reasoning over the semantic device it can deduct that by flashing the lamp repeatedly it can generate an alarm signal, so the lamp is included as part of the semantic heating system.

The basic idea behind semantic devices is to hide all the underlying complexity of the mapping to, discovery of and access to physical devices. The programmer just uses it as a normal object in his application, focusing on solving the application's problems rather then the intrinsic of the physical devices. The description of semantic devices are realised as device OWL [McGuiness, 2004] ontology, which will be outlined in the next chapter. The concept of semantic devices supports the semantic MDA approach. The semantic MDA in HYDRA is used in two ways. Firstly, it is relevant at the design-time, and it will support both device developers as well as application developers. Secondly, at the run-time any HYDRA application is driven from the semantic MDA.

3.1.1   Semantic MDA at design-time

Model-driven code generation for physical devices

Within HYDRA project a tool, called *Limbo*, has been developed, which takes as inputs an interface description ("Provide WSDL file") and a semantic description of the device on which a web service should run ("Provide OWL description") [Hansen, 2008]. The interface description is assumed to be in the form of a WSDL file and the semantic description is a link to an OWL description of the device (ontologies used are described in the next chapter). The semantic description is used to:

- *Determine the compilation target.* Depending on available resources of a device, either embedded stubs and skeletons are created for the web service (to run on the target device) or proxy stubs and skeletons are created for the web service (to run on an OSGi gateway).
- *Provide support for reporting device status.* Based on a description of the device states at runtime (through a state machine), support code is generated for reporting state changes. This should be also used as the support of self-* properties of HYDRA.

Model-driven code generation for Semantic Devices

The semantic descriptions of services can be used at the design time to find suitable services for the application that the HYDRA developer is working on. The descriptions of these services will be used to generate code to call the service, query the device that implements the service, and manipulate the data that the service operates on. The project team is currently aiming at making the HYDRA SDK available in an object-oriented language environment. Thus, SDK will provide objects a developer can use to access the services (service proxies) as well as objects from the device ontology connected to the service. HYDRA developer can specify a service to be used, and leave the device as generic as possible - any device that is capable of implementing the service. The necessary code will be generated both for the service and the device.

These device objects could be used when creating a semantic device or HYDRA application from the selected devices and services. The services could also be used by a service orchestration engine (however, presumption that some applications will be standalone and have a fairly small footprint may not be suitable for all HYDRA applications).

The way how the application uses the device ontology should be configurable, so that the middleware supports both standalone applications that only use the device ontology at the design time as well as applications that always query the device ontology for new types of services that match the descriptions.

3.1.2   Semantic MDA in run-time

Models for discovery

At the design time, the HYDRA application developer selects the HYDRA devices and services that will be used to implement the application. These devices may be defined at a fairly general level, e.g. the application may be interested only in "HYDRA SMS Service" and any device to be included into the network (or application context) that fits to these general categories will be presented to the application. The application will then work against more general device descriptions. This means that an application should only know of (types of) devices and services selected by the developer when it was defined. This also means that the application could use a device that was designed and built after the application was deployed - as long as the device can be classified through the device ontology as being of a device type or using a service that is known to the application, e.g., a HYDRA application built in 2008 could specify the use of

"HYDRA Generic Smart phone" and "HYDRA SMS Service" and thus use also a "Nokia N2010 Smartphone" released two years later.

When a device is discovered, the device type is looked up in the device ontology and if it can be mapped to a specific device model (perhaps it can always be mapped to a most generic type of devices).

A HYDRA Application may present an external interface so that it can be integrated with other applications and devices. It will do this by identifying itself as a HYDRA device with a set of services. This is transparent to other devices, which means that some devices or services used in the application will be composite ones - based on other HYDRA applications that have exposed external interfaces. When such an application is discovered, the applications interested in that type of device and its services will be notified.

The use of models for resolving security requirements

The dynamic and networked execution environment of HYDRA requires strong yet adaptable security mechanisms to be in place. In order to establish the ability to securely connect any application/device to any application/device, HYDRA also uses the semantic MDA to define and enforce security policies [Wahl, 2008]. A basic design objective for the HYDRA security model is to provide a secure information flow with a minimum of pre-determined assumptions, while being able to dynamically resolve security requirements. The security policies of HYDRA can thus be defined and enforced based upon knowledge in the device ontology as well as on knowledge of the context of devices, and also makes use of virtual devices.

The use of models for context-awareness

To support ambient intelligence applications, the models for context-awareness functionality are also provided. The models are created as a combination of OWL ontologies and SWRL [Horrocks, 2004] rules and serve as the basic mechanism supporting the self-* properties [Zhang, 2008]. At present, the context-awareness models are used in the self-management and self-diagnosis task. The ontologies contain the models of devices and the state machines representing the actual status of devices. The ontology containing possible malfunctions, which may occur on devices is also used. The context is modelled using the SWRL rules, which can be defined on the device level (monitoring and reacting to the state of the single device) and the system/application level (monitoring and reacting to the context created as a combination of multiple devices states). The continual execution of rules may lead to generation of several malfunctions containing the description of error and the related remedies, which are provided to application users.

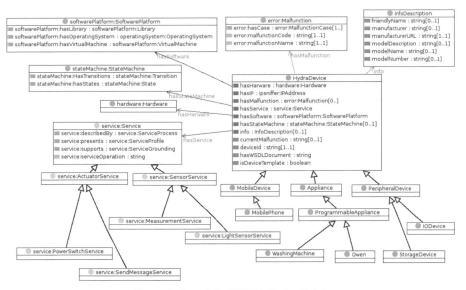

Figure 1. Part of the HYDRA Device Ontology.

3.2 Semantic Description of Devices

To achieve the vision of a Semantic Model Driven Architecture we have decided to base our approach on ontologies and related semantic technologies. HYDRA device ontology presents basic high level concepts describing basic device related information [Kostelnik, 2008]. The semantic device model can be viewed from two perspectives:

- *Design/development phase*: Every ontology module can be further extended by creating new concepts according to the needs of representation of the new information about new device types and models. The concepts can also be further specialized. For example, if the new device type is needed, the adequate concept in the device classification module can be further sub-classed by more specialized concepts and the new properties can be added. Specific device models are created as the instances of device ontology concepts and filled with real data.

- *Run-time phase*: Each instance created in the development phase represents a specific device model and serves as the template for run-time instances of real devices discovered and connected into HYDRA. In the device discovery process, the discovery information is resolved in ontology and the most suitable template is identified. Based on the identified template a new unique run-time instance is instantiated representing the given device. Each real device instance has an assigned unique HYDRA Id. Using this Id, it is possible to retrieve and update all the relevant information related to the general description of the device and its actual run-time properties.

The ontology structure was designed to support the maintainability and future extensions of used concepts. The ontologies have been developed using the OWL language. Figure 1 illustrates a part of HYDRA device ontology.

The Hydra Device Ontology presents the basic high level concepts describing basic device related information, which are used in both the development and run-time process. The core device ontology contains taxonomy of device types and basic device and manufacturer information. The description of the device properties and capabilities is divided into four interconnected modules:

- Device malfunctions ontology represents possible errors that may occur on devices. The malfunctions are divided in the taxonomy of possible error types according to the severity, such as error, warning or fatal. Each error model contains the human readable description and set of cause-remedy pairs. The connection of malfunction model and device state machine is used also for diagnostic purposes. Various faults related to specific ontology states can be, for example, used to predict or avoid fatal error states of device or to invoke related call-back events to handle the error states that may occur in the run-time.

- Device capabilities represent the extended device information mainly used for purposes of generation of embedded device services code and self-* properties. The device capabilities are divided into three modules:
  - o Hardware module includes the hardware related device properties such as connection and communication protocols (e.g. Bluetooth or various network bearers, etc.), description of hardware interfaces (such as camera, display, etc.). Device hardware capabilities are mainly used for generation of embedded device services code.
  - o Software module includes various software platforms, operating systems, etc. Software description is used by the Limbo compiler used for generating the codes for embedded device services.
  - o The special case of capability is the state machine model representing the concepts of states and transitions, which are updated in the run-time and represent the device/service actual status. The state machine ontology is also used by Limbo to generate state and transition related code.

- Device services ontology presents the semantic description of device services on a higher, technology independent level. The HYDRA service model enables the interoperability between devices and services, employing the service capabilities and input/output parameters. The semantic service specification is based on the OWL-S [Martin, 2004] standard, which is currently the most complete description of semantic mark-ups for services following the web service architecture. The OWL-S approach was taken as the starting point for HYDRA service model. The models of services may be automatically created using the SAWSDL annotations [Farrell, 2007] enabling automatic classification of device and its services into ontology. Service models serve as the semantic representation supporting the search of devices providing required functionality and also as the grounding information for service execution.

- Security capabilities ontology represents the security properties of devices and the services, such as protocols, policies, mechanisms or objectives. The NRL ontology [NRL, 2007] was selected as a starting point for this model and has been modified and extended to match HYDRA's requirements. The NRL ontology is a set of various security related models covering the representation of credentials, algorithms, assurances, but also the service security aspects directly supporting the SOA approach.

3.3 HYDRA end-user applications

The HYDRA middleware serves as a tool supporting efficient development of AmI applications in various end-user domains. System developers are thus provided with tools for easy and secure integration of heterogeneous physical devices into interoperable distributed systems.

The middleware includes support for distributed as well as centralised architectures, cognition and context awareness, security and trust and will be deployable on both new and existing networks of distributed wireless and wired devices that typically are resource constrained in terms of computing power, energy and memory. The middleware is validated in three application domains: Building automation, healthcare and agriculture.

The development is realised in an iterative way - four iterations are planned within HYDRA for the middleware development. After each cycle the middleware is progressively becoming more advanced – while learning more about developer as well as end-user requirements. Evaluation of experiences from the previous cycles is taken into account. At the end of each cycle a demonstrator is produced with a specific purpose to illustrate:

- Concept Demonstrator;
- SDK Demonstrator;
- DDK (Device Development Kit) Demonstrator;
- IDE Demonstrator.

For each cycle more and more of the end-user applications are implemented, so they become more sophisticated as the project progresses. For each cycle there is one user domain in focus but scenarios from the other two is also considered - in cycle (1) Building Automation is the main emphasis, in cycle (2) Healthcare and in cycle (3) Agriculture. Finally in the fourth cycle all domains will be fully demonstrated.

An example of the building automation scenario used for the demonstration of the proof of the concept can be outlined as follows (see Figure 2 for illustration):

The resident is living in a new flat in the "Krøyers Plads" housing complex in Copenhagen. In addition to the usual set of automatic lamps, computer and wireless network, the flat is equipped also with an automatic heating system.

While the resident is at his office, he receives an alert from his "Hydra Building Automation System" (HBAS) that the heating system has broken down. Since the temperature has reached sub zero level, HBAS categorized it as an emergency situation and tries to contact the resident until he replied to the alert.

Since the resident is having a contract with the service provider of the heating system to send out a service agent to repair the system in case of a break down, the resident sends a repair order to the service provider. The service provider sends out a service agent to the flat. The service provider has transferred the appropriate credentials to enter the house and to repair the heating system to the service agent's PDA.

When the service agent arrives at the complex, he authenticates himself to the door and is given access to the resident's flat after the validation was successful. The service agent checks the logs present in the heating system to identify the errors and uses the online help of the service provider to fix the problem. After finishing his work, the service agent leaves the flat and the HBAS system informs the resident that the heating system is working again and the service agent has left the flat.

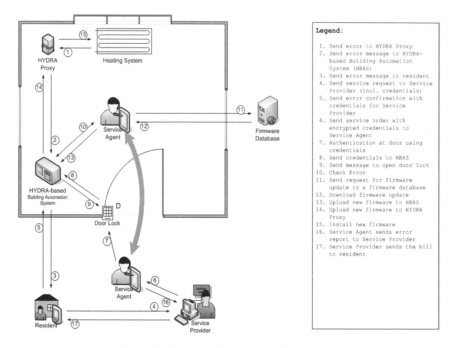

Figure 2. Example of home automation scenario.

4.   Conclusions

Semantic technologies represent a very promising approach to solving many problems in AmI applications. Coupling of these technologies with the MDA method generates many possibilities for incorporating semantics into the design of applications as well as into process of running AmI applications. Enabling semantics on the level of the description of AmI technological elements (mainly services and/or devices) results in enriched possibilities for matching operation (e.g. service to service, service to goal, device to service, device to device, etc.) not forced to rely only on syntactic similarity any more. Such matching can be found in the background of such essential tasks as discovery, composition, and mediation.

Regarding the future development within the HYDRA project, since the semantic MDA is built on ontologies we foresee a need for tools and methods for design and managing these ontologies. Therefore for the next development iterations the problem how the design and management of the three Hydra ontologies can be carried out efficiently will be investigated. The ontology management addresses mainly the following issues:

- Ontology design process: The initial HYDRA ontology design process is manual, performed by ontology engineering experts. The tools enabling the ontology design and refinement also for not expert users should be provided.
- Ontology extensions: To support the efficient development of applications in various end-user domains, ontologies should be extended also by descriptions representing the end-user domains. Such descriptions should lead to increased capability of semantic interopearability between devices, but also between applications.
- Automatic modification of ontologies: HYDRA should provide more tools for automatic extension of ontologies, mainly in the terms of automatic classification of the new devices into ontology, where the description of new device may be provided in various form, such as MS Word, PDF, HTML or XML. This process would require the development of transformation tools enabling the parsing and processing of this description forms.
- Mediation, aligning and merging of ontologies: A developer should be able to import an external (device) ontology and be provided with tools for its adaptation and use in application development.

There are also several issues to be further investigated regarding the management of the discovery process and management of semantic devices at the run-time. Actually, the whole service composition occurs at the design time. In the following iterations, the Hydra middleware may have to resolve this at the run-time when a set of devices and services that are present in the network constitute a composite device. The semi or fully automatic service composition may improve the system robustness mainly in the case of run-time device failures.

There will be also required various visualisation mechanisms supporting several development tasks, such as searching and retrieving the devices or services by functionality requirements or required capabilities. This functionality may be used in the tasks of semi or fully automatic creation of composite semantic devices and will require, as the addition to the ontology reasoning, also planning capabilities.

Acknowledgements

The work presented in the paper is partly funded by the European Commission through the IST Project HYDRA (Networked Embedded System Middleware for Heterogeneous Physical Devices in a Distributed Architecture), contract No. 034891 as well as by the Slovak Grant Agency of the Ministry of Education and Academy of Science of the Slovak Republic within the 1/4074/07 Project "Methods for annotation, search, creation, and accessing knowledge employing metadata for semantic description of knowledge".

References

[HYDRA D2.2, 2007] D2.2 Initial technology Watch report. Hydra Project Deliverable, IST project No. 034891, 2008.

[HYDRA D13.9, 2008] D13.9 Report on Projects Connected to HYDRA. Hydra Project Deliverable, IST project No. 034891, 2008.

[Farrell, 2007] J. Farrell, et.al. Semantic Annotations for WSDL and XML Schema, W3C Recommendation, 2007.

[Hansen, 2008] K.M. Hansen, W. Zhang, G. Soares, Ontology-Enabled Generation of Embedded Web Services. The 20th International Conference on Software Engineering and Knowledge Engineering (SEKE '2008), 2008.

[Horrocks, 2004] I. Horrocks, et.al. SWRL: A Semantic Web Rule Language. W3C Member Submission, 2004.

[Kostelnik, 2008] P. Kostelnik, M. Sarnovsky, J. Hreňo, M. Ahlsen, P. Rosengren, P. Kool, M. Axling. Semantic Devices for Ambien Environment Middleware. EURO TrustAMI, Internet of Things and Services Workshop, 2008.

[Martin, 2004] D. Martin, et. al. OWL-S: Semantic Markup for Web Services, W3C Member Submission, 2004.

[McGuinness, 2004] D.L. McGuinness, F. van Harmelen, OWL Web Ontology Language Overview, W3C Recommendation, 2004.

[NRL, 2007] Naval Research Lab. Nrl security ontology. http://chacs.nrl.navy.mil/projects/4SEA/ontology.html, 2007.

[Wahl, 2008] T. Wahl, J. Schütte, P. Kostelnik, Security Mechanisms for an Ambient Environment Middleware. ServiceWave, 2008.

[Zhang, 2008] W. Zhang, K.M. Hansen, Towards Self-managed Pervasive Middleware using OWL/SWRL ontologies. Fifth International Workshop Modeling and Reasoning in Context (MRC 2008), 2008.

Contributed Papers

Ambient Intelligence Perspectives
P. Mikulecký et al. (Eds.)
IOS Press, 2009

doi:10.3233/978-1-58603-946-2-27

Tangible Light Interaction
How light portrays the tangible action of things and spaces around us

Richard APPLEBY, Kees OVERBEEKE

Technische Universiteit Eindhoven, Netherlands

r.s.appleby@tue.nl

Abstract. The field of tangible interaction currently studies how the user interaction with physical products can be improved through physical feedback, as a more direct experience. Here we explore this subject further with particular emphasis on the elements of visual attraction of illuminated surfaces as an early factor in the interaction process. Richard Appleby is an experienced industrial designer who has developed many consumer products where the surface definition and visual language has had a significant impact on the perceived values and tangibility of the product. These changing surface interactions should not be difficult or challenging, but intuitive and enjoyable to live with. The systems may be complex, but the way they reveal and offer their actions can heighten our awareness and sensitivity in new and unique ways. It is a question of subtlety and detail. As the surfaces we interact with have the intelligence to appreciate a much wider range of human conditions and user feedback, their response can be attuned more closely to our different senses and feelings, particularly as this leads to more subjective and sensorial types of interaction, with varying dimensions and magnitude. These surfaces change through colour and form that attract the user we coin 'light tangible interaction'. Particularly within the field of intelligent technologies, project examples show design concepts that support social interaction and remote communications in new ways.

Keywords. Tangible Light Interaction, Pre-interaction, Surfaces

Introduction

The field of tangible interaction currently studies how the user interaction with physical products can be improved through physical feedback, as a more direct experience. Here we explore this subject further with particular emphasis on the elements of visual attraction of illuminated surfaces as an early factor in the interaction process. The first author is an experienced industrial designer who has developed many consumer products where the surface definition and visual language has had a significant impact on the perceived values and tangibility of the product.

Early contributors to the field of tangible Interaction, particularly by Stephan Wensveen, [1], have clearly established that considerable improvements in many aspects of interaction design are attributed to the awareness of and need to 'design with' the perceptual-motor and affective skills, in addition to the more traditional cognitive processes. As Wensveen questions, " How can we design for human product interaction, so that product gets information about what we 'know' and how we 'feel' from the way we 'do' this interaction, in order to adapt to this information?"

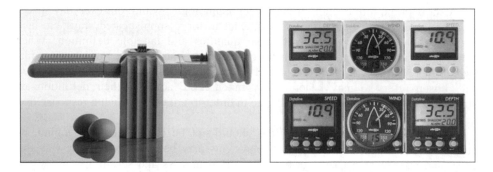

Figure 1. Pasta Maker = soft tangible surfaces, and Navigation Displays = high contrast surfaces
(product examples designed by Richard Appleby)

It's all about where the 'known' information is at any given point in time, in order to provide the most sensitive interaction. If products are simply seen as tools and designed as objects then they rely on people to provide all the information during the interaction process, with no capacity for the product to interpret these given commands. There is a functional interpretation, it's just very literal and follows the instruction given from its operator. Computers and other semi-intelligent products don't work like this, they provide some feedback and reactions to our input and so we appreciate this information exchange, (and sometimes we find it irritating). Nevertheless, this change in the way products are now equipped with more adaptive and re-active capacities, signify this shift in focus to the point where the information is and subsequently, this changes our perception of products and the way we interact with them. Using the tangibility of light builds expectations of how much more products and spaces around us can contribute to our experience and interaction, simply through the information and knowledge they make tangible through action Finally the beauty of this feedback loop between perception and interaction is manifest in the richer engagement, awareness and sensitivity to our spatial experience.

But how does light become tangible. . . .

To start with, Gibson [2], provides us with simple definition of light and surfaces. . . . ." Light comes from the sky and becomes ambient in the air. This is what makes persisting surfaces potentially visible as well as potentially tangible." . . . and then later on. . . " The surface is where most of the action is. The surface is where light is reflected or absorbed, not the interior of the substance."(p23) Within his theory of affordances, Gibson later describes surfaces as an invariant which do not change relative to the observer's viewpoint. . . ." the affordance of something does not change as the need of the observer changes. The observer may or may not perceive or attend to the affordance, according to his needs, but the affordance, being invariant, is always there to be perceived." (P.138) With these references in mind, when designing for more intelligent environments many questions arise that are concerned with the tangibility of form, colour and surface (and their illumination to the observer), that can change the user-attraction and interaction with many different products and situations.

Also, with the introduction of intelligent technologies within our everyday spaces, we are provided with opportunities to interact in more sophisticated ways. Surfaces might be able to change their reflective qualities and tangible definition. Where materials are conceived through genetic or artificial nano-technologies, surfaces may become more variable in their colour and form. Subsequently, the surface affordances that Gibson refers to may become very much more acute in their definition and attractiveness to the user. They can change in order to attract and elicit a response from the user during the interaction experience.

These changing surface interactions should not be difficult or challenging, but intuitive and enjoyable to live with. The systems may be complex, but the way they reveal and offer their actions can heighten our awareness and sensitivity in new and unique ways. It is a question of subtlety and detail. As the surfaces we interact with have the intelligence to appreciate a much wider range of human conditions and user feedback, their response can be attuned more closely to our different senses and feelings, particularly as this leads to more subjective and sensorial types of interaction, with varying dimensions and magnitude. This surfaces change through colour and form that attract the user we coin 'light tangible interaction'.

Cues and tangible responses.

Through our knowledge of construction and needs of high volume consumer markets, our built environment and physical products are traditionally designed in a way that facilitates the manufacturing process. The configuration and arrangements of these constructed artefacts have visual cues which are more to do with their 'history of making', rather than embodied design values for user interaction.

Now we can design specific 'cues and responses' which are more closely related to our human interaction at that moment, rather than design values that are centred around the object's construction. There will simply be various states of interaction – such as active or passive, collaborative or autonomous, and so on, where the character and resemblance of objects and the surrounding context depends on the type of human interaction. If we are concerned with physical elements and a physical space where we are designing for adaptive changes which happen frequently, then materials and dimensions used for designing and creating these environments need to maintain a simple geometric framework or 'design system' which can then contain interactive zones (functions and media) which may be highly complex. Such was the design exploration from the 'Light Story' project, by Guus Baggermans,[3], an Industrial Design Master Student at Eindhoven University (TU/e). He developed the product concept "Newsflash".

This project topic was about how people review news stories in the paper and other media. Since these stories are publicized 24/7, they are much more available to read in your free time, (rather than necessarily on the way to work or when the newspapers are available). Also, because this information is updated on worldwide databases (internet) with different interpretations appearing in many different papers across many continents, then comparisons between different opinions and political interpretation are easy to see. The project studied how light itself can become more physically tangible and how it can be influenced by the visual attraction and gestural movement when people are browsing or reading the newspaper stories. Projected light is deliberately chosen to deliver the image to the reading pane because it simulates the experience of a more typical reading situation. The light and dark parts of the image are reflected from the surface of the reading pane rather than being electronically emitted from a PDA type screen based product. The challenge was to form a more sensitive balance between the visual attraction and hand movement, to guide how the text flows across the 'reading plane'. In this way, the turning page action is replaced with a connected visual and gestural action.

Figure 2. Newsflash project by Guus Baggermans

The physical product was comprised of a book system, which opened to provide a two-page surface, with a laser projector positioned as a 'reading light' to project text based images onto the book surfaces. Incorporated within these surfaces, sensors were embedded and tuned to recognize proximal hand movements. The projector resourced the text from the internet, based on the direct interaction movements of the reader, which are sensed and transmitted to the projector light by Bluetooth connectivity. Holographic projector technology with infinite focus is used in order to maintain a sharp image across variable contoured surfaces of the book.

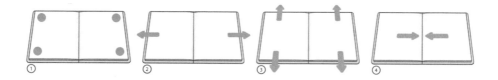

Figure 3. These illustrations show the four stages of interaction. (1) Four headlines are displayed and the reader can move his hand over the desired topic to select a more detailed story. Then within the selected category, two new stories appear, resourced from the web search. (2) By moving the hand from the centre of the page outwards to the edge, then this story is pushed off the edge of the page. (3) If the hands are moved either upwards or downwards, then this action discards the story and replaces it with another story in the same topic. (4) Finally, if two hands are brought towards the centre of the book, then this signifies closing and returns the page view to (1) the four headlines again.

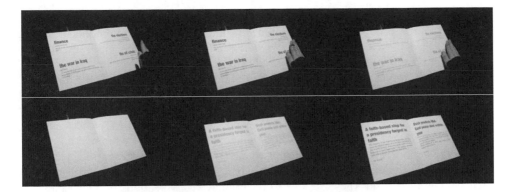

Figure 4. Four headlines are displayed and the reader can move his hand over the desired topic to select a more detailed story. Then within the selected category, two new stories appear, resourced from the web search.

Figure 5. Rather than considering the pure efficiency of the technology, this project links the human movement and feeling to the searching and reviewing gestures. The light projection provides the atmospheric tangibility with all the shadows and other influences of ambient light that contribute to the reading moment. The user's movement shapes the portrayal of stories. It only happens at human speed, however fast or slow that might be. Sample users were invited to inspect and play with the working prototype to provide some early qualitative feedback on the interactive design, readability, and browsing experience.

More tangible presence and proximity

With many interactive experiences such as those found in modern communication technologies, the form of interaction greatly determines the kind of experience a person feels. With simple voice telecommunications there were clear differences in the social protocols between business conversations and more casual 'gossip'. Business calls are generally functional in nature and once the questions have been answered, then the call ends. With more sociable conversations the objectives are different. It is not so important what the conversation is about, but pleasure is gained from simply talking to someone you know. Vodaphone identified in their consumer research that the network usage for these 'social' conversations was much higher, for each person, than the time spent on more direct functional calls. This research also indicates user preferences of difference technology products (wired versus wireless) because of the perceived reliability of the product makes a difference to the consistency and emotional feeling communicated between people. *(It is not a pleasant experience to be exchanging intimate comments in areas with intermittent bandwidth)*

Now with increased use of posted (email) and real time messaging, the 'presence' of the person you are communicating with becomes more abstract. It is more difficult to imagine where your friend is answering from, or what their situation is, are they at work or home, etc., exemplified by the telephone table interaction project entitled, 'ratphone' from Ab Rogers [4]. There are things that can be deduced in real time voice conversations but are somewhat disguised and missing from messaging and email services, more contextual information is missing. Also common in longer voice calls is that people multi-task. They are able to have longer conversations provided they can continue with other tasks in their daily routine, but this is a problem with communications services that require keyboard input. All of these issues steer towards questions about communicating 'context' and 'presence' between callers as an important factor that supports the interaction experience. (remote sociable interaction)

These notions are further supported by David Frohlich [5], which provides a survey that contrasts domestic calls with workplace conversations, and identifies different aspects and recommendations for further research in this field.

Such was the design exploration from the 'Follow me phone' project, by Joris Zaalberg, [6], an Industrial Design Master Student at Eindhoven University (TU/e). This project explores how light tangible interaction can replace forms of more physical manipulation of hand held phone products. By including a more multi-sensorial approach in the design process for social interaction, we are able to provide considerable freedom and preference in how people enjoy more continuous conversations. He developed product concepts for a multi-node domestic phone system that referenced the speaker's proximity within the immediate physical context and communicated that in real time to the respondent. Further research explores how we understand social voice conversations, how we perceive different forms of space, intimate space, personal space, social space and how that influences our notion of 'presence', between callers. Another important aspect of this project was changing the time dimension. Zaalberg observed that when people talk to each other in everyday situations, they do not start and stop conversations in a formal way. Rather they 'drift' in and out of a continuous sequence of conversations, where others join and leave at different times, but the main conversation continues. Conversely, normal telephone conversations have well established protocols of 'opening the call' and 'closure', which interrupt the general flow of any longer social interaction.

Subsequently the concept emerged as an 'open' conversation space (on 24/7), which determined the different aspects of human proximity and presence, with light tangible interaction embodied within the distributed nodal system. This meant that users can drift from room to room and simply adjust their interaction according to proximity to the speaking node. This distance and movement is made tangible through the colour, intensity and size, of light rings that surround the voice node. This is seen by the remote caller to register their presence and availability to talk. Obviously this can support multiple users where many people can freely join and leave the conversation, without interruption, and each can see the presence and proximity of other callers.

The technology is based on a network of a few nodes positioned in a domestic setting (perhaps one per room), and using a simplified version of short range radio frequency that senses the variance in received signal strength, thus determining the distance (proximity) between slave and master devices. This had the technical sensitivity at low range (close distance) and the advantage of relatively low power consumption for this kind of computing process.

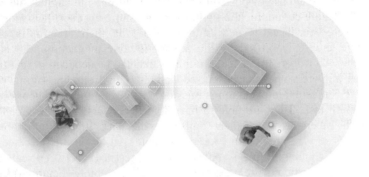

Figure 6. Distributed network of phones in domestic environment

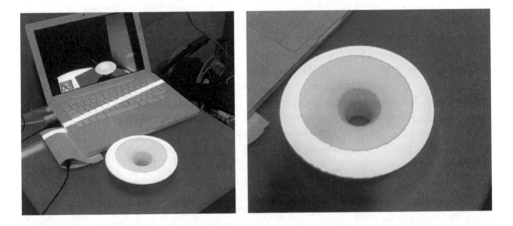

Figure 7. These pictures show a prototype set up where in the background you see one phone is in a remote environment being recorded on video and displayed on the computer screen. In the foreground is a similar phone connected directly. As people move closer or further away from the phones their proximity is registered and changes the visual response from the phone system nodes.

Figure 8. These four simulated images show how the visual indications (colour differences) can change according to the user proximity at both places.

Figure 9. The experiments

Experiments were conducted to test a variety of aspects of this prototype where users followed a scripted conversation. Whilst this research is not completed, we can draw some provisional; conclusions from the observations taken during the experiments. The original research question was concerned with: does an 'always on/visual proximity cues' phone system facilitate social interaction over distance'? Early findings showed: Always on audio looks like a very promising tool for social interaction over distance. People who talk a lot benefit from the voice and visual light interaction of this system, whereas quiet people tended to use the visual presence indication more frequently. The tests also indicate that the users find it easy to experience the system in their peripheral awareness and only address it when they wish to.

Light Tangible Interaction - In Space.

Designing for spatial interaction requires a more 'immersive' approach to the design process. This has been explored in many different ways already. . . design in context, designing movement, senses design. Spaces don't change to such a great extent. However the interventions of light, sound, movement and other media can radically change the 'feeling' and 'awareness' of the space around us and change the way we perform and move within a space. We are interested to explore these more adaptive elements that make the spaces more tangible and intuitive. These can be very direct and functional objects moving, or more ambient media that is more seductive and gradually changing. Our perceptual awareness and interactions within a space change according to the viewing position and depending on the type of ambient information provided. So, to what extent do your senses pick up the contextual media and how does this influence your interaction within the space? There are many meanings hidden in the background of the space and lighting of our environment. How is the spatial information delivered and presented? How can it be created and performed within the spaces we occupy, how can it intervene and change space. This is a more phenomenological approach to designing that appreciates conscious experiences and sensations that are immediate and peculiar to each person and place. Maurice Merleau-Ponty [7].

With recent intelligent technologies and various types of sensing tools we can develop 'adaptive spaces' which can do several things. They can sense the presence and movement of people and objects and change some elements to be more tuned to our perceptions. Or they can work the other way round and reverse and augment what we currently perceive as being 'normal' in our everyday environment. This can subvert our relational senses as a form of surreal and disorientating effect. This spectrum is a kind of dimension of adaptation, where the outcome of the created effects are directly relative to the senses of the individual person or object that is experiencing the change. There are many possible aspects and interpretations.

These surreal and imaginary scenarios may be quite theatrical. The tuning of contextual information can enhance the quality of experience, where ambient signals and reflections heighten or reduce awareness. The interconnection of different visual fields relative to each other and the observer, can propose a more directional 'teasing and seducing' approach, thus producing a more personable and persuasive context . Overbeeke, C.J., Wensveen, S.A.G. (2003) [8]. To explore this further, we conducted a short workshop for the ID Master students in the Faculty of Industrial Design, Eindhoven University. We also made comparisons to other design research work from Mathew Emmett [9] and Peter Dalsgaard [10].

Taking these explorations a step further, within such adaptations of light, sound or other media is the idea that they serve as 'monitors' of our perception (awareness signals) These effects influence our feelings creating attraction towards or distraction away from the source. In this way it helps us to measure these dimensions as relative values with our immediate environment in physical terms of distance, proximity, temperature, resonance, etc. So our senses 'monitor' our perception of effects around us. We watch how different media are rendered and presented and feel how this affects our emotional state. In this way we can estimate these proximal dimensions as a more intuitive reference. So instinctively, we are attracted towards sources of illumination, and brightness that allow things to reflect and be perceived in greater detail.

An example of this from the workshop is a design proposal for waiting areas within 'sHertogenbosch Railway station, created by Annegien Bruins Slot, [11]. Seasonal changes mean that some areas of the station are well lit during the summer months, whereas during the colder seasons they remain dark and rather uninviting. During rush hour there are sufficient people to provide a safe atmosphere, however in the times between or late in the evening, people hurry by, avoiding personal contact and are often frightened by the prospect of standing alone. Simple 'hotspots' of light were suggested, automatically activated by individual's presence on the platform, which provides a warm cocoon of light, appearing from above and below, to surround and protect the waiting person.

Figure 10. 'Railway Station Hotspots' by day and by night.

At a more precise level, objects with high contrast and high reflectance such as jewelry and precious metals, high contrast screen displays, black/white text, etc., all induce high levels of attraction. These things are very clearly seen and accurately perceived, where the media levels describe the physical attributes and boundaries of objects and contextual effects very clearly. On the other hand, when experiencing situations of low media sensitivity, our perception is blurred and diffused. There is nothing to sense and measure from. In this situation designed interventions for interaction can be introduced to heighten our perceptual focus and ability to measure our relative position. Arguably, within these examples there are known environments where the physical dimensions are evident and realized through frequent visits. In terms of how our awareness alerts our actions relative to our emotional feelings, this known physical information has a fairly low level of importance compared to more direct intervention of user specific media and light which has a much higher emotional effect and magnitude.

How tangible light experiences can contribute to the pre-attentive awareness of subsequent interactions.

Within the recent film 'Minority Report', Spielberg [12], the 'Pre-cognitives' were three characters portrayed as special people who could anticipate and see into the future. They were employed by the national crime agency in order to see and intercept crimes before they were committed. It isn't quite as simple as that but this is an aspiration that we all imagine would be interesting to happen. The term precognition from the Latin definition of 'prior cognitio' refers to a situation of 'getting to know' where there is a form of extra sensory perception that is required to perceive information about things before they are about to happen. This effect is rather paranormal, clairvoyant, and scientifically difficult to argue.

However, our explorations and experiments that involve 'tangible light' are about real time events that are a prelude to human interaction with objects and situations. It refers to the earlier part of the human interactive sequence that is often assumed or ignored. Early perceptions are formed about the objects that are seen, which contribute to the expectations and actions we subsequently perform. These early perceptions 'before the interaction' are quite clearly evident and can be observed in everyday scenarios. This phenomenon is about the quality and type of subsequent interaction. It is an information collecting and selection process for the preparation of the action. These early perceptions we coin 'pre-interactive'. Importantly, some are quite direct and intuitive, elicited during the performance of action. But there are also things observed that are relative or can be associated to other situations. The latter are concerned with more abstract perceptions like visual language, semantics, and other associative concepts. I have tried to distinguish the differences:

• Pre-Interaction is everything that immediately precedes a human interaction with other objects or media, where the purpose and values of the interaction are introduced, indicated by the pre-interactive state of the observer.

• Semantics is a definition of meaning that is achieved through the deliberate use of icons, symbols, or other indices that is relative to the observer in that particular situation. Some would argue that everything we create has some semiotic dimension or effect, simply through the process of being created or built. It is away of relating other known experiences and forms within the newly designed object (or interaction) that makes it more understandable. It conveys the meaning in several ways simultaneously. More abstract semantics can form a 'visual language' of particular objects and spaces.

• Gibson's 'affordance' of an object is a phenomenon that pre-interaction includes. In the sense that yes, affordances are visual signals that indicate the subsequent potential action and information available (and user orientation). Pre-interaction however, is a more deliberately designed experience, rather than an ecological definition, made up from both direct perception and more abstract observations.

So how do things become 'pre-interactive' Where more contextual information can be sensitive to human presence, movements, sounds, then this provides information which enable 'action possibilities' that determine and 'tune' the experience. Again, it is a sensitizing process where the more attractive the interaction the closer the sensitivity can be. With this in mind, further hypothetical project studies are evolving that review the material 'person to product' relationships and propose more layered and abstracted ways interact with material and projected media. The next paragraph introduces future projects that explore this research topic further.

Tangible light to communicate remote context

Many different types of media available today are able to support social communications in many different ways, particularly remotely. The direct, voice to voice conversation as it has evolved only provides a limited 'experience' value in terms of appreciating the wider emotional senses and feelings of users communicating with each other. The time spent in social communication has become more abstract. Many different services are now available that provide posted media as a background presence to support relationships – email, msn, facebook, etc. More economic travel services have led to need to support long distance relationships, particularly within a business environment. Communicating contextual information and media is seen as a key element of the communication of more social and emotional feelings, within everyday environments.

The 'Context Communicator Prototype' spatial design system is a hypothetical concept to explore these theories. The objective is to provide the 'point of view' of a remote person to another, transmitting different types of recorded media in real time. The important factor here is the positioning and selection of the communicated media and presentation to the receiver. These aspects can illustrate the actions, senses and feelings of one person to another, as a direct contextual link. You see what they see, and hear what they hear. This is seen as directly opposite to the picture postcard, or the holiday video that has a deliberately manufactured effect. This intends to capture more random but real experiences without edition, thus portraying the true experiences from one to another person. This will be much more interesting than a normal voice calls on current telephones or mobiles. It communicates your physical point of view (your seeing position and perspective) and articulates this image within the receiver's environment. It will communicate what the other person is looking at, both objects and contextual information in answer to the question – 'where are you?' and 'what does it feel like?' Deliberately only images and sounds sent at predetermined intervals (or indeed triggered by the caller) could provide rich information about the immediate surroundings and events to a distant friend. There can be many different abstractions that provide different interaction possibilities, from direct and literal information (media) in real time to adaptive and abstract media, with time dependencies. The spatial interpretation also has many variable parameters, which can be explored according to how the user interaction intervenes as a component of the communication. Because of the difficulty in seeing the complete 360 degree context at the same time, the captured data can only provide cues and suggestions of context and movement. This has "suggestive" and impressionistic" advantages. As individual elements they are quite random and abstract, but when reviewed collectively, these aspects can illustrate the actions, senses and feelings of one person to another, as a direct contextual link. Below is an example of context sample images to provide the feelings and impressions of being in the same location. The position as a 'viewpoint' is communicated through the height, position, movement, and angle of view. – Walking by the waterfall in the sun.

Figure 11. Context views, walking by the waterfall in the sun.

We depend on the surrounding context as a definition of the physical and material dimensions, according to how well or how occluded the immediate surroundings are. This is how we read our surroundings and explore location specific information. The surface geometry and materials also change how images may reflect the sense of location and experience and to what extent the visual detail can be perceived on the same plane or separate surfaces.

The physical aspect is also important. Ecologically we exist within a mixture of direct and ambient light, both daylight and artificial light behaves as a multiple source depending on the environment around us. In this respect screen displays on many technology products are too literal. They have a consistent back-light which is not particularly context sensitive and trying to create the right ambient lighting without glare or reflection is difficult for many products. However, projected images on the other hand, behave in a similar way to other lighting systems (both direct and ambient), where they are able to contribute to the general atmosphere – affording the observer visual dimensions from the physical and material surroundings. Smaller LED and laser technologies enable a much higher colour resolution, video image display, with a long focal range. Surfaces and object planes at different distances and angles can always maintain a clear image definition. The visual images are abstracted from the normal technology format in order to portray a more direct 'feeling' of the environment they are being retrieved. The impression of the remote location becomes more immediate and purposeful and thus a more direct and realistic 'shared experience'.

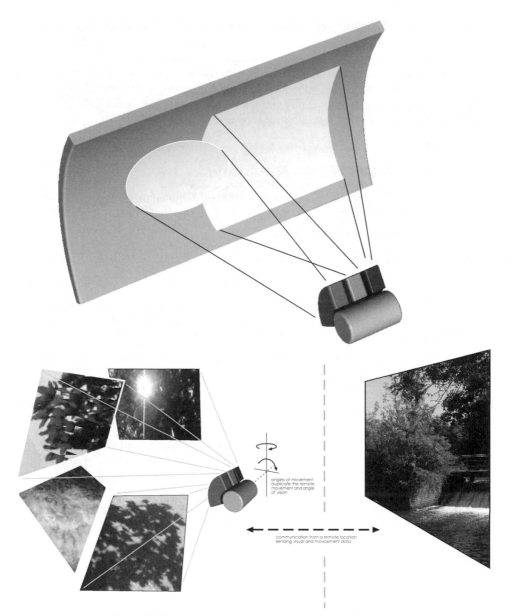

Figure 12. Basic projection system connected to remote location

To summarize, we have discussed the way surface definition and lighting reflection can influence our tangible perception and interaction with objects and environments around us. There are examples of projects that show cues and responses that are informed through tangible light. There are also examples of how these design concepts can integrate theories of presence and proximity as tangible light for communication. Then aspects of spatial context are discussed to explore feelings and awareness within larger scale locations and how lighting surfaces and effects provide a relative and tangible visual field. Finally, I note three supporting observations which contribute to these thoughts and ideas as; 'pre-interaction', 'semantics', and Gibson's [2] 'affordances' before concluding with a hypothetical concept of the 'context communicator' as a next step for this study.   I believe that the research and development of these theories and concepts will provide a platform to explore many different aspects of how media supports communication of feelings and actions more directly and sensitively. Subsequently, indicating how this can remotely support the social and emotional aspects of relationships over distance.

Acknowledgement:

I would like to thank all the master students who have included their work in this paper, Guus Baggermans, Joris Zaalberg, Annegeien Bruins Slot. I would also thank my colleagues within DQI for their support and confidence with my research projects.

References:

[1]   Stephan Wensveen, "A Tangibility approach to Affective Interaction," PhD thesis, Febodruk bv, 2005.
[2]   Gibson,JJ. Ecological Approach to Visual Perception.(1979) Houghton Mifflin. Boston.
[3]   Guus Baggermans, "Light Story" M11 Design Project, Technical University of Eindhoven, January 2008
[4]   Ab Rogers Design, "Rat Table Project" BOB, 2004   'Micro Office Monster RAT'
[5]   David Frohlich, Kathy Chilton, Paul Drew, Remote Homeplace Communication: What is it Like and How Might We Support It? Interaction Technology Department , HP Laboratories Bristol, July 1997.
[6]   Joris Zaalberg, "The Use of Social Space in Telecommunication" M1.2 Research Project, Technical University of Eindhoven, January 2008
[7]   Maurice Merleau-Ponty, Phenomenology of Perception (1945),
[8]   Overbeeke, C.J., Wensveen, S.A.G. (2003). From perception to experience, from affordances to irresistibles. In Jodi Forlizzi (Ed.), Proceedings of the DPPI. (pp. 92-97). Pittsburgh, PA, USA: ACM Press
[9]   Mathew Emmet, Plymouth University, http://www.mathewemmett.com
[10] Peter Dalsgaard, University of Aarhus. http://www.cavi.dk/projects/experienceapplications.php
[11] Annegeien Bruins Slot, "'Railway Station Hotspots", concept, from Master Module: Intervention and Interaction, Technical University of Eindhoven, November 2007.
[12] Steven Spielberg, "Minority Report" written by Philip Dick, Scott Frank, produced by Walter F. Parkes, Jan de Bont, Gary Goldman, (20th Century Fox), June 2002.

Ambient Intelligence Perspectives
P. Mikulecký et al. (Eds.)
IOS Press, 2009
doi:10.3233/978-1-58603-946-2-42

Knowledge Practices Laboratory

František BABIČ[a], Ján PARALIČ[a], Michal RAČEK[b] and Jozef WAGNER[a]

[a] Centre for Information Technologies, Technical University of Košice, Slovakia
[b] PÖYRY Forest Industry Oy, Finland

frantisek.babic@tuke.sk

Abstract. This paper presents some aspects of the IST project called Knowledge Practices Laboratory (KP-Lab), which aims at facilitating innovative practices of working with knowledge (knowledge practices) in education and workplaces. The project is based on the idea of trialogical learning that refers to the process where learners are collaboratively developing shared objects of activity (such as conceptual artifacts, practices, products) in systematic fashion. It is important do develop relevant flexible tools and functionalities for supporting this new innovative approach like semantic middleware with collaborative working or learning environment, etc.

Keywords: trialogical learning, shared objects of activities, virtual learning environment, ontology, web services.

Introduction

KP-Lab[1] is an ambitious project that focuses on developing a theory, appropriate knowledge practices and collaborative learning system aimed at facilitating innovative practices of sharing, creating and working with knowledge in education and workplaces.

Theoretical foundation of this project is trialogical learning approach. This approach has emerged from two others that have been adopted before in broader sense, i.e. monological and dialogical learning [3]. There are some other pedagogical approaches which are quite near the trialogical approach to learning, e.g. knowledge building, project-based learning, learning by design or progressive inquiry learning. Trialogical approach can be used to give a new focus on these existing pedagogical approaches. It is not tied to any of them but aims at given methods and features for supporting aspects of collaborative knowledge creation.

Technological goal of this project is represented by the KP-Lab System that consists of KP-Lab platform and the end-user virtual learning environment (KP-environment) with several integrated tools for collaborative knowledge practices (working with knowledge objects, managing knowledge processes, multimedia annotation, meeting support, visual modeling, etc.).

---

[1] www.kp-lab.org

1. Trialogical learning

Trialogical learning [3] refers to the process where learners are collaboratively developing shared objects of activity (such as conceptual artefacts, practices, or products) in a systematic fashion. It concentrates on the interaction through these common objects (or artefacts) of activity (see Figure 1), not just among people (as it is in dialogical learning) or within one's mind (as it is in monological learning).

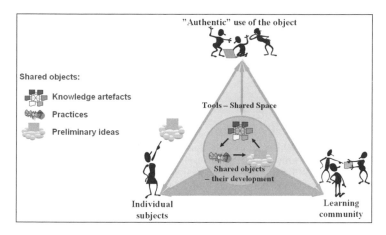

Figure 1. How individuals and a community develop shared "authentic" objects [6]

Trialogical learning means that individuals (or groups of people) are developing some shared objects of activity within some social or cultural settings. It is a combination of (or about transcending) a purely individualistic approach and a purely social approach on learning.

As a demonstrative example of trialogical activities can be mentioned the approach how the Wikipedia is being collaboratively developed. It is a long-term effort of developing something for communal use on the basis of individual enthusiasm and initiative. Individuals are important but only when orchestrated on a joint work. The interactions happen through shared objects (individual Wikipedia articles) following other people's efforts.

Theoretical as well as practical aspects of this innovative learning approach have origin in Finland, at the University of Helsinki[2] (UH). This innovation has been distributed from UH now in the (not only) European educational community, e.g. within the Knowledge Practices Laboratory (KP-Lab) project which is coordinated by them.

2. KP-Lab project

KP-Lab aims at developing theories, tools, and practical models that enhance deliberate advancement and creation of knowledge as well as transformation of knowledge practices. The main aim of this process is to provide a platform for creation of a shared

---

[2] http://www.helsinki.fi/behav/english/

understanding of current knowledge practices and to envision, design and evaluate novel applications and methods and thereby contribute to the facilitation of innovative knowledge practices.

The first three years of this 5 years long integrated EU funded project are devoted to the research and implementation of tools, practices and theories. Existing and/or newly developed tools are being designed and tested against user requirements in real cases within various pilot cases (in e.g. Israel, Netherlands, Finland, or Hungary). The last two years will be devoted mainly to finish longitudinal experiments, dissemination activities and exploitation planning.

The multinational consortium integrates expertise from various domains, including pedagogy, psychology and engineering as well as end-users and key representatives from the corporate/business sector to provide authentic environments for research and piloting. The project involves 22 partners from 14 countries providing a suitable variety of universities, companies, work places and other prospective end-users.

KP-Lab technology builds on emerging technologies, such as semantic web and web2.0, web services and SOA, real-time multimedia communication, ubiquitous access using wireless and mobile devices, and interorganisational computing. Essential part of the KP-Lab System is also a non-technological tool called Change Laboratory.

3. KP-Lab System

KP-Lab System has been designed and developed with the aim to effectively support the innovative knowledge practices based on ideas and principles of trialogical learning, accompanying also knowledge practices that also need to be changed when using this new approach to learning, supported by new type of tools provided within the KP-Lab project. Architecture of the KP-Lab System is based on the platform and user environment.

3.1 KP-Lab platform

The KP-Lab platform (see Figure 2) is based on interoperable and integrated tools and on a support of semantic web models and standards. It is composed of several groups of services and libraries, e.g.:

- Semantic Knowledge Middleware Services (**SWKM Services** in Figure 2), providing storage and management of the metadata created by the KP-Lab tools. This metadata are stored into RDFSuite that is used as the knowledge repository [1]. RDFSuite[3] is being developed at FORTH -ICS in Greece and comprises the Validating RDF Parser (VRP), the Schema-Specific Data Base (RSSDB) and interpreters for the RDF Query Language (RQL) and RDF Update Language (RUL).
- Content Management Services (**Repository Services** in Figure 2) are dedicated to creation and management of regular content (documents in various format) used in knowledge artefacts (content described by metadata), either towards KP-Lab's own content repositories or external content repositories. KP-Lab content repositories are implemented through Jackrabbit

---

[3] http://139.91.183.30:9090/RDF/

for the compatibility with the JSR-170 standard. Access to them is provided by G2CR (Gateways to content repositories) that have been implemented in cooperation with Silogic[4] (now AKKA) and TUK[5].

- The Multimedia Services (**MM Services** in Figure 2), oriented towards the manipulation and management of dynamic content such as streamed material for audio and video function to be supplied to the KP-Lab tools.
- **Technical services** cover those middleware support services, dedicated to the authorization and identity management, the user management, routing etc.

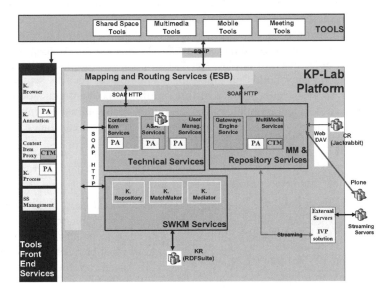

Figure 2. Logical view of the KP-Lab architecture [4]

The KP-Lab platform is a set of services that are based on heterogeneous technologies, which provide interoperability that is neither language nor platform dependent. For these reasons, the KP-Lab platform is based on web services. This set of services will be addressed by the KP-Lab Service Bus, implementation[6] of Enterprise Service Bus that is a centralized, scalable, fault-tolerant, service-messaging framework and provides necessary functionalities as service registration, routing, process orchestration, service choreography security, transaction management.

3.2 KP-Lab ontology architecture

One of the KP-Lab platform important components is the "common language" for the communications and functionalities around knowledge artefacts in the KP-Lab System. The software model relies on the three-layered ontology architecture (see Figure 3) that consists of:

---

[4] http://www.kp-lab.org/partners/silogic
[5] http://web.tuke.sk/fei-cit/index-a.html
[6] http://servicemix.apache.org/home.html

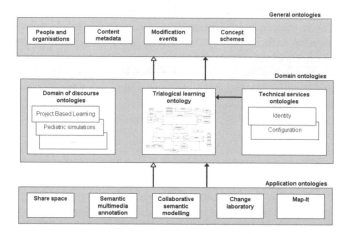

Figure 3. KP-Lab ontology architecture [5]

- **Trialogical learning ontology** (TLO) defines core concepts and principles of trialogical learning. This ontology is shared by all applications and tools in KP-Lab System, providing the common semantics needed for the data interoperability.
- **Domain of discourse ontologies** that model the concepts and their relations in project priority applications domains, e.g. project-based learning ontology that describes educational practices in Finnish and Dutch pilot courses. This ontology provides framework to think in meta-terms about performed processes, to visualize different relationships between shared objects, to group various types of these objects into several categories, etc.
- **Technical ontologies** that model technical concepts related to the services provided by the KP-Lab platform, integration of tools, etc.
- **Application ontologies** specialize and integrate the above mentioned ontologies based on the requirements of the given application or tool.

3.3 KP-environment

All the user actions and activities with various shared objects (knowledge artefacts) are mediated by the KP-environment. This virtual environment offers various end-user applications, which are built on conceptual ideas underlying the proposed learning approach (TL), such as collaboration, shared objects, boundary crossing, etc.

Examples of such end-user applications are Shared space, Semantic multimedia annotation tool, Collaborative semantic modeling, Change Laboratory or Discussion-support tool - Map-It. It can be said that user environment consists of a set of tools that enable collaborative knowledge practices around shared knowledge artefacts.

3.3.1 Shared Space

Shared Space application (see Figure 4) is a learning system aimed at facilitating innovative practices of sharing, creating and working with knowledge in education and workplaces based on trialogical learning theory. It supports users' collaboration according to different working practices and allows viewing of shared knowledge in flexible manner.

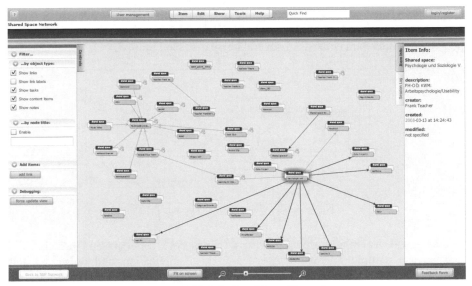

Figure 4. KP-Lab Shared Space Network

Current release of the Shared Space provides several necessary and interesting functionalities, as:

- working with the knowledge artefacts; e.g. for creating, editing, storing, sharing, commenting, discussing, annotating semantically using existing vocabularies and/or using users' own tags;
- managing the knowledge processes; e.g. creating, changing and executing process models composed from several elements that are described with metadata and relations between them;
- managing the shared space itself; e.g. configuring the tools available
- displaying a status information about each logged user, status information about actual working environment, present and performed user action, etc;
- context-based chat;
- visualization of "knowledge objects" through various views
- possibility to use some integrated tools as meeting tool called Map-It, SMAT (Semantic multimedia annotation tool) or Change Laboratory (CL).

3.3.2 Change Laboratory Application

The Change Laboratory (CL) application is a tool that provides functionalities and shared working environment to realize knowledge (working or learning) practices based on an intervention method called DWR (Developmental Work Research [2]). This method is based on basic theoretical and methodological ideas that are presented by trialogical learning. DWR is a reflective method. This reflectivity is actualized by forming a "mirror" in front of the participants by presenting concrete material about their work. The "mirror" is used by the participants for analyzing and evaluating their way of working. Simultaneously an assumption of the developmental phases and contradictions of the work is formed by a historical analysis of the work.

One of the CL main parts is Virtual Whiteboard (VW) that is developed to facilitate the visual construction of new models and solutions in DWR process with some extended features such as flexible editing and linking of created materials (shared objects). CL whiteboard consists of several key parts (see Figure 5):

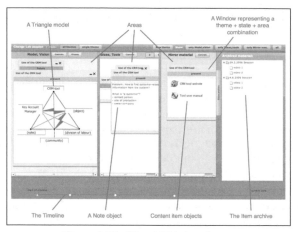

Figure 5. The Virtual Whiteboard

- Three main **Areas** of VW are: *Model & Vision*, *Ideas & Tools* and *Mirror material*. These are used to classify data items based on their use in the context of a specific session. VW represents state of a single CL session within CL process. CL process is mainly composed of sessions. All sessions contain three areas as mentioned before and may contain any number of themes. Themes are objects of discourse (or groups thereof) that are being discussed in the session. All themes have three **states**: *past*, *present* and *future*.
- A **Window** is a representation of a specific state of a specific theme. All created themes have windows for each of its three states in each of the three areas, thus having total of nine windows. When a data item is set as belonging to a specific theme/state/area combination, it is visualized inside the corresponding window.
- The **Timeline** is a visualization of all the sessions in the process that the currently viewed session belongs to. It can be used to navigate between different sessions.
- The **Item Archive** contains all material that is available in a list of tree format. This list can be used to drag and drop items into the VW and it is only visible to members with sufficient access rights to modify the current VW – CL session. With its tight integration to the KP-Lab environment CL Application not only works with objects that are specific only to the CL but facilitates objects which are common to other tools as well (Shared Space, SMAT, Map-It, etc.):
- A **Note** object represents simple text notes that can be of any length.
- The **Content Item** objects are basic concepts of a piece of material with arbitrary content in the Shared Space.

- **Triangle Model** describes objects that represent performed activities during session and consists of following components: *Instruments* (in Figure 5 it is concrete CRM-tool), *Object*, *Subject* (in Figure 5 it is Key Account Manager), *Rules*, *Community* and *Division of labor*.
- **Four Field Model** enables to create four *boundaries* upon objects/themes of disclosure and by enriching them with *entries* it is easy to represent state in which current object is in.

4. Conclusion

One of the main results of the KP-Lab project will be integrated system that provides collaborative working or learning environment with flexible tools for supporting collaborative knowledge creation in systematic fashion, like Shared Space and CL, which have been presented in this paper.

Acknowledgment

The work presented in this paper was supported by: European Commission DG INFSO under the IST program, contract No. 27490; the Slovak Research and Development Agency under the contract No. APVV-0391-06 and the Slovak Grant Agency of Ministry of Education and Academy of Science of the Slovak Republic under grant No. 1/4074/07 and 1/3135/06.

The KP-Lab Integrated Project is sponsored under the 6th EU Framework Programme for Research and Development. The authors are solely responsible for the content of this article. It does not represent the opinion of the KP-Lab consortium or the European Community, and the European Community is not responsible for any use that might be made of data appearing therein.

References

[1] Alexaki, V., Christophides, G., Karvounarakis, D., Plexousakis, K., Tolle. The ICS-FORTH RDFSuite: Managing Voluminous RDF Description Bases, In Proc. of the 2nd International Workshop on the Semantic Web (SemWeb'01), in conjunction with Tenth International World Wide Web Conference (WWW10). Hongkong, (2001) 1-13

[2] Engeström, Y., Virkkunen, J., Helle, M., Pihlaja, J., Poikela, R. The Change laboratory as a tool for transforming work. Lifelong Learning in Europe, 1(2), 10-17, 1996.

[3] Hakkarainen, K., Paavola, S. From monological and dialogical to trialogical approaches to learning. A paper at an international workshop "Guided Construction of Knowledge in Classrooms", February 5-8, 2007, Hebrew University, Jerusalem, 2007.

[4] Ionescu, M., et. al. KP-Lab Platform Architecture Dosier. KP-Lab public deliverable D4.2.3. November, 2007.

[5] Markkanen, H., Holi, M. Ontology-driven knowledge management and interoperability in trialogical learning applications. Article in the KP-Lab book, 2008.

[6] Paavola, S., Lipponen, L., Hakkarainen, K. Models of Innovative Knowledge Communities and Three Metaphors of Learning. Review of Educational Research 74(4), 557-576, 2004.

Ambient Intelligence Perspectives
P. Mikulecký et al. (Eds.)
IOS Press, 2009
doi:10.3233/978-1-58603-946-2-50

Emulation of an Active Tag Location Tracking System

Razvan BEURAN [a,b], Junya NAKATA [a,b], Takashi OKADA [b,a], Tetsuya KAWAKAMI [c],
Ken-ichi CHINEN [b,a], Yasuo TAN [b,a], Yoichi SHINODA [b,a]

[a] *National Institute of Information and Communications Technology, Japan*
[b] *Japan Advanced Institute of Science and Technology, Japan*
[c] *Matsushita Electric Industrial Co., Ltd., Japan*
razvan@nict.go.jp

Abstract. In this paper we present the emulation of a location tracking system that uses active tags to identify the position of the active tag wearer. Using emulation we were able to carry out live experiments with such active tag applications. Emulation is done using QOMET, a wireless communication emulator, and the active tag processor emulator. Experiments are performed using the experiment-support software RUNE. Emulation is used during the development of the pedestrian localization system so as to perform large-scale experiments easily and in a repeatable manner.

Keywords. active tag, location tracking, emulation

Introduction

Active tags are being researched actively in connection with numerous applications. For example, active tags are used in transport and distribution industries, for factory automation or asset tracking. The communication characteristics of active tags allow for a wide range of applications. One of such applications is that of determining the location of moving objects or people. Location tracking of persons is an important issue related to several events such as disaster situations, public surveillance, etc. For instance, during the evacuation of a school following an earthquake, it is important to be able to determine whether evacuation was completed successfully. If persons are in the disaster perimeter, their location should be identified.

We are developing an emulation system for active tags to make it possible to carry out realistic experiments during the development of active tag applications by running the real active tag firmware within a virtual, emulated environment. Real-world experiments with wireless network systems, and active tags in particular, are difficult to organize and perform when the number of nodes involved is larger than a few devices. Problems such a battery life or undesired interferences often influence experimental results. Through emulation much of the uncertainties and irregularities of large real-world experiments are placed under control. In the same time, using the real active tag firmware in experiments enables us to evaluate exactly the same program that will be deployed on the real active tags; this is a significant advantage compared to simulation.

The active tag emulation experiments are done on StarBED, the large-scale network experiment testbed at the Hokuriku Research Center of the National Institute of Information and Communications Technology (NICT), located in Ishikawa, Japan. To use the testbed for active tag emulation we developed several subsystems, and integrated them with the existing infrastructure. The subsystems were developed on the basis of existing tools that are already used on StarBED, namely the wireless network emulator QOMET [1], and the experiment support software RUNE [2].

To the best of our knowledge this may be the first attempt to emulate active tags so as to perform live experiments in realistic conditions. Active tags were so far mainly studied through simulation, such as the work presented in [3]. We created an experimental platform for active tags in which emulation plays an essential role in:

- Recreating the wireless communication conditions between active tags, so that the information exchanges between them are similar to the reality;
- Emulating in real time the active tag processor, so that the same firmware that is developed for the active tag prototype system can be run and tested.

Matsushita Electric Industrial Co., Ltd. is involved in the development of a pedestrian location tracking system that employs active tags. This system makes use of the data communication and processing features of active tags so as to provide to a central pedestrian localization engine the information needed to automatically calculate the trajectory to date and the current position of the active tag wearer. Using the prototype of the pedestrian localization system, real-world experiments were carried out in March 2007, as reported in [4]. The experiment consisted in the orchestrated movement of 16 pedestrians both in indoor and outdoor environments. The results of this experiment are currently being used as a basis for improving the prototype of the pedestrian location tracking system. One of the conclusions was that it is very difficult to organize a real-world experiment for such applications of active tags. The number of people involved, and the accuracy of their movement following the predefined scenario, are only a few of the issues encountered. Moreover, the pedestrian localization application is intended for use with large groups of people. The active tag emulation system plays an essential role at this point, since it makes it possible to continue the experiments in the development phase with ease.

1. Active Tag Emulation

Using emulation to carry out experiments in a repeatable manner and in a wide-range of conditions implies creating a virtual environment in which the movement, the communication, and the behavior of active tags are all reproduced.

1.1. Emulation System Overview

The active tags used for the pedestrian localization system by Matsushita Electric Industrial Co., Ltd. are based on the AYID32305 tags from Ymatic Corporation [5]. These active tags use as processing unit the PIC16F648A microcontroller made by Microchip [6], which has 4096-word flash memory, 256-byte SRAM and 256-byte EEPROM. Its frequency is configured at 4 MHz for this application. The wireless transceiver of the active tag operates at 303.2 MHz, and the data rate is 4800 bps (Manchester encoding), which results in an effective data rate of 2400 bps. According to Ymatic, the active tags have an error-free communication range of 3-5 m, depending on the antenna used.

The active tag communication protocol was custom designed by Matsushita Electric Industrial Co., Ltd. The prototype system uses a very simple protocol based on time-division multiplexing. Each tag will select at random one of the available communication slots, and advertise its identifier and the current time. The random selection may induce reception errors if two tags choose the same slot. Currently the number of available communication slots for advertisement messages is 9. Message exchanges take place at intervals of about 2 seconds. There are additional communication slots that can be used on demand to transmit location tracking records.

An overview of the system that is currently used for active tag emulation experiments and the development of the pedestrian localization prototype is given in **Figure 1**. RUNE (Real-time Ubiquitous Network Emulation environment) [2] is designed to support emulation of large ubiquitous networks, having features such as: emulate the surrounding environment, support real-time concurrent execution of numerous nodes, provide multi-level emulation layers, etc. RUNE Master and RUNE Manager are modules used in all RUNE-based experiments for controlling the experiment globally and locally, respectively. The active tag module was specifically designed and implemented for this application. This module includes:

- Active Tag Communication and *chanel* spaces, used to calculate and manage the communication conditions between active tags;
- Active Tag Control space, which is powered by the active tag processor (PIC) emulator, and runs the active tag firmware in real time to reproduce the active tag behavior.

The experiment itself is performed using standard PCs (running the FreeBSD operating system) that are part of the StarBED testbed. They are labeled as Execution Units in **Figure 1**.

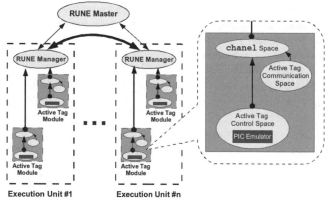

Figure 1. Active tag emulation system overview

1.2. Active Tag Communication Emulation

The active tags employed in the pedestrian localization experiment use wireless communication to exchange information with each other. Therefore we must be able to recreate with sufficient realism the communication between the emulated active tags. This was accomplished by extending the WLAN emulator QOMET [1] to support the wireless transceiver used by active tags. QOMET uses an XML scenario-driven architecture that has two stages. In the first stage, from a real-world scenario representation we create a network quality degradation (ΔQ) description which corresponds to the real-world events (see Figure 2). This is done by modeling the effects at the different layers of the communication protocol, from physical to data link layer. Then we apply in real time the ΔQ description to the traffic communicated during the effective emulation process so as to replicate the user defined scenario.

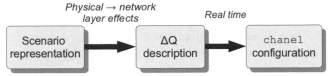

Figure 2. Scenario-driven two-stage emulation

The model used in QOMET to obtain the ΔQ description that corresponds to the active tag communication conditions in a certain user-defined scenario is an aggregation of several models used at the various steps of the conversion needed to recreate that scenario's conditions; more details on these models can be found in [7].

Given that the active tags do not generate IP traffic, as usual PC applications, we decided to implement *chanel* (CHANnel Emulation Library). This module is inserted between the space emulating the tags (Active Tag Control Space in **Figure 1**) and its connection to the other spaces. The main role of *chanel* is to recreate scenario-specific communication conditions based on the ΔQ description (FER probabilities) computed by QOMET. A second function of *chanel* is to make sure the data is communicated to all the systems that would receive it during the corresponding real-world scenario.

1.3. Active Tag Processor Emulation

We emulate the active tag processor so that the active tag firmware can be run in our emulated environment without any modification or recompilation. Processor emulation in our system had to take into account the following aspects that we implemented: (i) instruction execution emulation; (ii) data I/O emulation; (iii) interrupt emulation.

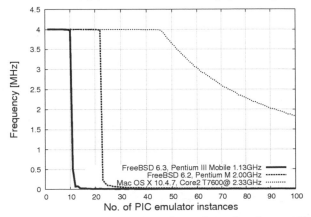

Figure 3. PIC emulator frequency accuracy depending on the number of executed instances

When emulating active tag applications such as ours it is important to introduce cycle-accurate processor emulation. In our case active tags use the time information contained in messages to synchronize with each others autonomously. Incorrect time information may lead to artificial desynchronization problems and potentially communication errors, therefore it must be avoided. In Figure 3 we show how emulation accuracy changes depending on the computing platform used and the number of instances of the PIC emulator that are run in parallel. We remind that the intended execution frequency is 4 MHz. Given a sufficiently powerful platform, good accuracy is obtained for up to about 45 instances running in parallel. Nevertheless, even with the less powerful platforms we still managed to have at least 10 PIC emulator instances running at the intended execution frequency.

2. Real-world Experiment

The real-world experiment was carried out in March 2007 by Matsushita Electric Industrial Co., Ltd. Each experiment participant was equipped with an active tag based pedestrian localization system prototype, as the one shown in Figure 4(a).

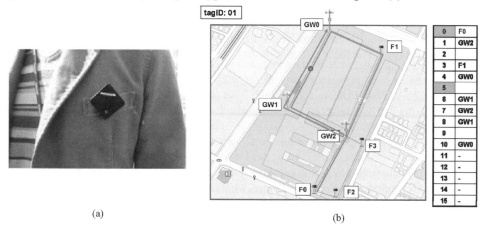

(a)   (b)

Figure 4. Real world experiment: (a) participant wearing an active tag; (b) movement instructions as received by participant #1

2.1. Experiment Description

The 16 participants were each provided with instructions regarding the path they should follow in the 100 x 300 m experiment area. The instructions indicated the experiment topology, as well as the time in minutes when each known location should be reached. An example of instructions, as received by participant #1 is shown in Figure 4(b).

The experiment was scheduled to last 15 minutes, and followed a scenario in which a disaster situation leads to the necessity of area evacuation. After 5 minutes of unrelated walking patterns for each of the individual pedestrians and couples of pedestrians, it was considered that an event took place, such as a fire or earthquake, which required an evacuation procedure. Following this event all pedestrians' instructions were to proceed to an assembly point located in the upper left corner of the area (GW0 in Figure 4(b)). Participants also received a stopwatch, to try to ensure they follow as closely as possible the indicated scenario, and a GPS receiver for an external confirmation of their position.

The real-world experiment also included a number of tags with known position. These tags are divided into two classes: fixed and gateway tags, denoted in Figure 4(b) by F0 to F3, and GW0 to GW2, respectively. Fixed tags cannot communicate information except by using the tag protocol and wireless network. They are placed at 4 known locations, both outdoors and indoors. The role of fixed tags is to communicate with the mobile tags that come in their vicinity and makes it possible to determine the absolute location of those tags. Gateway tags, in addition to tag communication, also allow information to be transferred to the outside world by using the IEEE 802.11j standard. The gateways are placed at 3 known outdoor locations and are connected to each other in an ad-hoc style network. Gateways are also connected to the Internet; the log data they receive from mobile tags is used to determine the trajectories and positions of pedestrians.

2.2. Localization Technique and Discussion

The real-world experiment was successful in the sense that data collected from the active tags could be used to localize the pedestrians in most cases with sufficient accuracy. The tag log information is used to predict the trajectory of tag wearers and track their position. The basic equation used to calculate the position P_x of a pedestrian at moment of time t_x is:

$$P_x = P_i + (P_j - P_i)\frac{t_x - t_i}{t_j - t_i}, \tag{1}$$

where P_i and P_j are the known positions of the pedestrian (from tag logs) at moments of time t_i and t_j, with $t_i \leq t_x \leq t_j$. For more details about the experiment and the pedestrian localization engine one may consult [4] (in Japanese).

While experimenting with the prototype active tag based localization system under various circumstances, a series of problems were identified:

- The wireless communication between the prototype active tags was not always reliable; in addition, battery depletion was relatively fast and caused signal to weaken during and between experiments;
- Orchestrating a real-world experiment using even as few as 16 people is a cumbersome task (to perform the 15 minutes experiment it took actually a few hours of preparation);
- The off-the-shelf GPS receiver used had difficulties in providing a reliable location for small scale movements; in addition, they could not be used inside buildings.

Table 1 below shows a summary of the main differences between position localization using cellular phones with GPS capabilities (that transmit their position via the cellular phone network), and our active tag based technique.

Table 1. Comparison between cellular phone with GPS and active tag based location tracking techniques

Cellular phone w. GPS	Active tag system
Snapshot of position	Track movement continuously
Paging each terminal	Track many tags at a time

Not available in disaster	Potentially more reliable
Outdoors use only	Outdoors/indoors/underground
High power	Low power

3. Emulation Results

The emulation experiment shown below uses exactly the same conditions as the real-world experiment described in Section 2, and was used to validate the emulation system. For simplicity each active tag and the associated *chanel* component were run on one PC. Movement of the nodes in the virtual environment is visualized using an interface based on MOMOSE [8], for which a screen caption is shown in Figure 5(a). We obtained a good agreement between the trajectory of the pedestrian and the positions localized by the system. As it can be seen in Figure 5(b), the emulated trajectory on which pedestrians moved in the virtual environment during the emulation experiment (cf. Figure 4(b)), and the trajectory tracked by the localization engine correspond very well.

Moreover, in our emulation system, communication between mobile nodes and fixed nodes only takes place when the mobile node is in the vicinity of a fixed node, exactly as it would happen in reality due to the short communication range of active tags. This proves that mobile node motion in the virtual space and wireless communication condition recreation (using QOMET and *chanel*), as well as tag execution (using RUNE) are perfectly synchronized and in accordance with our expectations from the real-world experiment. By emulation experiments we were also able to identify some issues in the active tag firmware, for example related to time synchronization.

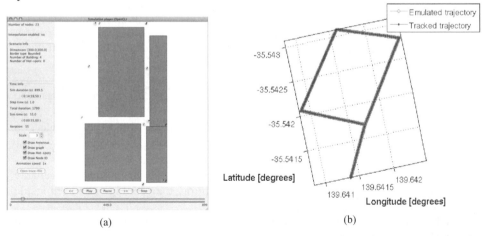

(a)   (b)

Figure 5. Experiment visualization: (a) interface; (b) trajectory of pedestrian #1

4. Conclusions

In this paper we presented an emulation system that we designed and developed for active tag applications. This emulation system is currently employed for the development phase experiments of a pedestrian localization system by Matsushita Electric Industrial Co., Ltd. By using our system it was possible to simplify the development and testing procedures of the localization engine, and identify several firmware implementation issues.

In order to validate the emulation system we carried out tests that reproduced a real-world 16 pedestrian experiment that took place in March 2007 using the prototype of the active tag based pedestrian localization system. The emulation experiment results show the good agreement that exists between the virtual motion patterns of pedestrians, reproduced according to the real-world scenario, and the actual conditions that were recreated in our emulation experiment.

Our future work has several main directions, such as improving the scalability of the system so as to enable experiments of pedestrian groups as large as 1000; improving the realism of the wireless communication emulation by using more accurate 3D models for topology and electromagnetic wave propagation. For large-scale experiments, we intend to combine a behavioral pedestrian motion model with a GIS-based urban area description to create a realistic urban environment.

Acknowledgment

This work was supported in part by the Japan Science and Technology Agency (JST) under a grant of the 2007 3rd round of the Innovating Industry-University Collaboration Seeds project.

References

[1] R. Beuran, L. T. Nguyen, K. T. Latt, J. Nakata, Y. Shinoda, "QOMET: A Versatile WLAN Emulator", IEEE International Conference on Advanced Information Networking and Applications (AINA-07), Niagara Falls, Ontario, Canada, May 21-23, 2007, pp. 348-353.

[2] J. Nakata, T. Miyachi, R. Beuran, K. Chinen, S. Uda, K. Masui, Y. Tan, Y. Shinoda, "StarBED2: Large-scale, Realistic and Real-time Testbed for Ubiquitous Networks", TridentCom 2007, Orlando, Florida, U.S.A., May 21-23, 2007.

[3] A. Janek, Ch. Trummer, Ch. Steger, R. Weiss, J. Preishuber-Pfluegl, M. Pistauer, "Simulation Based Verification of Energy Storage Architectures for Higher Class Tags supported by Energy Harvesting Devices", 10th Euromicro Conference on Digital System Design Architectures, Methods and Tools (DSD 2007), Lubeck, Germany, Aug. 29-31, 2007, pp. 463-462.

[4] Y. Suzuki, T. Kawakami, M. Yokobori, K. Miyamoto, "A Real-Space Network Using Bi-Directional Communication Tags – Pedestrian Localization Technique and Prototype Evaluation", IEICE Forum on Ubiquitous and Sensor Networks, technical report, October 30-31, 2007.

[5] Ymatic, Inc., http://www.ymatic.co.jp.

[6] Microchip Technology, Inc., http://www.microchip.com/.

[7] J. Nakata, R. Beuran, T. Kawakami, K. Chinen, Y. Tan, Y. Shinoda, "Distributed Emulator for a Pedestrian Tracking System Using Active Tags", 2nd International Conference on Mobile Ubiquitous Computing, Systems, Services and Technologies (UBICOMM2008), Valencia, Spain, Sep. 29–Oct. 4, 2008 (accepted for publication).

[8] S. Boschi, P. Crescenzi, M. Di Ianni, G. Rossi, P. Vocca, "MOMOSE: A Mobility Model Simulation Environment for Mobile Wireless Ad-hoc Networks", 1st International Conference on Simulation Tools and Techniques for Communications, Networks and Systems (SIMUTools 2008), Marseille, France, March 3-7, 2008.

Ambient Intelligence Perspectives
P. Mikulecký et al. (Eds.)
IOS Press, 2009
© *2009 The authors and IOS Press. All rights reserved.*
doi:10.3233/978-1-58603-946-2-58

Enabling NFC Technology to Public Services

J. BRAVO, R. HERVAS, G. CASERO, R. PEÑA, M. VERGARA, S. NAVA,
G. CHAVIRA and V. VILLARREAL

MAmI Research Lab – Castilla-La Mancha University, Spain
jose.bavo@uclm.es

Abstract. Ambient Intelligent are usually emerged in contexts like health, education, business and so on. However there are not many researches focusing on social aspects as public administrations. In these kinds of contexts, some problems are continuously in our minds. Especially these that people waste time on clues or solving dubs about the required documents. In this work we present a proposal through the adaptability of the Near Field Communication technology (NFC). With it, some tags and readers can interact with the mobile phones, running different applications according to the places, contexts and users' requirements.

Keywords. Ambient Intelligence, RFID, NFC, Natural Interaction, Context-Awareness

1. Introduction

Ambient Intelligence vision proposes a shift in computing. In front of the traditional desktop computer emerge the idea of many devices placed around us [1][2]. This vision promotes embedding technology into everyday objects, attaining effortless and closer interaction and, finally, supporting a means for getting needed information anywhere and at anytime. For creating intelligent environments unobtrusive hardware, wireless communications, massively distributed devices, natural interfaces and security are needed. To attain this vision it is fundamental to analyze the concept of context. A. Dey defines this concept as "*any information that can be used to characterize the situation of an entity. An entity is a person, place, or object that is considered relevant to the interaction between a user and an application, including the user and application themselves.*" [3]. This fact encourage researches look for contexts in order to model them according with this vision. Some of these contexts like healthcare, education or transport are traditional and others are arising. In this case, we have found a special context much extended but not very studied. We mean the Public Administrations. In it, traditional the everyday document management, presentations, registers, access, etc. have to be considered. This reality made us focusing on the technological adaptability with the purpose of solving daily activities in this kind of environment.

We agree with the idea of natural interaction that AmI proposes. However, we have changed the ideal interaction by using RFID technology. It means, only wearing tags, the user can obtain services from the environment. This interaction is categorized like implicit or embedded [4]. However it is necessary to mention that the hardness of the RFID kits in fixed places, the cost of infrastructures and finally, the responsibility of the "when" aspect of the environment have guided us to adapt the NFC technology. With it, the interaction is not implicit but, a simple touch is needed. Moreover, this change supposes some advantages that they have to be mentioned [5]. With the first technology users wear tags, readers are fixed and the interaction with the environment is centralized due the information stored in tags is small. The NFC allows the reader is mobile, tag is fixed or mobile and the interaction is through a touch. In addition, the mobile phone offers process, storage and communication capabilities. So, with this technology we have discovered multiple functionalities thorough the most extended electronic device in the world, the mobile phone.

Applying NFC technology in a public administration environment, we distinguish some kinds of users. Some of these equipped with mobile phone achieving a great variety of services. For example, it is possible to manage documents (showing, printing, sharing, moving, etc.), access (public and private), location, payment and ticketing, register and so on. Others refer to a user with fewer services like access or payment. In the first case the interaction can be through the mobile phone with reader or tag. At this point, we have to mention the idea or "tagging context". For that, we provide each tag with the adequate structure. It means, information about how activate the mobile phone application, the place identification, the near server for providing services, etc. In the second class, the user with the tag, maybe embedded in a credit card, interacts with the fixed readers or mobile phones by people in the public administration.

Under the next heading, we present the proposed technology NFC. In the following section a context and our approach can be seen. This paper finishes with conclusions and future works.

2. NFC Technology

As we said before, the NFC technology totally changes the way of thinking about how to understand traditional RFID installations. The reader is now mobile and the tag can be fixed or mobile. The tag will contain contextual information, solving the problem of the small amount of space that was available for the information storage in RFID.

The change of way towards a mobile reader logically goes ahead for needing a contact interaction. This process is very simple because, the only required action is bringing a mobile phone near the tag. In addition, this tag may be embedded anywhere, allowing different services can be activated into the environment.

NFC technology was developed by Philips and Sony in 2002 and is being propagated by Nokia, Samsung and the Philips Company itself. Consisting of the integration of the mobile telephony with identification by radiofrequency, it provides an intuitive communication between electronic devices, which is at the same time simple and secure, it works at a distance of between 5 – 10 cm. to 13.56 MHz and transfers data up to 424 Kbits/seg. [6].

NFC technology consists of two elements:

- Initiator- as its name indicates, it begins and controls the information interchange.
- Target- this is the device that replies to the initiator's requests.

Two forms of operation exist in an NFC system: passive or active. In the passive way (figure 1a), only one of the devices generates the radiofrequency field of short reach, providing energy to a tag that was inactive, allowing it to be able to read or write data in its memory. In the active way (figure 1b), both devices generate their own radiofrequency field to broadcast the data, recognizing each other automatically (Harold 2005). In addition Figure 1 shows the four NFC modes of operation.

Figure 1. Passive and active forms and four modes of operation

Figure 1a, a mobile phone with NFC technology can be observed (the one in charge of generating the radiofrequency field of short reach), and to its right the electronic tags that are used with this technology. Figure 1b shows two devices that generate the radiofrequency field of short reach, a mobile telephone with NFC technology and to its right a reader.

Two characteristics which distinguish NFC technology from RFID technology are that:

- A NFC device can function as Initiator or Target (figure 1c).
- Two NFC devices which recognize each other automatically can only work at a short distance from each other (figure 1d).

In Figure 1c we can see an initiator device (reader) and a target device (tag), and in Figure 1d, two NFC devices that recognize each other automatically, by just bringing them close together. A similar case would be that of a reader and a mobile with NFC technology, as we have shown in Figure 1b.

3. The context

In this section we describe the context, that is, an example of public administration: a city council. In it, we describe through a scenario, our proposal for not waste a lot of time handling administration processes. Then, we explain the simple proposed architecture. Finally, our vision through NFC technology in order to improve public services is presented.

3.1 A scenario

Peter has hurry this morning because he has to arrange some documents that will be present in the city council. Also, he has to be at 10h for an important meeting 20 km. distance from there. He arrives at 8.45 at council reception asking to the receptionist about the process to payment fees for an authorization for improvement of his house. Worker says Peter that he has to go to the third floor and look for the desk number four. Then, in the desk, an auxiliary give Peter a form giving him information about the improvement and, also, some documents are required. It means that, after getting these documents, Peter has to back to the council, filling this form and, in a few days is going to receive a notice about the council decision.

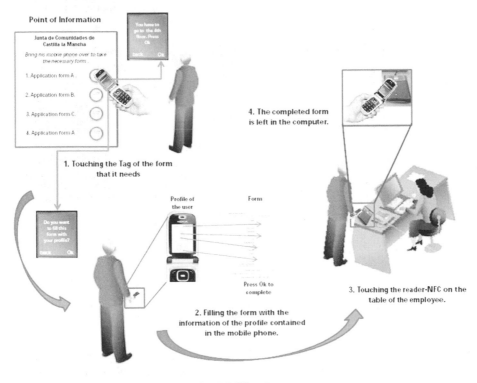

Figure 2. NFC filling form process

3.2 Our NFC proposal

With this technology it is possible to realize the process mentioned before more easily and quickly. For that people have to introduce the citizen profile into the mobile phone. It consists in personal data concerning to obligation of citizens, e. g. date and place born, address, house and car references, taxes, and so on. This data have to be stored into the mobile phone adequately. The reason is the matching process between data profile and the form requirements. This fact make needed a standardization of public administrations but, we think it is not difficult because there is a powerful mechanism to define formal vocabularies in order to reduce the ambiguity.

In figure 2 we show the process described into the scenario. In a point of information the user obtain the information about the place that he has to go and the correspondent form. This place is a desk with some tags, each one run an application for the required document. Next, this form is automatically filled with the information enclosed into the user profile. After that and, only passing the mobile phone next to the reader, the filled form is transmitted to the database. In a few days, the user will receive the document in the mobile phone by GPRS or attached to an e-mail.

Finally, to complement this kind of processes, we have implemented a variety of mobile-desktop applications. With these, each user exchange information from and to the PC, printer or visualization devices. These applications help users to obtain the information adequately into a display or paper. Additionally, it is a simple mode to carry out all kinds of documents and exchange then in public administration processes.

At this point it is needed to mention another device allow users to interact with the environment in the filling process: the tag. With that, it is possible to send information to the computer through the correspondent reader. The application in the computer matches data from the tag and form concluding the filling process. So, in some cases, a combination of a computer, reader and tag can substitute the mobile phone.

3.3 Meta-information

In the public administration processes and, in general, in many daily administrative tasks it is necessary a matching between data values and semantic labels. The citizen profile is an example of reusable and shared data that need to be standardized to improve administrative processes. Semantic Web languages can be used as meta-languages to define other special purpose languages such as communication languages for knowledge sharing [7] In general, the application of ontologies in AmI environments is important because provide an explicit representation of semantics and a means for independently developed context aware systems to share context knowledge, minimizing the cost and redundancy

We propose Resource Description Framework to define the necessary metadata in AmI solutions. In fact, RDF is intended for situations in which this information needs to be processed by applications, rather than being only displayed to people [8]. RDF provides a common framework for expressing this information so it can be exchanged between applications without loss of meaning. It is important to differentiate RDF and RDF-Schema, the fist one is general-purpose language for representing information and defines how to use RDF to describe vocabularies using RDF-Schema specification.

The definition of vocabularies is a core benefit of RDF. In our case of study, a vocabulary about citizen profile is expected. There are domain-centered vocabularies that can unify metainformation about users. For example, FOAF (Friend of Friend) [9] is a machine-readable ontology describing persons, their activities and their relations to other people and objects. Anyone can use FOAF to describe him or herself. FOAF allows groups of people to describe social networks without the need for a centralized database. The public administration systems can share this information using well-known vocabularies and publishing their own RDF vocabularies in order to define specific concepts (e.g fine number identification, tax-deductible value, etc.).

```
<?xml version="1.0"?>
<rdf:RDF
    xmlns:rdf="http://www.w3.org/1999/02/22-rdf-syntax-ns#"
    xmlns:rdfs="http://www.w3.org/2000/01/rdf-schema#"
    xmlns:foaf="http://xmlns.com/foaf/0.1/"
    xmlns:time-entry = "http://www.isi.edu/~hobbs/damltime/time-entry.owl"
    xmlns:loc=http://simile.mit.edu/2005/05/ontologies/location#
    xmlns:contact="http://www.w3.org/2000/10/swap/pim/contact#"
```

```
<foaf:Person rdf:ID="694659345T">
<foaf:title>Sr</foaf:title>
<foaf:givenname>Ramon</foaf:givenname>
<foaf:family_name>Hervas</foaf:family_name>
<foaf:phone rdf:resource="tel:+34-926295300-Ext-6332"/>
```
Personal information vocabulary

```
<adss:improvementID>CR9876234</adss: improvementID >
<adss:feesRange>B2</adss: feesRange >
<adss:feesQuantity>127</adss: feesQuantity >
```
Specific Administration Vocabulary

```
<time-entry:CalendarClockDescription  rdf:ID="meetingCR9876234">
    <time-entry:unitType rdf:resource="&time-entry;unitMinute" />
    <time-entry:year rdf:datatype="&xsd;gYear">2008</time-entry:year>
    <time-entry:month rdf:datatype="&xsd;gMonth">06</time-entry:month>
    <time-entry:day rdf:datatype="&xsd;gDay">5</time-entry:day>
    <time-entry:hour rdf:datatype="&xsd;nonNegativeInteger">9</time-entry:hour>
    <time-entry:minute rdf:datatype="&xsd;nonNegativeInteger">30</time-entry:minute>
    <time-entry:timeZone rdf:resource="&tz-us;EST" />
 </time-entry:CalendarClockDescription>
```
Time Ontology

```
<contact:Address>
<contact:city>Ciudad Real</contact:city>
<contact:country>Spain</contact:country>
<contact:postalCode>13004</contact:postalCode>
<contact:street>Paseo de la Universidad 4</contact:street>
<loc:coordinates>42.361860,-71.091840</loc:coordinates>
</contact:Address>
```
Location Ontology

Figure 3. Example of RDF description

Figure 3 shows an example of RDF description for the explained scenario in the subsection 3.1. The description includes personal information using FOAF specification, the date of the process, that are described by means of a time ontology [10] and, finally, the user house location applying the MIT SIMILE [11] project specification for geographical points.

3.4 Public Services

At this point we presented some services that can be supported by this technology and the way in which the user easily interacts with the environment only augmenting the capability of mobile phones. It means the idea of interaction by touch and executing an application automatically.   Table 1 shows some services and the needed NFC devices. These devices are readers, mobile phones and tags. In addition, some tags are distributed in a Din-A4 surface form called "Wall tags". These can be placed near to Public Displays or desktops. Some examples of tags covered by icons are printing, displaying, share & get documents from the computer, and so on.

Service	Description	NFC Devices
Point of Information	Reception desk	Wall tags
Registry	Register Documents	Reader
Official Documents	Filling forms	Mobile phone / user tag & Reader
Public Display	Announcements	Wall tags
Public Services	Identity card for gym, swimming pools, etc.	Tag / Mobile phone
Public Schools	Inscriptions, events, etc.	Tag / Mobile phone
File Council	For all generated documents	Reader
Documents	Print, Display, Share, etc.	Tag / Mobile phone
Time Control	Workers Clock in/off	Reader
Security	People-Identification entering into the council	Reader
Access - Control	For worker restricted areas	NFC - lock
Event Organizations	Fair, Congress, Concerts, etc.	Tag / Mobile phone
Financial	Sponsorships	Tag / Mobile phone

Table 1. Passive and active forms and four modes of operation

3.5 Users

As we said before, in a Public Administration we distinguish three kinds of users. For that we propose three kinds of devices for them: 1K tag, 4K tag and mobile phone. The first group corresponds to worker with low qualification e. g. caretaker, auxiliary worker, etc. Also, people who going to solve steps, identification cards for gym, swimming pool, getting information of public displays, etc. In addition, we have to say that we have created a profile for occasionally people. For that it is necessary to download a middleware to interact with the Public Administration context. The second group is the semi-specialized workers. They interact with the environment carrying out document, sharing, printing, visualizing and so on. Additionally, access and home automation processes are contemplated in this state, e.g. when a worker enters into the office the open-door and the luminosity controls are offered. Finally, the thirst group is the specialized one. Workers carrying out theirs mobile phones, can interact with the environments but, in a best structure that the previous group. For example, to carry out documents with 4K tags it is only possible to put in it the reference of the document. In this case, thanks to the micro-sd target, it is possible to store a great amount of information (over 2 Gb.).

4. Conclusions and future works

We have adapted the Near Field Communication technology in a public context with the main goal to complement and the traditional exchange of information. In it, some advantages are clear. For that, the public documents' management can be solved, in some cases, immediately. All processes are managed by the simple interaction that supposes approaching the mobile phone to a tag or reader. This means that everyone can handle the required public documents without any extra effort and knowledge.

In order to standardize these processes it is necessary to define adequately the user profile. That is, all the user information has to be stored into mobile form at the way that, all public statements can interact with data contained into the user mobile phone through the forms. This fact supposes a regularization effort by administrations. However, we think that will be a beneficial method to manage public documents.

Acknowledgments

This work has been financed by the FIT-350300-2007-84 ALIADO project of the Industry Ministry.

5. References

[1]   Weiser, M., The Computer for the 21st. Century. Scientific American, 1991. 265(3): p. 94-104.
[2]   ISTAG, Scenarios for Ambient Intelligence in 2010. Feb. 2001. http://www.cordis.lu/ist/istag.htm.
[3]   Dey, A. (2001). "Understanding and Using Context". Personal and Ubiquitous Computing 5(1), 2001, pp. 4-7.
[4]   Bravo, J., R. Hervás, I. Sánchez, G. Chavira & S. Nava, (2006). "Visualization Services in a Conference Context: An approach by RFID Technology". Journal of Universal Computer Science. Vol. 12-3. pp. 270-283.
[5]   Bravo, J., Hervás, R., Chavira, G., Nava, S. & Villarreal, V. (2008). "From Implicit to Touching Interaction: RFID and NFC Approaches". Human System Interaction Conference (HIS'08). Krakow (Poland).
[6]   ECMA_International, Near field Communication –white paper-, 2004
[7]   Chen, H., T. Finin, and A. Joshi. Semantic Web in a pervasive context-aware architecture. in Workshop on Ontologies and Distributed Systems. IJCAI. 2003. Acapulco, Mexico.
[8]   W3C, RDF Primer. Frank Manola and Eric Miller, Editors, W3C Recommendation, 10 February 2004. http://www.w3.org/TR/rdf-primer/
[9]   Brickley, D., Miller, L. FOAF Vocabulary Specification 0.91, http://xmlns.com/foaf/spec/
[10] Hobbs, J.R. and F. Pan, An ontology of time for the semantic web. ACM Transactions on Asian Language Information Processing (TALIP), 2004. 3(1): p. 66-85
[11] Mazzocchi, S. Minimalistic Location Ontology. MIT SIMILE project. http://simile.mit.edu/2005/05/ontologies/location#

Ambient Intelligence Perspectives
P. Mikulecký et al. (Eds.)
IOS Press, 2009
© *2009 The authors and IOS Press. All rights reserved.*
doi:10.3233/978-1-58603-946-2-66

Reputation Building for Electronic Marketplaces

Radoslav DELINA

Faculty of Economy Technical University of Kosice, Slovakia
radoslav.delina@tuke.sk

Abstract. Reputation mechanisms are considered as trust-building processes which are highly relevant in e-commerce marketplaces. The different forms of reputation building mechanisms have different level of significance and necessity for trust building. The paper presents results from pilot research, where the significance and necessity of particular trust building mechanisms esp. reputation building services for electronic marketplace was analyzed. Together, the possibilities of service model are discussed.

Keywords Trust building mechanisms, reputation, e-marketplaces

Introduction

In electronic commerce, where the buying and selling of goods or services is conducted online (eMarketServices 2004a), trust has received significant attention, as it is related to growth in this area of business. The Commission of the European Communities noted that, in order to win consumers as well as businesses over to e-commerce, it is necessary to build trust and confidence.

Trust usually is conceptualized as a cumulative process that builds on several, successful interactions (Nicholson et al. 2001). Each type of process increases the perceived trustworthiness of the trustee, raising the trustor's level of trust in the trustee (Chopra and Wallace 2003). It is not known exactly what trust-building processes are relevant in an ecommerce context. It is suggested that, in this setting, trust-building is based on the processes of prediction, attribution, bonding, reputation and identification (Chopra and Wallace 2003). According to Atif, the reputation has a very high relevance in a trust-building process on e-commerce markets.

1. Reputation mechanisms

With reputation is understood the process of transmitting an image of an actor in a network of other actors (Conte and Paolucci 2002). Reputation is defined as an estimation by others of an "entity's willingness and ability to repeatedly perform an activity in a similar fashion" (Herbig, Milewicz, and Golden 1994).

In e-commerce specifically, reputation concerns both buyers and sellers. It is obtained from offline sources and online ratings (Chopra and Wallace 2003). Offline sources are presented by references.

1.1 Rating

Online ratings could be presented as positive or negative ratings according to the experience with individual business case. Feedback presented by rating is trust-building mechanism with some empirical support for its effect on buyer-seller trust. Feedback refers to a mechanism for providing reliable information to buyers about sellers' past trading activities (Pavlou 2002, Ba & Pavlou 2002)

According to Sundaram and Webster (1998), negative messages have a detrimental effect on unfamiliar brands. Lee et al. (2000) report that higher negative feedback ratings lead to lower bidding prices in Internet auctions. Given that most sellers have not established any name recognition, negative feedback is likely to have a very strong negative effect on a buyer's trust perceptions, which is most likely to supersede the effect of positive feedback. Thus, the negative ratings have a greater opposing weight than positive ratings in shaping buyers's trust in a seller's credibility.

Buyers will calculate that a more reputable seller is less likely to destroy a good name to exploit a single transaction (Scott and Derlaga 1983). They will assume that sellers who have accumulated a good reputation would incure a high cost from cheating behaviours, and thus would be less likely to act opportunistically. It means, a greater number of positive ratings induces stronger buyers trust in the seller's credibility when there is no negative feedback.

In order to make better decisions in partner selection, buyers are naturally asking and looking for negative ratings or references. This issue is very sensitive because of the fear of unfair partner's activities.

1.2 Forum

A platform feedback forum is another tool for building trust between buyers and sellers. Users can evaluate the services provided by their business partners. A user can leave feedback to its partners based on the business outcome. By reading these feedbacks users are able to form a baseline of trust required before a contract could be made.

The provided ranking mechanism must not be biased to the positive or to the negative assessment. Potentially, the party being commented can also be allowed to explain the situation and problems regarding to the comments made by another party.

1.3 Approaches to the construction

For the reputation mechanisms implementation, three basic approaches will be presented - 1) statistical analysis of past transactions, 2) network of trust models, and 3) rule-based mechanisms:

Statistical analysis of past transactions - The best known methods presenting methods that aggregate ratings based on statistical analysis of past transactions are collaborative filtering mechanisms. The major problem with methods that statistically analyze past ratings is that they require a substantial amount of data to obtain useful results. This may not be a problem for C2C e-commerce merchants, such as Amazon.com, but could pose some difficulties in B2B e-commerce, especially during a start-up phase.

The "network of trust" - Some researchers (Zacharia et al., 1999) have proposed formalizing people's "networks of trust" – the concept of trusting a friend of a friend – into rating applications. It results from the assumption that people tend to trust the friend of a friend more than someone unknown. The strength of such a solution is that it can build upon existing relationships, which could be important for a B2B community. This solution has problems however. It is difficult to measure the trust that a user attributes to the members of his or her "Network of Trust." In interviews with industry decision-makers, it was found that the attitude towards the idea of a network of trust varies considerably. For some interviews, the concept of trusting "a friend of a friend" seemed intuitive, while others did not consider it to be relevant whether they and an unknown rater turned out to have a common friend. A second problem is that the most common approach (e.g., (Zacharia et al., 1999)) is to use a single dimension to model trust, combining both a party's trustworthiness as a business partner (Will he cheat in business?) and credibility as an evaluator (Can I trust what he is saying?).

"Rule-based mechanisms" constitute another important type of rating filters. Abdul-Rahman et al. (2000) propose the deployment of rules to determine and update rater weights. These rules assess whom the user trusts based on outcomes of previous interactions. The problem with this approach is that the rules tend to be ad-hoc. For example, if user A believes that rater B's rating of Supplier C is inaccurate, should A's trust in B decrease by 0.6 or 0.4?

Source credibility theory (Ekström 2003) can serve to overcome the three above listed problems associated with alternative approaches to rating mechanisms. First of all, source credibility theory provides tested frameworks (e.g.,Birnhaum and Stegner, 1979) for aggregating ratings from different sources. These frameworks decrease the dependence on ad-hoc operators. It also provides validated scales for measuring a source's (rater's) credibility (McCroskey, 1966); these can serve as the key input parameter in a rating system based on source credibility. Finally, the weights in a rating based on source credibility theory depend on user preferences and not on rater's behaviour, which decreases the amount of data required to calibrate the rating application. The opportunity to measure the credibility of the rater's organization as well as the person further decreases the amount of user input needed.

2. Survey results

The questionnaire survey (sample 100 companies) within Seamless project carried out in several European countries focused on the impact of potential trust building mechanisms and minimum necessary components for joining e-markets[7]. One of the most important mechanisms the reputation building was identified.

In this field, we have identified following sub-mechanisms useful as trust building mechanisms:

---

[7] See complete report from
http://www.seamless-eu.org/deliverables/TrustedOperationalScenarios.pdf

- Positive and negative ratings (feedbacks)
- Discussion forums
- Historical data
- Rating

Companies were asked whether mechanisms like feedbacks, discussion forum, historical data and rating will increase trust in the platform and if it is necessary to be implemented for joining the e-marketplace. Feedbacks were divided into "Positive only" and "Positive together with negative (combination)" feedbacks.

The survey showed that all companies prefer "Positive and negative feedbacks" rather than "Positive only feedbacks". "Positive and negative feedbacks" significantly increase trust for 45% of all companies instead of "Positive only feedbacks" with only 23%. The need for "Positive and negative feedbacks" was at the level of 39% and at the level of 20% for "Positive only feedbacks". 50% of e-skilled companies consider that "positive and negative feedbacks" significantly increase trust and necessity for these feedbacks is at the level of 43%.

It exists an assumption that seller would prefer more "only" positive feedback before combination of both types. According to the correlation analyses between type of the company (seller, buyer, combination) and type of feedback, this assumption was not confirmed. Together hypotheses "Sellers will trust less in the combination of positive and negative feedback as other types of companies" and "Sellers will request more positive feedback as the combination of both types of feedbacks" were analyzed. Although, first hypothesis was confirmed, only small differences between types of companies emerged. According to the contingency table test, second hypothesis was rejected. It supports the recommendation for e-market makers, that it is more suitable to implement the combination of positive and negative feedback into the e-marketplace environment.

A "Discussion forum" significantly increases trust for 24% of all companies and for 36% of e-skilled companies. 21% of all companies and 29% of e-skilled companies consider a discussion forum as necessary.

"Aggregated historical data" significantly increases trust for 39% of all companies, but 46% of e-skilled companies marked this data as significant for trust building. The data is necessary for 39% of e-skilled and for 29% of all companies.

The last question for building the trust through reputation mechanisms was usefulness of "rating presented as a simple symbol". 54% of e-skilled and 37% of all companies consider that rating will significantly increase trust and also this mechanism was necessary for 50% of e-skilled companies and for 35% of all companies, making it the second most popular and trustworthy of all analyzed mechanisms.

3. Possibilities for reputation building services implementation

Reputation building mechanism can provide a self-regulation function of trust on electronic business platform. According to source credibility theory (Ekström 2003), it will be suitable to calculate aggregated ratings and feedbacks by weighted average where the weight is determined by the rating of raters (companies providing feedback).

Feedbacks from business partners could be split into positive only feedbacks and combination of positive with negative feedbacks. Positive only feedbacks could deform information ability and according to several surveys, companies usually tend to look for negative feedbacks. In our survey, only 19% of all companies said that positive feedback is necessary. 45% of all companies said that this model would significantly increase trust and more than 40% of them marked this model as necessary for joining the platform, a combination of positive and negative feedbacks should be implemented. Feedbacks should be provided on several business areas, as for example payment, service, product quality... The companies should have the option of evaluating business partners after a transaction. We propose to use the scale from 0-1, weighting by rating of rater and also present the number of total ratings.

A *discussion forum* can be established in the company section, which means that if a business partner is unsatisfied, he can add comments about a company on the discussion forum. These comments have to be non-anonymous and public, the concerned company could react to these comments and describe the situation from its point of view. Comments cannot be translated so it is necessary to use common language. Although only 21% of companies would require this service as a pre-requisite for joining the platform and for only 24% would this information significantly increase trust, the implementation is ease, therefore it would be useful to implement.

Historical aggregated data as statistical support can increase trust in business partners, as well as the platform, where companies could see useful aggregated data about their partner as well as the number of tenders in which the company was involved, the average time of reaction, in how many tenders was the company selected as winner, the total number of transactions, the frequency of platform presence, number of Online Dispute Resolution or Escrow service activities, etc. This information can be implemented into the traditional section "Company profile". Although only 29% of companies replied that this information is necessary, 39% said that it would significantly increase trust. Therefore, it would be positive to implement such information into any electronic business platform. Together, appropriate model of aggregated e-marketplace data would help to improve market research for all e-marketplace participants.

Rating is presented as a simple mark or number and is calculated on the basis of feedbacks and weights of raters. Although only 35% of companies request rating as necessity, 50% of e-skilled companies responded, qualifying rating as a necessary tool and 54% of the same type of companies found that rating is very important. For that reason, rating would be beneficial to the trust issue for any business platform. A general rating mark could be made public to all participants on the platform. An important issue is also to indicate and publish the number of business partners which rated this company (e.g. number of unique companies / number of rated businesses). This helps indicate unfair practices like multiple rating from related partner. Rating can be always visible for all references on the platform sites.

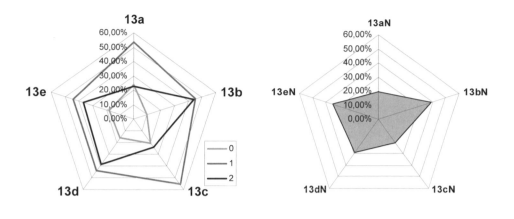

Figure 1 Different level of trust in reputation mechanisms

Figure 2 Necessity of relevant elements of trust building mechanism

Comments:

13a Positive-only feedback from the partners; 13b Positive and negative feedback from the partners; 13c Discussion forum; 13d Reports with aggregated historical data about the platform business activities of the company; 13e Rating presented as a simple symbol; N means Necessary element for joining the e-market; 0 no increase of trust; 1 medium increase of trust; 2 significant increase of trust

Generally, the survey showed that trust in the reputation mechanism is increasing by increased e-skills (skills in electronic commerce and e-marketplace functionalities) and is very important to provide at least feedbacks and rating in an easily understandable way.

Acknowledgements

This work has been funded by the Slovak Research and Development Agency under the contract No. RPEU-0025-06.

References

Atif, Y. (2002). Building Trust in E&-Commerce, IEEE Internet Computing, Jan-Feb (2002), pp. 18-24

Birnhaum, M. H. and Stegner, S. E. (1979) Source Credibility in Social Judgment: Bias, Expertise and the Judge's point of view, Journal of Personality and Social Psychology, 37, 48-74.

Blois, K. (1999). Trust in Business to Business Relationships: An Evaluation of its Status, Journal of Management Studies, Vol. 35, No. 2 (1999), pp.197-215

Castelfranchi, C., Tan, Y.(2002). The role of Trust and Deception in Virtual Societies, International Journal of Electronic Commerce, Vol 6, No. 3 (2002) pp.55-70

Chopra, K., Wallace, W., Trust in Electronic Environments, Proceedings of the 36th Hawaii International Conference on Systems Sciences (HICSS), (2003)

Conte, R., Paolucci, M., Reputation in Artificial Societies, Kluwer Academic Publishers, (2002)

Deelmann, T., Loos, P., Trust Economy: Aspects of Reputation and Trust building for SME:s in e-business, Eight Americas Conference on Information Systems (AMCIS) (2002), pp. 890-898

Delina, R., Vajda, V., Bednár, P. (2007). Trusted operational scenarios: trust building mechanisms and strategy for electronic marketplaces [on-line]. August 2007. Kranj: Moderna organizacija, 2007. 78 p. ISBN 978-961-232-205-2 Accessible from:
http://www.seamless-eu.org/deliverables/TrustedOperationalScenarios.pdf

Dellarocas, C., 2000, Immunizing online reputation reporting systems against unfair ratings and discriminatory behavior, Proceedings of the 2nd ACM Conference on Electronic Commerce. Association for Computing Machinery, Minneapolis, MN, 150-157.

Dellarocas, C., 2001, Analyzing the economic efficiency of eBay-like online reputation reporting mechanisms, Proceedings of the 3rd ACM Conference on Electronic Commerce. Association for Computing Machinery, Tampa, FL, 171-179.

Dellarocas, C., 2003a, The Digitization of Word-of-Mouth: Promise and Challenges of Online Feedback Mechanisms, Management Science 49 (10), 1407-1424.

Dellarocas, C., Fan, M., and Wood, C., 2003b, Self-Interest, Reciprocity, and Participation in Online Reputation Systems, 2003 Workshop in Information Systems and Economics (WISE), Seattle, WA.

Dellarocas, C., 2004, Building Trust On-Line: The Design of Robust Reputation Mechanisms for Online Trading Communities. G. Doukidis, N. Mylonopoulos, N. Pouloudi, eds. Social and Economic Transformation in the Digital Era. Idea Group Publishing, Hershey, PA.

Ekström, M.A. et al: The Impact of Rating Systems on Subcontracting Decisions. CIFE Technical Report #135, February 2003, Stanford University

eMarketServices (2004a), eMarket Basics, [Online], Available at: http://www.emarketservices.com [April 15, 2004]

eMarketServices (2004b), Cases & Reports: Naples Goes North, [Online], Available at: http://www.emarketservices.com [December 10, 2004]

eMarketServices (2005), eBusiness Issues: Building Confidence, [Online], Available at: http://www.emarketservices.com [April 2, 2005]

EU Commission (2002). Open consultation on "Trust barriers for B2B emarketplaces" Presentation of the main results, [Online], Available at: http://europa.eu.int/comm/enterprise/ict/policy/b2bconsultation/consultation_en.htm [November 5, 2002]

Herbig, P., Milewicz, J., Golden, J., A model of reputation building and destruction, Journal of Business Research, Vol. 31, No. 1, (1994), pp. 23-31.

Kuttainen, Ch.: The Role of Trust in B2B Electronic Commerce - Evidence from Two e-Marketplaces. Doctoral Thesis. Luleå University of Technology, 2005. ISSN 1402-1544.

Lee, Z., Im, I., S. J. Lee, 2000, The Effect of Negative Buyer Feedback on Prices in Internet Auction Markets. W. J. Orlikowski, S. Ang, P. Weill, H. C. Krcmar, J. I. DeGross, eds. Proc. 21st Int. Conf. on Information Systems (ICIS 2000), Association for Information Systems., Brisbane, Australia, 286-287.

Ambient Intelligence Perspectives
P. Mikulecký et al. (Eds.)
IOS Press, 2009
doi:10.3233/978-1-58603-946-2-73

Harnessing "Fair Trade" metaphor as privacy control in Ambient Intelligent

Abraham ESQUIVEL, Pablo A.HAYA, Manuel GARCÍA-HERRANZ
and Xavier ALAMÁN
Escuela Politécnica Superior, Universidad Autónoma de Madrid, Spain
abraham.esquivel@estudiante.uam.es

Abstract. Ambient Intelligence is a promising research area that opens attractive perspective for improving human-computer interaction. Since AmI systems require knowing user's private information, privacy issues are especially relevant. This paper follows a two-fold approach. Firstly, a privacy framework for AmI systems is introduced. We analyses the elements involved in privacy management and the nature of personal information. Mainly we will focus on control privacy for short-term information. Secondly, this work presents a privacy management solution, simple enough for the common understanding, but rather flexible to fulfill users and services expectations. This proposal, named as "Fair-Trade" metaphor, relays on trading quality of service for information. This strategy combined with optimistic access control and a logging mechanism, enhances users' confidence in the system while encouraging them to share their information, with the consequent benefit for the community.

Keywords. Privacy, "Fair Trade", Ambient Intelligence

Introduction

Ambient Intelligence (AmI) success relies on gathering user personal information. The interaction between the environment and its inhabitants provides personal information that may be private and can be originated in multiple physical sensors, or elaborated from raw data. Many of this information correspond to what Dey [1] identify as context, that is, information about the particular circumstances surrounding an entity. Identity, location, activity and time are classical examples of context variables. This context information is acquired autonomously to enable the integration of adaptive services. Although technological achievements in this area have been of outstanding importance, social factors will also be key roles in the success or failure of pervasive environments. In this sense, a major step in leveraging AmI comes from overcoming their ethical and psychological issues [2].

Privacy is a dynamic phenomenon [3] depending on the user and its context: each individual has as many privacy issues as different situation he/she is involved in. In general, we can say that privacy management is a permanent negotiation where the private and public boundaries are constantly changing in response to the circumstances. Furthermore, we pose that a particular privacy configuration depends on the user sharing a service, and the service itself. In consequence, depending on the users and services involved, user's privacy needs will change.

One immediate problem arising from those considerations is privacy management. It seems reasonable that users would like to control their privacy boundaries. However, a very dynamic context can frustrate user's expectation due to an overwhelming amount of information. This is particularly true in AmI systems which are populated by heterogeneous technologies, multiple and varied sensors in multiple and varied situations. Applying this definition to these systems is a challenging problem since users must decide privacy configurations for every data gathered or deduced from sensors.

But, how can the user establish those limits? A first approximation can be to manually set up privacy, assigning the desired level to each source of information. The key problem of this solution relays on the nature of privacy and AmI systems: the degree of privacy desired for a source of information depends not only on the user and the source but also on the context. In other words, for every source and every person there can be as many different privacy configurations as diffrent contexts they can be involved in. To configure a priori each possible arising situation for every source of information can be an overwhelming task that justifies the use of automatic management solutions. On the other hand, the success of such automatic management solutions depends directly on the trust the user place on them. This trust depends directly on the following requirements: a) The model must be simple enough to be understood by a non-technical user, and b) The user must be able to modify the automatic configuration at any moment. In developing our framework we focused particularly on the importance of usability. Especially in this case, confidence and trust are synonyms of usability.

This paper is organized as follows: We first provide a privacy framework for AmI systems. Following this framework, section 2 describes a semi-automatic privacy management approach based on the "fair trade" metaphor. Section 3 summarizes the previous and related work. Finally, section 4 offers the conclusions.

1. Privacy Framework

Privacy can be seen as a matter of information, entities and their relation. Every privacy solution has to deal with these factors and their characteristic problems. In this section we will analyze the elements and factors involved in our privacy world.

1.1 Elements involved in privacy management.

From the privacy management point of view, several elements can be distinguished:
- **User**. An entity with administrative rights. It can be a single person or an organization.
- **Agent**. A software module that acts on behalf of others persons or organizations.
- **Space**. A physical or virtual area.
- **Data Source**. A resource providing information about environment's entities. Data can vary from a single value such as temperature to a multimedia streaming.
- **Data Source Owner**. The user with administrative rights on the data source.
- **Inquirer**. Agent or user inquiring a data source.

– **Receiver**. Agent or user receiving the answer of the inquirer. In some instances, it is possible that the receiver and the inquirer are not the same entity, as for example when the inquirer's answer is broadcasted to a group of receivers.

In Figure 1, we provide a high-level illustration of our design framework. As shown, we consider multiple spaces organized hierarchically. Each of them represents a physical or conceptual space serving as container of data sources [4].

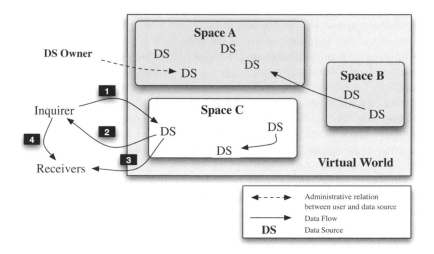

Figure 1. Graphical representation of the privacy framework.

We assume that every data source providing information of a user is controlled by him/her. Additionally, every data source is represented in the virtual world, where it can also store information (see Figure 1).

1.1.1 Interaction between information and users

Besides spatial and administrative relationships, Figure 1 also shows an example of interaction between data sources and agents playing diverse roles. The procedure is as follows:

1. The inquirer requests some information to the data source.
2. The data source, according to privacy rights, returns the answer to the inquirer. The answer may contain the whole data, or it can be filtered. In the latter, the inquirer will only receive a partial view of the data.
3. When the answer is delivered, other agents or users may receive it. This may happen with or without an explicit indication of the inquirer. For instance, an answer may be broadcasted to unsolicited receivers if a speaker is used as output device.
4. Once a user obtains data from a source, he may freely distribute it to other users.

The privacy management approach presented in this paper deals with the first and second phase. The third and four phases are beyond the scope of this work.

1.2 Taxonomy of personal information

Information is probably the most important element of privacy. In fact, privacy can be summarized as protecting information loosely enough to permit interaction but sufficiently tight to preserve confidentiality. When talking about AmI, in which all the information is digital -and thus storable- it is important to think about the use that can be made with some information not only in the present but also in the future.

According to the nature of the user's personal data, we classify information in two categories: long-term information and short-term information. The former comprises information with a low changing rate -e.g. telephone number, social security number, name, surname or postal direction- The latter, on the other hand, contains information of changing nature -e.g. location, activity or cohabitants. These two types of information have their own strengths and weakness. Thus, since static information is probably valid in the future, a single unwanted access will endanger the information in the long term. Consequently we can categorize this information as especially sensible in a time line. On the contrary, dynamic information may change with time, for what it could seem less sensible, on the other hand, is precisely this kind of information what really describes a person's way of living -e.g. where you are, doing what and with who. Therefore, even not especially sensible in a time line, this kind of information is more directly related to what we understand by privacy than the previous one.

1.2.1 Long-term personal data

As we described before, privacy data could be split on two categories. One kind of information is named long-time personal data. This means that the value of this data remains constant with time.

In our environment model [5] each entity has a set of properties and relations associated. Regarding privacy issues, each property or relation must be included in one of the previous groups (i.e. long-term or short-term information). Depending on the assigned group, each property or relation will require a different privacy management policy. Long-term data are insensible to context changes, meaning that once the value is revealed to an unwanted receiver, the data is compromised forever. In this case, the main concern must be who has rights to access the information while when, where, or how is accessed are not relevant. Accordingly, the privacy mechanism associated to long-term personal data is based on a restrictive approach, in which the user must specify which individuals can access each piece of long-term information.

1.2.2 Short-term personal data

Contrary to long term information, properties or relations more likely to change over time are classified as short-term information. Many examples can be found in an AmI systems in which sensors are constantly gathering information about the inhabitants and the environment itself. Similarly, information inferred from short-term raw data can be categorized as short-term information too. As a result, there is a huge amount of available information categorized as short-term, from inhabitant spatial-temporal coordinates such as location or activity information, to environment information such as temperature, humidity, lighting levels and appliances' status and so on. We consider only three types of short-term information: identity, location and activity. Even though identity can be considered –as it is in fact- as a long-term information, it must be also kept within the short-term ones due to the indexing function it bears. Thus, without identity, nor location neither activity has any sense.

Short-term information is classified according to two discrete axes: privacy level and personal data. As illustrated in Table 1, the accuracy of the information varies with the privacy level. This accuracy is characterized by different degrees of granularity of each variable. Although different scales and values can be considered, our three levels approach is motivated by simplicity of use. We believe that more levels could lead to a non-feasible approach partly due to technical issues, but more importantly, because the model should remain simple enough to be comprehensible by non-technical user. Nevertheless, as we will suggest in future work, we will study if a four level approach is also reasonable.

The three privacy levels are:
1. **Restricted**. In this level a non-disclosure of information is achieved. Thereby, user's information is not distributed to the community.
2. **Diffuse**. Personal data can be retrieved with some level of distortion. Thus, for each variable, an intermediate value is established hinting at the real one without revealing it. This distorted value can be automatically obtained from the real one or hand-written in the user preferences.
3. **Open**. The information is revealed without any modification. Hence, the community receives the information as accurate as possible. Besides privacy configuration, the accuracy of the data will depend on the sensors' quality and deployed infrastructure.

Table 1. Context variables are filtered using different granularity depending on its privacy level.

Privacy Levels	Identity	Location	Activity
Restricted	Anonymous	Not available	Not available
Diffuse	Alias	Building level	High level activity
Open	Real	Roo level/GPS data	Raw data

2. An alternative approach to AmI privacy management.

The main challenge relies on how to assign these privacy levels to short-term information. One possible approach would be to apply the same strategy that for long-term information. However, due to the constantly changing nature of context, an approach that requires full-control over privacy will force the definition of particular privacy settings for each situation, meaning that users must anticipate every possible situation, or review their privacy preferences every time the situation changes. While the former is non-feasible the latter can be achieved by following an incremental approach, with the system asking for new privacy settings every time a new situation occurs and then remembering it. In this way, the system acquires, step-by-step, privacy settings close to the ideal. A real example can be found in firewall applications. On the other hand, the main problem with this kind of solutions is that users might find annoying –as they truly are in the case of firewalls-the repeated interruptions of the system, even more if we consider that notifications might be sent through ambient interfaces such as speakers. A completely opposite approach would be to consider totally automatic privacy control as an option. This implies that the system automatically infers the privacy configuration for each situation in behave of the user, whom stays aside. However, we believe that it will be hard for end-users to feel comfortable in delegating control over their privacy to an automatic system, unable to explain its behaviour [6]. Although automatic decision-control techniques can be very competent, user direct control is particularly relevant when the variables to be controlled are personal data.

Summarizing, and following P. Maes [7] guide on trust and competence as main issues in developing software applications, we would like to emphasize the importance of choosing a **comprehensible** and **useful** solution. Where comprehensible means that the user has enough knowledge of the how, when, and why the system reacts to trust it; and useful means that the system is sufficiently easy to use and powerful to achieve a high degree of competence over the problem.

2.1 "Fair Trade" Metaphor

Dealing with the requirements stated above, we present a model based on the "fair trade" metaphor. Our proposal relies on the following assumption:

> Users will accept to harm their privacy if, on return, they receive valuable services and they are able to track the flows of their disclosed information.

Our information management protocol is among those referred to as "fair trade politics", in other words, a user can see another user's context variable (identity, location, activity, time) -with the degree of privacy established by the owner- if he harms his privacy equally. This model comprises only what we called dynamic information for what opening or closing the static one to some, none or all others is up to the information's owner through manually configuring so.

For example, following the previous approach, if a user defines his privacy level as Diffuse, his personal data will be shown after being filtered but he would only be able to retrieve filtered information from others in the best case, even from those with an Open privacy level. At the end, the amount of shared information grows information needs, making context-aware services more useful and valuable.

Four different mechanisms are used to support our privacy control system. These mechanisms, when together, are able to deal with all the factors identified in previous sections.

2.2 Optimistic access control

Access control in AmI systems must stimulate the cooperation between users and groups. In addition it must guarantee that individual's access rights are not lost when joining a group in a collaboration process. Now, most systems use pessimistic access controls, based on the principle that the user restricts his information from the beginning, granting access later to those considered reliable. Conversely, an optimistic access control allows free access to information, with strict registration of whom, what and when accedes to it. This registration acts as a dissuasive mean to prevent abuses within the system i.e. The only fact that user B is aware that A can know if he consults A's information, and how many times, prevents B from abusively consult A's information.

2.3 Templates to model degrees of privacy.

Templates, combined with default configurations, help users in controlling their privacy and modifying it when necessary. The goal is to promote user's interest in protecting his/her static information in a practical and simple way. Thus, if a user wants to show his/her telephone number he/she will explicitly specify, through a template, to which user or group of users must be shown. Contrary to dynamic information, templates for static information use a restrictive configuration.

2.4 Punitive measures

As mentioned in the subsection 2.2, optimistic access control provides a logging service to maintain informed users about who accesses their information and in what degree. This mechanism provides a way to detect inappropriate, suspicious or abusive conducts (for instance, to detect a user consulting activity and location of others excessively in the course of the day). The punitive measures can consist in applying a restrictive privacy to that specific user, expelling him/her from users' groups of confidence and in consequence, limiting the quality of services he/she may receive. Additionally, a voting system could be applied in which those conforming the community maintain a list of unpleasant users to which deny services in the environment.

2.5 Manual override

The user can manually modify his/her privacy. This is particularly useful when talking about long-term information.

3. Background

A project sharing a vision similar to the one that we propose in this paper is Babble [8]. This IM provides a graphical representation of the community social activity. They pose the idea of "Socially Translucent Systems". People have tendency to imitate others individual behaviour through observation. The key point is social conventions and rules supporting the cooperation will emerge, if systems facilitate the exposure of community activity. Therefore, these translucent systems aim to the creation of open communities.

In relation to optimistic access control, Grudin and Horvits mention in [9] the use of shared calendars as a good alternative to detect abuses on the system through optimistic access control. Povey in [10] affirms that an optimistic access control is valid for emergency situations in which security and privacy policies must be ignored like, for instance, a medical emergency. Kuening and Popek in [11] referred to one of the few practical implementations: they tried to learn the behavior of users in validating his access in real time, preventing the loss of information due to the disconnection of mobile devices.

Regarding to the use of templates, Myles has already used a similar idea in the Privacy System project [12], calling them "user preferences". Some other systems use them in user interfaces design in which they try to administer and feedback privacy configurations. This is the case of RAVE [13] and the Faces Metaphor project of Lederer [14].

The use of anonymity and pseudonyms has also been influenced by the work of Lederer [15] about the development of a user interface to control privacy in an active environment.

4. Conclusions

The idea behind the "Fair Trade" metaphor is the stimulation of sharing information, hypothesizing that users will accept to harm their privacy if, on return, they receive valuable services. In addition to the services they obtain in exchange of their information, users must be able to track the flow of their disclosed data. Our approach emphasizes the "fair trade" metaphor in the following way: users configure their privacy settings according to the amount of information they would like to know from others, assuming that others would be able to access their own information in the same terms.

Summarizing, our privacy management proposal relays on trading quality of service for information. Users give their context information data in exchange of better services. A recording mechanism is proposed to mitigate the risk of personal information disclosure. Users can revert their privacy preferences to a more restricted one if they believe somebody is misusing their context information.

Despite all this, another issue of considerable importance for the success of the metaphor has been the optimistic access control, which acts as a dissuasive measure to prevent abuses combined with the punitive actions that can be taken.

Acknowledgement

This work has been partly funded by HADA project number TIN2007 – 64718 and the UAM – Indra Chair in Ambient Intelligence.

References

[1]   Dey, K. A.: Understanding and Using Context. Personal Ubiquitous Computing, 5 (1), (2001), 4-7.
[2]   Stone, A.: The Dark Side of Pervasive Computing. IEEE Pervasive Computing, 2 (1), (2003), 4-8.
[3]   Palen, L., Dourish, P.: Unpacking "Privacy" for a Networked World. In: ACM Conference on Human Factors in Computing Systems (CHI). ACM Press, New York (2003), 129–136.
[4]   Dix,A., Rodden, T., Davies, N., Trevor, J., Friday, A., Palfreyman, K.: Exploiting space and location as a design framework for interactive mobile systems. ACM Trans. CHI, 7(3), (2000), 285-321.
[5]   Haya, P. A., Montoro, G., Alamán, X.: A prototype of a context-based architecture for intelligent home environments. CoopIS, OTM, LNCS 3290, (2004). 477-491.
[6]   Norman, D. How might people interact with agents. CACM, 37(7), (1994), 68-71.
[7]   Maes, P. Agents that Reduce Work and Information Overload. CACM, 37 (7), (1994), 31-40.

[8]   Erickson, T., Smith, D. N., Kellogg, W. A., Laff, M., Richards, J. T., Bradner, E.: Socially Translucent Systems: Social Proxies, Persistent Conversation, and the Design of "Babble". CHI, (1999), 72-79.

[9]   Grudin, J., Horvitz, E.: Presenting choices in context: approaches to information sharing. Workshop on Ubicomp communities: Privacy as Boundary Negotiation, 2003.

[10] Povey, D.: Optimistic Security: A New Access Control Paradigm. Highlights of the 1999 New Security Paradigms Workshop. (NISSC). Arlington, Virginia, 1999, 40-45.

[11] Kuenning, G. H., Popek, G. J.: Automated Hoarding for Mobile Computers. Proceedings of the 16th ACM Sym. on Operating Systems Principles (SOSP), Saint Malo, France, (1997), 264-275.

[12] Myles, G., Friday, A., Davies, N.: Preserving Privacy in Environments with Location-Based Applications. IEEE Pervasive Computing, 2(1), (2003), 56-64.

[13] Bellotti, V., Sellen, A.: Design for Privacy in Ubiquitous Computing Environments. In Proc. of the Third European Conference on Computer-Supported Cooperative Work (ESCW'93), (1993), 77-92.

[14] Lederer, S., Dey, A., Mankoff, J.: A Conceptual Model and Metaphor of Everyday Privacy in Ubiquitous Computing. TR UCB-CSD-02-1188, University of California at Berkeley, 2002.

[15] Lederer, S., Hong, I. J., Jiang, X., Dey, A. K., Landay, J. A., Mankoff, J.: Towards Everyday Privacy for Ubiquitous Computing. TR UCB-CSD-03-1283, University of California at Berkeley, 2003.

Ambient Intelligence Perspectives
P. Mikulecký et al. (Eds.)
IOS Press, 2009
© 2009 The authors and IOS Press. All rights reserved.
doi:10.3233/978-1-58603-946-2-82

Variability in AmI Middleware Context-Awareness Service

Lidia FUENTES, Nadia GÁMEZ, Pablo SÁNCHEZ
Universidad de Málaga
lff@lcc.uma.es

Abstract. AmI technologies are mainly based on the combination of concepts from ubiquitous and pervasive computing and the production of software embedded in everyday objects and devices, for many kind of users and supporting different applications types. A Software Product Line approach would be very appropriate to express the different requirements of either devices or applications in terms of commonalities and variabilities defining a family of AmI middleware platforms. One of the main services that an AmI middleware has to provide is the management of the context. There are several properties that affect the current context of the middleware: device constraints, applications restrictions, user preferences and runtime environment state. A feature model will help to specify and reason about the different middleware configurations tailored to either devices or application constraints. This feature model will enable different versions of a specific middleware for AmI to be generated, with the minimum number of services being required by the specific context properties.

Keywords. AmI, Context-awareness, Middleware, SPL

Introduction

Ambient Intelligence (AmI) represents a new generation of computing environments equipped with a wide range of small devices and [1] present everywhere, available for everyone and at all times. One of the main challenges of AmI domain is to be able to produce software embedded in everyday objects and devices, tailored for many kinds of users and supporting many types of applications. Thus, AmI applications have to deal with a wide variety of devices, applications, users and so on. Middleware platforms could play a key role in hiding the complexity and heterogeneity, by providing specific services (e.g. location, context-awareness, device discovery, etc.) to support and facilitate AmI application development. There are several properties that affect the current context of the middleware: device constraints, applications restrictions, user preferences and runtime environment state. So, one of the services that the middleware has to provide is the management of the context.

The large number of the possible contexts (for example, heterogeneous devices, the diversity of communication technologies and AmI application requirements) make it unfeasible to construct a single middleware platform that can be deployed and configured on all kind of devices and providing services that fulfil the requirements of any AmI application. Instead, the developer of an AmI middleware platform should define *families* of middleware platforms that can be instantiated according to the different constraints imposed by the current context. Thus, the application of a

Software Product Line (SPL) approach would be very useful to express the different requirements in terms of commonalities and variabilities defining a family of AmI middleware platforms [2]. Since device resource constraints (e.g. in memory, processor throughput, etc.) is an important consideration in AmI, only a specific middleware platform configuration that is suitable for the device capacities must be installed.

In this paper we present a feature model for the AmI domain, which will help to specify and automatically derive different configurations of middleware tailored according to a high diversity of context. (e.g. device capacities, user preferences, application requirements, etc.). A feature model allows specifying where the variability is independent of the core asset, and enables reasoning about all the different possible configurations. Middleware for AmI should benefit from the SPL approach in terms of configurability, reusability and evolution management [3]. AmI applications will benefit from a highly-optimized and custom middleware, which will offer appropriate services consistent with device configuration and resource constraints.

There are several middlewares that try to manage the context. For example, GREEN [4], CARISMA [5] and the work of Yau et al. [6] are middleware platforms for pervasive systems focused on context-awareness. GREEN [4] is a configurable and re-configurable publish-subscribe middleware for pervasive computing. CARISMA [5] is a mobile computing middleware which exploits the principle of reflection to enhance the construction of adaptive and context-aware mobile applications. In [6], a reconfigurable context-sensitive middleware for pervasive computing is presented. These platforms use different technologies for dealing with context-awareness, but none of them use SPL, as we do.

In this paper we focus in the management of the context in order to instantiate a specific middleware as minimum as possible that fits with the current context properties. Following this introduction, this paper is structured as follows. In Section 1 we show the AmI middleware feature model and architecture. In Section 2 we explain the Context-Awareness service. In Section 3 is detailed the process of instantiation of a particular middleware of the family, how we solve the dependence between features and a possible dynamic reconfiguration of the middleware. Finally, in Sections 4 some conclusions are outlined, respectively.

1. AmI Middleware

Product Line Software Engineering (PLSE) exploits commonality and manages variability among products from a domain perspective [7]. Consequently, adopting this approach seems to be appropriate in order to encompass all the variability present in a middleware for Ami applications. In a feature-oriented approach, commonalities and variabilities are analyzed in terms of features. A feature is any prominent and distinctive characteristic that is visible to various stakeholders.

The features can be organized into a feature model that represents all possible products of a software product line. Commonalities are modelled as mandatory features and variabilities are modeled as variable features which are classified as alternative or optional features. In feature diagrams three kinds of relationships are found: compose of (when the feature is composed of several sub-features), generalization or specialization (when the feature is a generalization of the sub-features), and implemented by (when the sub-feature is needed to implement the feature).

Furthermore, for each variable feature, feature dependency analysis can identify dependencies between features.

A feature model can be used as input for generating an architectural representation of a product line. Thus, in this section firstly, we detail the feature model that will be used as input for the middleware product family architecture later depicted in the last subsection.

1.1 AmI Middleware Feature Model

In order to instantiate a particular product of the middleware family it is necessary to know all the features that influence the specific configuration of the middleware that fits the specific characteristics of each possible context.

- **Device driven features.** The distinctive characteristics of each device strongly influence the size and the implementation version of the middleware services,.
- **Applications driven features**. Final applications may require only a subset of the available middleware services. Considering the resource limitations of AmI devices, only those services that will be invoked by final applications will be part of a specific middleware configuration.
- **User driven features**. The typical user preferences also affect the middleware configuration. For example, the user may enable or disable optional middleware services (e.g. resource monitoring).
- **Runtime Environment driven features.** If during the middleware instantiation process it is detected that some device resource (e.g. a Bluetooth communication protocol) is not working properly, then the corresponding middleware service will not be present in the resulting configuration.

Since the idea is to define a highly flexible configuration process, the middleware for AmI must be structured in fine-grained components (Services in Figure 1) decoupled from a base infrastructure (Microkernel in Figure 1). The basic services are a mandatory feature but the extra services are optional. Looking up remote applications and the discovery of distant devices are examples of basic services. Extra services will be instantiated only if this is required by an application (e.g. logging, context-awareness, position location, etc.).

According to the applications restrictions one particular implementation of the microkernel and some specific services must be instantiated. The microkernel is composed by the container, factory, and service manager. The container is the responsible to search the required services. The factory element creates and instantiates such services. The last sub-feature of the microkernel is the service manager that manages the architecture of the middleware, composes the instantiated service with the microkernel and runs the service. On the other hand, the context-aware services is the responsible of be aware of any change in the context. We will detail this service in next section.

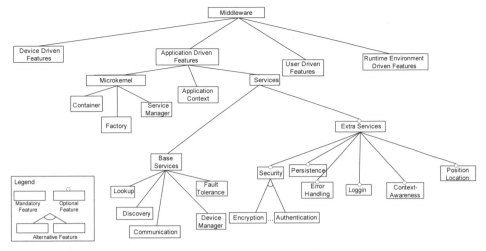

Figure 1. Middleware Feature Model.

1.2 AmI Middleware Architecture

Using the feature model as input we will design the architecture of our middleware product family. Likewise most traditional middleware platform architecture, we follow a layered approach as shown in Figure 2. The application level is at the top and the middleware itself is underneath.

The microkernel is responsible for loading and destroying applications and services. Also in order to run the application, the microkernel has to compose or weave the applications with the rest of services provided by the middleware. The middleware follows a microkernel and services structure. The microkernel term describes a form of operating system design in which the amount of code that must be executed in privileged mode is kept to an absolute minimum [8]. As a consequence, the rest of the services are built as independent modules that are plugged and executed by the kernel by demand. In this way, we obtain a more modular and configurable system. On top of the microkernel, the application services sub-layer provides the optional context-awareness, security, position location, and so on services. These services use the base services that are in the next layer, such as communication, lookup, etc.

Furthermore, before running an application, during the middleware instantiation process, the context properties and constraints about the user preferences, device, application restriction and runtime environment have to be known. With this information and with the architectural description of the application, the particular middleware architecture of the middleware family will be instantiated.

As mentioned previously, due to resource limitations the particular middleware instantiated has to be the minimum possible that fits the constraints. For example, if the device type is a sensor, only the middleware services which are really needed must be instantiated. In this case, the user context-awareness service may not be necessary, so the specific middleware will not provide this service. Furthermore, only the correct implementation of the services, considering either the hardware and software infrastructure has to be instantiated. For example, in the case of sensors network the device context-awareness monitoring only has to monitor the resources contained in a mote, temperature sensor, humidity sensor, and so on very different to the ones contained in mobile phones or PDAs. Additionally, the sensor networks usually work with TinyOS, and all the middleware components, the microkernel and services that have to be instantiated must run with TinyOS.

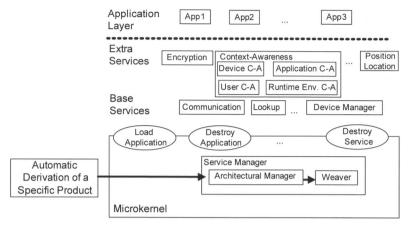

Figure 2. AmI Middleware Architecture.

2. Context-Awareness Service

The Context-Awareness Service is the responsible of (1) being aware of the context changes and (2) adapting the middleware to deal with these changes. As we said before, we have found four entities that trigger context changes: devices, applications, users and runtime environment. As is shown in Figure 3, the middleware has different context-aware services for each kind of context.

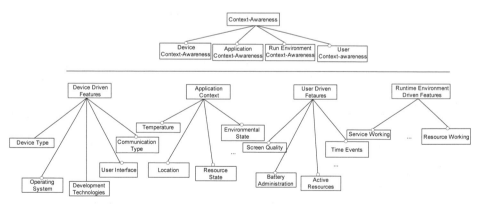

Figure 3. Context-Aware Service and Features Dependent of Context.

-   **Device Context-Aware**. This service has to monitor the current capacity and status and the correct functioning of all the devices that are using the applications and when one change is produced in one resource (e.g. the

Bluetooth do not work properly, the battery is under a minimum value) has to react and adapt the middleware to deal with the current context.

- **Applications Context-Aware.** This service is the responsible to be aware of the application restriction that can vary along the application execution. For example, the application may use some resources or not depending of its execution. The application may use the wifi connection at the beginning of the execution, but after this connection will not be used anymore, consequently the middleware can switch off the wifi car in order to save resources.
- **User Context-Aware.** The user preferences also have influences in the context. For instance, the user may want that in some kind of applications or at certain hours, the screen light will be high or low. Then, this service has to be aware of the user preferences and adapt the middleware to them.
- **Runtime Environment Context-Aware.** This kind of context contains the properties of the execution environment. For example, if one device is missing, the environment may change and some services may not be executed in the same way as before. In this case, this service has to adapt the middleware to work in the best way possible without the missing devices.

3. Instantiating a Particular Middleware

3.1 Instantiation Process

Figure 4 shows the application of an SPL Engineering process to the development of a family of middleware platforms for AmI applications.

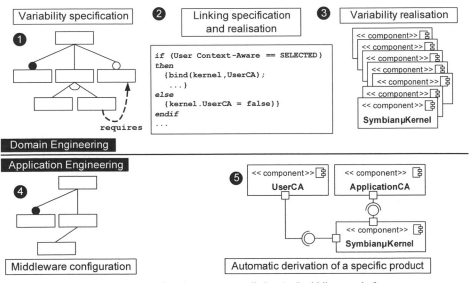

Figure 4. SPL Engineering process applied to AmI middleware platform.

1. The feature model for middleware platforms plus the constraints between features (i.e. dependencies and interactions between features) represent the 'variability specification', or, using SPL terminology, the *problem space*.

2.   Software engineers and architects must design a flexible architecture that enables its customisation, including and excluding functionality and components as required. As a result of this process, a reference architecture and implementation are obtained. These contain all the components that are required for implementing any product within the SPL family covered. This step represents 'variability realisation', or, using SPL terminology, the *solution space*. In this phase, all the different context aware services are implemented.

3.   The connection between a feature model and a reference architecture is rarely a trivial one-to-one mapping.Different SPL tools and languages, such as pure::variants [9], Gears [10], VML [11] or fmp2rsm [12], support the definition of mappings between a feature model and a reference architecture/implementation, often called *family model*.

4.   Middleware platforms for specific devices with a customised number of services, can be automatically derived. The first step in this process is the creation of a well-formed configuration that specifies which features must be included in the specific product being engineered. In our case, the selection of features will be firstly influenced by the device where the middleware platform is going to be deployed. Then, different features are selected according to the application requirements. This phase is related with deciding the services to be included in the middleware, for example the kind of context aware services.

5.   Finally, using the configuration created in the previous step, and the mapping created in Step 3, SPL tools, such as *pure::variants*, are able to automatically generate the specific product that corresponds to the desired configuration. This is achieved by interpreting and executing the rules that specify the mapping between the feature model and the reference architecture. As a result of executing these rules, the components that will comprise the specific middleware platform, plus their appropriate instantiation, initialisation, configuration and compilation files are automatically obtained.

3.2 Dynamic Reconfiguration

If the context changes (user properties, device constraints, ...) may be needed that the middleware has to be reconfigured in order to adapt the new context. For instance, a new service must incorporated this can carry out dependencies between features or service and may be needed add or remove other service. For example, in sensor networks, if the application at the beginning only uses the temperature sensor, but in some execution point it needs the humidity sensor, the device context-awareness services has to be aware of this sensor also. Then, a new device monitoring has to be added.

When the the middleware has to be adapted and reconfigured, to the new context the instantiation process would be running again and a new particular middleware architecture of the product line architecture of the middleware will be derivate. As our middleware will be driven by architecture, the architectural representation will be taken as input to the weaver in order to compose the middleware elements. This composition is made at runtime and changing the architectural description the middleware will change also, allowing in this way the dynamic reconfiguration of the middleware. The

Service Manager of the Microkernel has a weaver that is the responsible of making the composition between the selected services, the microkernel and application.

It should be noticed that may exists architectural configurations not allowed, because the feature selection imposed by the device and the feature selection demanded by the application that uses the middleware, or even by the user, may conflict. For instance, a device with limited processor capabilities would not be able to run security services that imply complex encryption algorithms. This kind of conflicts involves trade-offs that must be negotiated depending on whether end-users prefer to use better and probably more expensive device or they prefer to use cheaper devices but at the expense of certain application requirements.

4. Conclusions

In this paper we have considered the problems relating to AmI applications and how a middleware approach can solve them. We have adopted a layered middleware structure, using a microkernel and several services in order to obtain a more reusable and adaptable middleware. Furthermore, we have proposed the use of a middleware that allows dynamic reconfiguration, because this is a very important issue for context-aware AmI applications. In this paper we have focussed on the design of the context-awareness service of the middleware. The context-awareness service has been divided into several categories and each one has is the responsible to be aware of the context changes and to adapt the middleware.

As future work, we are working on the development of the rest of the services that the middleware will provide and on the internal structure of the microkernel.

References

[1]   Weiser M.:The computer for the Twenty-First Century, Scientific American 165, 1991.
[2]   Sven Apel et al.:Towards the Development of Ubiquitous Middleware Product Lines (2005) by In ASE'04 SEM Workshop, volume 3437 of LNCS.
[3]   Jules White and Douglas C. Schmidt: Model-Driven Product-Line Architectures for Mobile Devices, Proceedings of the 17th Annual Conference of the International Federation of Automatic Control, Seoul, Korea, July 6-11, 2008.
[4]   T. Sivaharan et al.: A configurable and re-configurable publish-subscribe middleware for pervasive computing. In Procceedings of Symposium on Distributed Objects and Applications, 2005.
[5]   L. Capra et al. Carisma: Context-aware reflective middleware system for moblie applications. IEEE Transactions on Software Engineering, 2003.
[6]   S. Yau et al.: Reconfigurable context-sensitive middleware for pervasive computing. IEEE Pervasive Computing, 1(3):33–40, 2002.
[7]   Kwanwoo Lee and et al.: Concepts and guidelines of feature modeling for product line software egnineering. Number 2319 in LNCS, pp 62–77. Springer-Verlag, 2002.
[8]   Phil Greenwood and et al.: Reference architecture. AOSDEurope NoE Public Documents (AOSD-Europe-ULANC-37), January 2008.
[9]   Danilo Beuche: Variant management with pure::variants. Technical report, pure-systems GmbH, 2003.
[10] Charles W. Krueger. Biglever: Software Gears and the 3-tiered SPL Methodology. In OOPSLA '07: Companion to the 22nd ACM SIGPLAN conference on Object oriented programming systems and applications companion, pages 844–845, New York, NY, USA, 2007. ACM.
[11] Neil Loughran, Pablo Sánchez, Alessandro Garcia and Lidia Fuentes: "Language Support for Managing Variability in Architectural Models". Proc. of the 7th International Symposium on Software Composition (SC), LNCS 4954:36-51, Budapest (Hungary), April 2008.
[12] Krzysztof Czarnecki e al.: fmp and fmp2rsm: eclipse plug-ins for modeling features using model templates. OOPSLA Companion 2005: 200-201.

Ambient Intelligence Perspectives
P. Mikulecký et al. (Eds.)
IOS Press, 2009
doi:10.3233/978-1-58603-946-2-90

Agent Based Risk Patient Management

Diego GACHET, Manuel de BUENAGA, Ignacio GIRÁLDEZ, Victor PADRÓN

Grupo de Sistemas Inteligentes, Universidad Europea de Madrid, Spain

gachet@uem.es

Abstract. This paper explores the role of information and communication technologies in managing risk and early discharge patients, and suggests innovative actions in the area of E-Health services. Treatments of chronic illnesses, or treatments of special needs such as cardiovascular diseases, are conducted in long-stay hospitals, and in some cases, in the homes of patients with a follow-up from primary care centre. The evolution of this model is following a clear trend: trying to reduce the time and the number of visits by patients to health centres and derive tasks, so far as possible, toward outpatient care. Also the number of Early Discharge Patients (EDP) is growing, thus permitting a saving in the resources of the care center. The adequacy of agent and mobile technologies is assessed in light of the particular requirements of health care applications. A software system architecture is outlined and discussed. The major contributions are: first, the conceptualization of multiple mobile and desktop devices as part of a single distributed computing system where software agents are being executed and interact from their remote locations. Second, the use of distributed decision making in multiagent systems, as a means to integrate remote evidence and knowledge obtained from data that is being collected and/or processed by distributed devices. The system will be applied to patients with cardiovascular or Chronic Obstructive Pulmonary Diseases (COPD) as well as to ambulatory surgery patients. The proposed system will allow to transmit the patient's location and some information about his/her illness to the hospital or care centre.

Keywords: Ubiquitous computing, ambient intelligence, telecare, mobile location.

1. Introduction

The model for delivery of health services in Spain is organized into a hierarchical structure of health facilities centres, where professionals provide services to their patients. The health professional's contact with the patient begins in primary care centres, while the specialized care and management of the disease are performed in hospitals of first, second and third level, according to the level of specialization in treatment and patient care.

In the hospital environment, given the high volume of activity and mobility, both medical doctors and nurses need technological tools that facilitate access to patient medical information and aid them to make clinical decisions, with a new form of interaction necessary among professionals, more natural and closer to the user, i.e. embedded in the working environment.

Moreover treatments of chronic illnesses, or treatments of illnesses with special needs, such as treatments of cardiovascular diseases, are conducted in long-stay hospitals and in some cases in homes of patients with a follow-up from the primary care centre. The evolution of this model is following a clear trend: trying to reduce the time and the number of visits of patients to health centres and deriving tasks, so far as possible, toward outpatient care. As a result, the number of Early Discharge Patients (EDP) is growing, thus enabling a saving in the resources of the care center [1].

This is largely due to certain structural aspects that encourage this trend [2]. The demographics of the population have changed, not only because of its growing aging but also because of the increase in chronic diseases. Moreover, these developments have an impact on the geographical characteristics of our environment, to do that there is a need to bring health services to rural populations and disconnected from the cities on the one hand and the need to decongest and decentralize health services.

1.1 Early discharge and remote monitoring of patients

Early discharge permits patients to return to their home for the completion of their recovery. Telecare and telemedicine aim to accelerate discharge from hospital and to provide rehabilitation / support in the home setting, providing services to the patients as shown in figure 1:

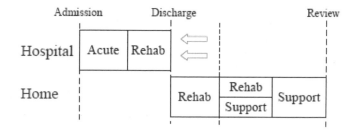

Figure 1: Services at patient's home for a early discharge

The early discharge service (EDS) enables health professionals to deliver more proactive care and support for patients, who can live independently, with the reassurance that help is at hand should they need it. Telemedicine units enable them to carry out early intervention, helping to adopt a more preventive approach to care, which has helped to reduced hospital readmissions [3].

The EDS is applicable to a large list of diseases, such us cardiovascular, chronic obstructive pulmonary (COPD) or stroke diseases. The criteria used for patient inclusion in an Early Discharge Program is highly dependent of medical team but in general we can take in account the following information:

- Age no more than 70 years old depending on the grade of disability
- Living not farther away than 100 km from hospital
- Stable clinical condition
- Sociofamiliar suitable environment
- Informed consent
- Capability to understand the program

The advantages for an early discharge program include better rehabilitation at home for the patient, increased availability of hospital beds and 85% cost reduction for the care centre [4] . Recent developments in ICT's have, however, opened up the prospect of creating a far more customised and integrated approach to care provision, where telecare is used to monitor people at risk within the wider, non-institutional environment. Two main types of telecare can be distinguished: systems designed for information provision and those designed for risk management [5]. The first approach aims to provide information about health and social care issues more effectively to individuals who need it. Our focus is on telecare for risk management, i.e. supporting activities for daily living.

2. System's Description and Operation

Health care processes and services take place in a variety of locations and involve multiple persons. Consequently, the software architecture of a computer system, designed to implement those processes and to support those services, should be distributed; and should also allow for the cooperation among persons and among remote computing devices. To meet these requirements, a multi agent system is proposed, where software agents are executed on desktop as well as mobile computing devices. The software agents play different roles (shown in figure 2):

- the **patient's agent** is executed in the smart phone carried by the patient. It monitors the patient's evolution, and informs other agents about its progress. It also provides directions to the patient as to how to follow the prescribed treatment, and assesses deviations from it.
- the **doctor's agent** is executed in the smart phone carried by the doctor. For every patient under the doctor's supervision, the agent is in charge of instructing the patient's agent on what treatment is to be followed by the patient, what are the appropriate and the alert values of the patient's vital variables, what are the emergency preconditions that should trigger the emergency protocol for the patient, and what are the guidelines to be followed (and transmitted to the patient's agent) should an emergency arise. Under regular operating conditions, the doctor's agent can work autonomously following instructions previously specified by the doctor or following standard-practice protocols. The doctor's agent contacts the doctor proactively in case an emkergency arises. Otherwise, it waits to provide the doctor with a summarized daily report of activity on demand.
- the **controller agent** is executed on the hospital's mainframe computer. It is in charge of, first, recording the activity regarding every patient in his/her medical record. Second, to produce a cost estimate of the resources spent in the patient's care, for accounting and billing purposes. And, third, to perform a quality control monitorization. This means, to check against medical records and a domain theory that the patient is not subjected to any unadvisable action from the standpoint of allergies, medical malpractice or others.

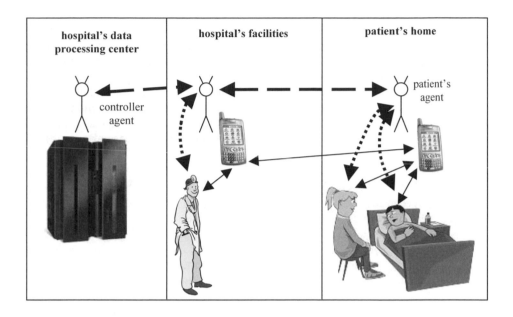

Figure 2: Global Concept of the System. Solid arrows indicate inter-personal communication, dotted arrows indicate communication between person and agent, and dashed arrows indicate inter-agent communication.

In our proposal we take measurements from the surrounding environment (mainly patient's location) and then transmit them along with other information to a health centre which will then act appropriately, permiting a care professional to provide support remotely, notify the patient about the medication, ask patient about some special condition, trigger an emergency response or alert a relative or neighbour.

In effect, telecare can form part of the risk management that every clinician undertakes, by transforming a previously unsuitable environment into one that is sufficiently safe for a patient to be discharged to.

As we can see from figure 2, from the hardware point of view the system includes mobile devices with processing and location capabilities, we think that this device may be a PDA with mobile phone characteristics with an integrated GPS receptor and Wifi capability, also, it might also be interesting if the device has an RFID (Radio Frequency Identification) reader for indoor location. From the communications networks point of view we are assuming at least GSM coberture in the patient's area of movement.

The illness information to be transmited to the health centre would include a questionnaire with information about the global condition of the patient, taking as example patients with stomach ambulatory surgery, the questionnaire may contain, among another, the   information shown in Table 1. This medical information will change depending on the type of ambulatory surgery and must be determined by the medical personnel.

As communication system to ensure a correct transmission of information between patient and health centre we will use the GSM/GPRS public mobile networks that also may provide the possibility for patient's location through the mobile device in case of necessity, i.e. when GPS service is not available.

The servers at the health centre must include the capability for visualizing map and location information and also the possibility for sending and receiving information to and from the patient, also this infrastructure has the possibility to contact inmediatly and in an automatic form with emergency and ambulancy teams in case of necesity.

Table 1. Questionarie about illnes condition to be transmitted to the care center

Surgery Problems	Answer
Pain in the afected body area	Nothing/ Tolerable / Much
Needed to take painkillers	Yes / No
Has bleeding	Yes/ No
Fever	Yes/ No
Deposition	Yes/ No
Vomited	Yes/ No
Headache	Yes/ No
Feeling dizzy	Yes / No
Tingling	Yes/ No
Blurred vision	Yes/ No
Has urine	Yes/ No
Pruritus or rash skin	Yes/ No
Dyspnea	Yes/ No
Difficulty swallowing	Yes/ No

In our case, the patient's location is very important due to medical personnel necesity to know at all times where is the patient, this is specially necessary for patients with an early discharge as a consequence of ambulatory surgery.

For obtaining location information we might mention the existence of mature technology such as the outdoor location through mobile phone networks that are based on   triangulation The possibility of   locating a mobile terminal has already led to numerous information services, tracking, route selection and resource management.

Because of the nature of the signal and network used, there are basically four types of mobile location systems: location through mobile pone networks, satellite networks, wi-fi networks and RFID devices.

There are several location techniques using the cells of mobile telephone systems, but they are based mainly in two principles: the measurement of the transmission time of the signal or the measure of the reception angle of the signal [6]. On the other hand the most used method for outdoor location is GPS (Global Positioning System). It is a fact that GPS is embedded in more and more devices: GPS receivers, PDAs and last generation mobile phones.

Nevertheless, the application for of GPS for indoor location is not so efficient. It is due to the lost and attenuation of the GPS signals because the lack of direct vision with the satellites and the attenuation that these signals suffer through building walls and roofs. The location using mobile phone terminals presents similar drawbacks. For these reasons in this proposal other variants of location have been taken into account: location using Wi-Fi networks and RFID-based location.

Location using Wi-Fi networks is obtained using several techniques. The simpler of which is determining the network access point close to the device to be located. Other very used technique consists in storing the measurement of the power of the network signal in different points of the indoor environment. The technique known as Wi-Fi mapping is more precise than the cell triangulation, reaching a precision in the range from 1 to 20 meters.

RFID-based location can be used in a big number of applications, because the data transferred from the label can provide information not only about location, but also identification or any other information that had been stored in the label.

3. Interface elements and methods

The system we are proposing consists in two main parts, a patient part and a health centre part, each with its own interface: the mobile device interface used by the patient and the hospital information system interface used by the medical personnel to access the information about the patients and make decisions about them.

Figure 3 shows a simplification on the interactions between users and subsystems. Figure 3 also shows the interface needs for each subsystem, where we can see that the mobile device's interface is pretty much simpler than the Hospital information system interface, that should allow the medical personnel to access and visualize patient's medical records and other related information about patients.

The Hospital information system interface will be implemented as a standard web interface to access the data, but the interface in the mobile device used by the patient needs more attention, it must be simple and usable by any possible risk patient as for example elder people with little knowledge about technology. The patient's location andctracking subsystem at the Hospital Information Servers could be based on Google Maps API, as it can be seen in the right part of Figure 4.

This interface would allow an easy location of patients showing the most important data for managing a possible emergency: the name of the patient, the state of the emergency and a summary of the clinical history, which can give some clues about the problem. This interface allows the medical personnel to access more data about the patient in a very simple way, by two links to the last recorded patient's questionnaireire and to all the data about the patient recorded in the system.

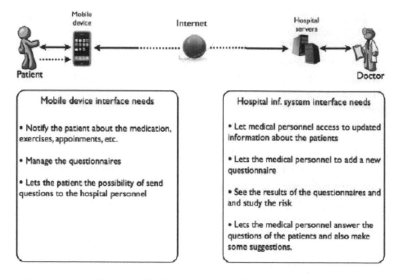

Figure 3: Interaction between patient's mobile device the hospital infrastructure in order to let the medical personnel access the data.

Figure 4 also shows (left image) a screenshot of the possible interface, it shows all events and reminders in an ordered list, which is very simple to manage by any possible patient. To fill out the questionnaires or to get more information about an event or a reminder the user only needs to select the desired option.

4. Future Work

The ideas presented in this paper are parts of a feaseability study and not a final system, but show interesting questions about the problem that we are trying to solve. The final implementation of the system must be designed to work on a real medical environment, which presents some differences and challenges:

- It must be able to manage different security profiles as the patient's information is confidential and only authorized personnel should access to it.
- It must be able to manage a huge volume of information, allowing a lot of connections between the HIS and the patient's mobile devices.
- The mobile device's interface should be standard or implemented for a large variety of systems.

The final system should also be evaluated in a real environment in a qualitative approach. We plan to evaluate the system with the final users: real patients and medical personnel. In this evaluation, we will study the usability and the satisfaction of the final users with the final system.

Figure 4: Screenshots of the interfaces of the system. The left image shows the patient's interface on a mobile device showing all the possible options. The right image shows a detailed view of the interface of the location subsystem in the Hospital Information Server.

References

[1] Hailey D, Roine R, Ohinmaa A. Systematic review of evidence for the benefits of telemedicine. J Telemed Telecare Vol. 8 pp. 1-30. (2002)

[2] Mechanic D. Improving the quality of health care in the United States of America: the need for a multi-level approach. Journal of Health Services & Research Policy. Vol. 7 suppl 1. pp. 35-39. (2002)

[3] C. R. Torp, S. Vinkler, K. D. Pedersen, F. R. Hansen, T. Jorgensen, and J. Olsen Model of Hospital-Supported Discharge After Stroke. Stroke, June pp 1514 – 1520 (2006)

[4] Ilias Iakovidis, Ragnar Bergström. European Union activities in e-Health http://europa.eu.int/information_society/ehealth (2006)

[5] Barlow, J., Bayer, S., Curry, R. Integrating telecare into mainstream care delivery. IPTS Report. See www.jrc.es (2003)

[6] Aranda E., De la Paz A., Berberana I., González H. Sistemas de localización en redes móviles: el servicio de emergencias 112. Comunicaciones de Telefónica I+D, número 21, pp. 117-131. (2001)

[7] Barlow, J. and Venables, T. Smart home, dumb suppliers? The future of smart homes markets. In Harper, R. (ed.) Home Design. Social perspectives on domestic life and the design of interactive technology. Springer Verlag. (2003)

[8] Brownsell, S.; Bradley, D.; Bragg, R.; Catling, P.; Carlier, JAn attributable cost model for a telecare system using advanced community alarms. Journal of Telemedicine and Telecare Vol. 7, 63-72. . (2001)

[9] Bull, R. (ed.) Housing Options for Disabled People. London, Jessica Kingsley. (1998)

[10] Cabinet Office E-government. A strategic framework for public services in the information age. London, Cabinet Office. (2000)

Ambient Intelligence Perspectives
P. Mikulecký et al. (Eds.)
IOS Press, 2009
© 2009 The authors and IOS Press. All rights reserved.
doi:10.3233/978-1-58603-946-2-98

Services provider for transport public customers based on mobile local devices

Carmelo R. GARCÍA, Francisco ALAYÓN, Ezequiel BELTRAMO, Ricardo PÉREZ
and Gabino PADRÓN
Universidad de Las Palmas de Gran Canaria
Edificio de Informática y Matemáticas, Campus Universitario de Tafira, Spain
rgarcia@dis.ulpgc.es

Abstract. In this article we describe a system whose purpose is to provide services, such as payment information at route, etc to the passenger public transport. The system carries out its mission integrating the mobiles local devices of the passengers (pdas and mobile telephones) and using wireless local communications (Bluetooth and Wifi IEEE 802.11). It addresses three important aspects of the system: its architecture, the scheme for implementing the applications that run on mobile devices and its security mechanisms.

Keywords: Pervasive systems and intelligent transport systems.

Introduction

Nine of each ten Spaniards have a cellular phone; at the beginning of the 2005, the statistic said that there was more than one cellular by each citizen Altogether, 44.3 million cellular lines were declared in Spain, whereas the census was 44,1 million the number of inhabitants; therefore, already in 2005 had more mobile phones than citizens. Independently of the exactitude of this affirmation, it is evident that we can consider the mobile phone like a "manhold-electrical" device (in similarity of the nomenclature for "household-electric" the electrical devices at the home) completely implanted between the Spanish citizenship.

Not only the communications have enjoyed a great impulse from the development of the wireless communications, this push has allowed that more and more soon the electronic advances of last generation arrive at the hands of the generic users not specialized nor particularly interested in the high technology. Every year, the users are induced to get rid of an "old" cellular phone (devices that would surpass the performance of any computer twenty years ago) in exchange for a new device with more sophisticated characteristics. This fact entails another detail of crucial importance: these characteristics, enormous in comparison with the technical knowledge of the most of the users, wisely have been hidden by a friendly interface that it facilitates the use and enjoys of these benefits without putting to the user in the "commitment" to have to learn complicated instructions of handling.

The other field in expansion derived from the progressing of the wireless communications and the wide unfolding of mobile devices between the populations are the development of applications for those devices. Most of applications developed for mobile devices are directed to the satisfaction of the playful necessities. Lately have been arising applications related to the commerce [1]: use of the mobile device like payment instruments, and also it is growing, mainly in the scope of the public administrations, the use of information systems that take the mobile devices like addressee of certain flows of information: administrative, tourist [2],[3],[4]. In this paper we present a system that belongs to this last field.

This system provides a platform for the development of services to the user of the public transport; that can be accessible via mobile terminal devices: phones, pdas, etc. The particularity of our proposal is that it exploits the availability of local communication (bluetooth, Wifi) into mobile devices that at the moment we consider underused - almost exclusively dedicated to the connectivity of accessories or the use of the device like access interface to the wire net and from there to the data network - occasionally interconnecting instances of cooperative games.

Our goal consist of providing the functionality of mobile devices to put itself in direct bonding with the information system of the public transport operating company and interacts with it without requiring the access to the wire net and therefore without the costs that the use of such services entails.

1. System's Goals

The object of the proposed system is to provide a platform that allows the development and the later distribution of information services to the user of the public transport. In order to reach this aim, first, the system will have to provide a model and a development and running environment, and second, the model must be sufficiently generic to include a wide range of target devices, no matter what operating system or communication technology be used. It will be necessary to describe an application model client that can adapt itself to the running and communication characteristics of device, offering to the user the best service that is possible given the device limitations. Bearing in mind this aims, we have derived next requirements:

We have decided to develop in Java platform; because is independent of operating system underlying. At the device side it has been widely deployed, chiefly between Symbian devices, with a wide range of API's of common use that permit access to hardware resources and communication technologies [5]. At the server side we adopt Linux OS that has a good support to this platform.

We must establish security levels adapted to different kinds of services we foreseen. A simple information service, that offers details about transport services, doesn't need the same requirements than a payment system, that it demands careful treatment of critical information.

The interface to the user must to have operative schemes simple, friendly and with reasonable response times depending on the type of services. And it must pay attention to the necessities of users with some type of difficulty, such as: linguistic specific needs disability.

The system that is described next fulfils these requirements. This Implements an offering services system adopting the server-client architecture.

2. Description of the system

In this section we will approach the description of the system. First we will describe the general principles of the system: its architectonic model and the general scheme of access to the services. Next, we will describe with some detail the three main components: the architecture model, the execution scheme of the applications and the security module.

2.1 Architectonic Model

The developed system is a case of distributed system based on the client-server model. Some applications run on different elements at the infrastructure of the transport company and others on the mobile devices of the users. The roles of each application are established based on a criterion of dependency of data. For example, in order to offer information services to the traveller it is necessary the participation of one application in the mobile device owned by a user. This application acting as client requesting information to another application running on onboard system that it receives and it manages such requests, acting as server. This server needs obtain information about actual localization of vehicle and so it asks for this information to other application, also running on the onboard system. It could need, too, obtain information about the client itself, that it is managed by a fourth application, in order to determine the characteristics of service requested by this client.

Another type of application are the interfaces that have to do with the communication technology, in order to separate the server from specific via of communications by which receives requests. The interfaces allows the free localization of different elements from distributed system, even allowing dynamic configuration depending on resources availability (the embarked system can consist on an only computer or a computer and a constellation of specific devices) or strategies of handling information (if vehicle remains in the bus station, could be more interesting request updated information to the central system).

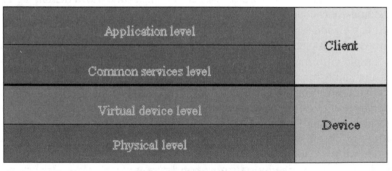

Figure 1. System functional levels

Figure 1 shows the configuration of the distributed environment for any service developed by the system. It's structured in functional levels likes Symbian structure [6], where at highest level is the user's application that request the services and it's running in the user's terminal. However, the functions provided by the rest of layers don't need to be assigned to a specific hardware:

Physical level: It is the inferior level and it includes to all the necessary resources hardware so that any service can be carried out, consists of three types: processor resource, storage resource and communication resource.

Virtual device level: In this level an abstraction is made from physical level providing a common extended machine for the execution of all the programs taking part in the execution of any service. This extended machine is formed by four units: archive's unit, security unit, communications unit and unit of administration of software.

Common services level: In this layer are provided all the common functions required to the execution of applications. The repertoire of functions is grouped in two categories: primitive for the accomplishment of basic operations and handling of data, and primitive for communicating and security aspects of the applications.

Application level: In this level are developed the different applications associated with each service. Each application running on this level represents a service offered by the system. The archives managed by each application are divided in two types: the data files and the archives of orders.

2.2 Common scheme for access to the services

Like the systems based on contactless card [7], in our system an application is defined as a set of data files and a set of commands. Application commands can only access data stored in the archives that are part of the same application. Basically, these commands permit us to perform: communications with other remote applications, simple arithmetic and logical operations and storage operations. The application data files are characterized by two attributes: a symbolic identification and an access mask. Each application is associated to a context, such as payment, traveller information, etc. There are services that have associated different contexts, for example, in a service payment system we can find different contexts. In each of these contexts, the associated application allows the client to pay the service in different modalities depending on the parameters stored in the application data. The extreme case of context dependent implementation we can find is when the application user is linked to his personal attributes. In general, a client application is executed following a common executing scheme:

Context identification: The local infrastructure sends context identification packets.

Context information request: When a client application identifies a context, it sends an information context request, producing an exchange of information between the client application and the local infrastructure.

Data transformation: A subset of the client application data is modified and generated by the client application or by an application running on the local infrastructure.

Transaction confirmation: The client application confirms the complete execution of the client application to the infrastructure.

The fourth phase, data transformation, is the stage that can be run in a distributed manner, emphasizing that the programs belong to this phase can execute both on the user mobile device, and on a specific station of the local infrastructure. Thus, the client application commands can be executed in a distributed way. This distributed computing capacity is motivated by several reasons: First, with this execution scheme the client applications are independent of the client devices capabilities. Second, in order to improve the security, we can ban the execution of certain operations on client devices. Third it allows us to support the dynamic nature of certain aspects of the user services.

2.3 Security aspects

As we have already mentioned security is one of critical aspects of the system. In general, according Gianluigi et al [8], security features should address the following issues:

- Eavesdroppers misusing collected data.
- Mobile fishing.
- Malicious users (payers or payees) which hack their own system.
- Lost or stolen mobiles devices.

Next we'll explain functionalities related to this concept, these capabilities are available to be used by applications.

Running on an only: There is a primitive that guarantee the running of an application in exactly the one device for which was downloaded. This primitive must be used by those client applications that offers personalized services, with particularized characteristics – for example a payment service modality adapted to a specific user.

Service Identification by UUID: By using this primitive is possible identify operation context. Each service has assigned an identifier and the applications that intends to use this service needs to know this identifier.

Safe connection, authentication and enciphering: There are a primitive that allows establish connection between application using authentication and enciphering protecting all data transferred.

Files enciphering: We can encrypt the data files that are going to be stored into user devices in order to maintain that information not accessible to the user but only to the application. It's a second level of information protection. The algorithm uses AES (Advanced Encryption Standard), encrypting by 128bits blocks with key size from 128, 192 or 256 bits and symmetrical key. The client application only stores the ciphered file, without access to it. The key it's only known by server that uses that information. In order to use the AES algorithm we use OpenSSL tool using Cipher-block chaining cipher. Another option is to use Base64 using alphanumeric characters.

How obtain keys for encrypting. In order encrypting is so necessary a good algorithm as a robust key. We have constructed a encrypting key that fulfills three essential characteristics: length, randomness and limited period of use. The primitive generates the key using a static part based on user identification and variable part based on circumstance data.

Hide files. It could be necessary maintain some hidden files to prevent access and avoiding modifications non permitted.

3. An example of service: a payment system

This example illustrates how the system has been applied to build a payment system based on cellular phones. Specifically the payment system uses an modality of electronic ticket of fixed numbers of travels. It consists of finite number of trips with fixed departure point and arrival point. Every time the client uses this ticket, one trip is decremented from the electronic ticket. Next we describe a situation where the user selects the payment option:

Context detection: The client application is waiting for the context detection; to achieve it is necessary that server application sends a packet of identification context.

Authentication: This step consists of authentication process between a client application and an element of the infrastructure. If the authentication is successful, then the client application can to continue executing. If the authentication is not successful, then it goes to the context detection (step 1).

Context information request: This step is reached when the authentication is successful; in this executing phase the client application can to request some context data needed by any command.

Payment validation: The client application sends to an element of the infrastructure two packets containing data and commands in order to execute the commands remotely.

Confirmation: An element of the infrastructure sends to the client application the confirmation of the validation if the requirements of the payment. If not, for example if the client terminal belongs to a blacklist, a warning is sent to different elements of the infrastructure, such us console driver.

Registered: If the confirmation step is successful, then the client application registers the updated data in the application files stored in the memory of the client terminal.

Transaction notification: This is the last step and it consists of sending by the client application of packet informing about the completed transaction. If this packet is not received by the infrastructure, then the transaction is considered as an incomplete transaction and it must be completed in the next use of the electronic ticket.

In this example, the data used by the client application are stored in the following files: keys data file which contain two keys associated to the client and to the application respectively, the second file contains the configuration data of the electronic ticket specifying the type of ticket and other specific parameters needed by the electronic ticket, and finally, the third file contains the movements history of all uses of the ticket.

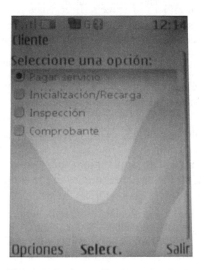

Figure 2. Device application main Display

Figure 2 shows initial screen after running application on a user device. As you can see the options are: pay a trip, recharge of number of trips, consult of data and, at last, show a ticket from last trip.

4. Conclusions

We have described a model of a system oriented to the development of information systems based on mobile terminals of telephony with local communication capacities. Our model is principally oriented to a public passengers transport infrastructure but can be easily generalized to other contexts. The system has a distributed architecture where modules can be running on different devices and the data communications can be achieved by wireless technology or other means depending on a dynamic configuration. The users can access to the information system using their mobile devices (pdas, mobile phones, etc) acting as clients. Some of the services that can be offered imply the necessity of transfer and maintain secure information and the system considers this aspects.

The main benefits of this system consists of exploiting the characteristics of local communication of users devices to access a Company Services reducing the costs both the Company that deploy at minimum costs its services and users that can access this services without added costs.

References

[1] http://wiki.forum.nokia.com/index.php/Nokia_6131_NFC_-_FAQs
[2] Arikawa, M., Konomi, S. and Ohnishi, K. "NAVITIME: Supporting Pedestrian Navigation in the Real Word. IEEE Pervasive computing, mobile and ubiquitous systems, Vol. 6, Num. 3, IEEE Computer Society pp.21-29. (2007)
[3] Reades, J., Calabresse, F., Sevtsuk, A. and Ratti, C. Cellular Census: Exploration in Urban Data Collection. IEEE Pervasive computing, mobile and ubiquitous systems, Vol. 6, Num. 3, IEEE Computer Society pp.30-38. (2007)
[4] Bassoli, A. et al. Underground Aesthetics: Rethinking Urban Computing. IEEE Pervasive computing, mobile and ubiquitous systems, Vol. 6, Num. 3, IEEE Computer Society pp.39-45 (2007)
[5] http://www.symbian.com/symbianos/index.html
[6] Stichbury, Jo. Symbian OS explained. Symbian Press (2004)
[7] ISO/IEC 14443 Proximity cards. International Standard Organization (2001)
[8] Me, G., Strangio, M.A. and Shuster. A. Mobile Local Macropayments: Security and Prototyping. IEEE Pervasive computing, mobile and ubiquitous systems, Vol. 5, Num. 4, IEEE Computer Society pp.94-100 (2006)

Ambient Intelligence Perspectives
P. Mikulecký et al. (Eds.)
IOS Press, 2009
doi:10.3233/978-1-58603-946-2-106

Ubiquitous platform for vehicles of passengers´ public transport

Carmelo R. GARCÍA, Francisco ALAYÓN, Daniel ÁLVAREZ, Ricardo PÉREZ
and Gabino PADRÓN
Universidad de Las Palmas de Gran Canaria
Edificio de Informática y Matemáticas, Campus Universitario de Tafira, Spain
rgarcia@dis.ulpgc.es

Abstract. In this article we describe a ubiquitous system developed and implanted in a public transport company. The system provides services to different actors inside and outside the vehicle as: drivers, operation maintenance and staff and travellers control. The main benefit of the system is that it solves the traditional problems of current systems installed on vehicles of road transport companies, providing the typical features, and also makes possible to develop new ones. This article describes the main features of the system: objectives, overall structure and operating principles and, finally, two examples of ubiquitous applications that run on it.

Keywords. Ubiquitous systems, automotive systems and intelligent transport systems.

Introduction

For several years, different technological advances have proved that the ubiquitous computing model, proposed by Mark Weiser [1], can be applied to develop computer systems that operate not only at the personal or household level, but also in the field of the corporate business. This paper explains an ubiquitous system working in the business context, specifically in the public passengers´ transport by road and describes how the system solves classic problems that these companies have, due to limitations and characteristics of their onboard information system. These problems basically are: limited capabilities of computing, storage and interconnection, hardware based on proprietary technology. As a consequence, they are closed systems. Using the paradigm of ubiquitous computing in its development, our system has solved these problems, resulting a system that supports not only all the traditional functions of such systems, but also new features based on their ability to interact with different users mobile devices using different communications infrastructures (wired and wireless).

1. System goals

Assuming the problems of traditional onboard systems of public transport companies by road and the keys non-functional requirements of the automotive domains (security, privacy, usability and reliability (SPUR) [2] [3]), the goals of the ubiquitous system proposed are:

- Improving the man-machine relationship, creating a system that allows easy interaction with the system users: drivers, travellers, supervisory and maintenance staff.
- Efficiency, stability, security, self-sufficiency are properties that must be associated with the operation of the system. To achieve these properties, the communication system plays a critical role; the system must be equipped with the communication resources required to interact with different ubiquitous devices that can work in the vehicle. The system should be able to recover from failure and return automatically to a proper state.
- Portability; the system software must run on different mobile users platforms on the onboard system.

Specifically, the system must be capable of:

- Providing appropriate interfaces to different users. Very important is the interface with the drivers of the vehicles, because it facilitates their work and the safety is increased. In this regard, the possibilities that provide positioning systems and multimedia resources are aspects to be taken in account.
- Processing all the information related to the planning. The system will have access to all the information that describes the operations to be carried out by the vehicle, controlling any deviation from the planned ones. It also has to provide the data required by the driver and travelers.
- Recording all the data related with the relevant events produced in the vehicle.
- Adapting to different environmental situations that occur in vehicles in an autonomous and spontaneous manner. Especially relevant are changes occurred in the availability of different communications infrastructures.
- Handling secure and intelligent communications from a technical and costs point of view, minimizing risk of data loss and not allowed access; so, it must use secure and connection-oriented protocols.

2. System description

Our system integrates ubiquitous mobile devices used by different users in the information system of the company. Users can obtain information using PDAs, mobile phones or personal computers. For example, travellers can use contactless cards or cellular telephones. Maintenance staff and control operations staff can use personal mobile phones or PDAs to access to the information required to carry out its task. The devices involved in the system are divided into two groups: those devices that are installed permanently on the vehicle, such as cards read/write terminals, positioning devices, environmental conditions sensors, etc. and, by the other hand, those which integrate spontaneously using wireless communications (IEEE 802.11, and Bluetooth). The connection of fixed devices of the system has a star topology, as described in Figure 1. The central element is the computer and it connects with the rest of fixed devices of different subsystems, for example: the payment subsystem (devices that allow different modes of payment), the positioning subsystem, the communications subsystem that connects the onboard system with the corporate information system, and the sensing subsystem, that provides data from the vehicles sensors.

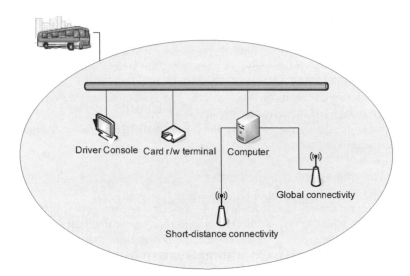

Figure 1. Hardware onboard system

The main functions of the system are: operation control of the vehicle, billing through various modes of payment (money, contact and contactless cards, mobile phones, etc.), and dealing with all relevant events occurred on the vehicle. These events range from operations carried out by drivers and travellers, to exceptions caused by hardware and software failures. The events are stored in archives, reported in real time if an event requires an urgent intervention, or reported at the end of the service. All these features produce an area of shared data, conceptually modelled through a set of entities with an hierarchical structure. This pervasive data model follows the model explained by Saha [4]. Nowadays, the system provides the following information contexts:

- System context. It is formed by all the entities needed to manage the communications and data flow. This environment is only handled by the applications with the appropriate privileges.
- Traveler context. It is formed by all the entities required by the passengers' information subsystem.
- Production context. It is formed by all the entities related to operations in the production and collection tasks.
- Control context. It is formed by the entities required to perform the control of the vehicles fleet planning.

The figure 2 shows the relationship between software elements. The system has service-oriented software architecture, so it provides the following benefits [5]:

- Uniform interfaces for applications, to facilitate the development and implementation of new functionalities.

- Flexible human-machine Interfaces, to adapt to different types of users of the system. For example, the driver interfaces are quite different from those used by travelers.

Ability to implement policies that establish which services are provided and how they depend on the type of user and context system

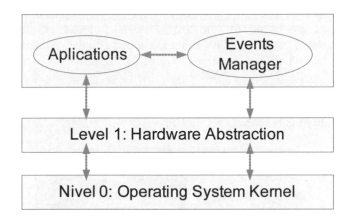

Figure 2. Structure of software elements

3. Examples of system ubiquitous applications

This section describes two examples of pervasive applications developed to run on our system. The first one, called Driver TPV, is a Java program, which plays the role of a driver interface device in the onboard system. Currently, it has been developed to execute on a Table PC. The second one, called Inspector, is a Java application based on J2ME specification and it is used by control operations staff to verify the operations of the drivers in route. It has been developed to execute in a cellular telephone.

3.1 Driver TPV application

This application allows the driver to enter data associated with the events of production, as well as ascertaining the occurrence of alarms linked to breaches of operational planning and technical errors (hardware and software). It also interacts with the system through onboard IEEE 802.11 infrastructure. It has access to different data contexts of onboard systems, specifically related to: production, planning, positioning and technical. The Driver TPV program is able to work in off line mode when the communication channel is broken and to put on line spontaneously when the communication channel is restored. Because of its capacity to execute in off line mode, this program admits direct connections with other applications, such as the Inspector application.

This application is a Java multithread program and it has three threads: the thread that implements the driver interface, the thread that supports the communication protocol and the thread which supports the interaction with the Inspector application. Basically, this protocol works as follows:

1. The protocol thread of the Driver TPV application periodically sends a status packet to the onboard infrastructure. This packet contains data produced by Driver TPV, which are relevant to the onboard information system, and so they are integrated in the ubiquitous data space.

2. The Driver TPV is integrated into the onboard infrastructure, so the infrastructure sends to Driver TPV an infrastructure packet as a response to the status packet sent in the previous step. The infrastructure packet contains data that are useful for the driver interface thread of the Driver TPV application. If the Driver TPV is not integrated into the onboard infrastructure, then it runs on off line mode.

When a relevant event is produced in the Driver TPV and it is integrated into the infrastructure, then it sends an event packet to the onboard information system to update the ubiquitous data space.

Figure 3. A screen of the Driver TPV application

3.2 Inspector application

Using this application, the inspectors can verify production operations performed by the drivers. As the Driver TPV program can not be integrated into the infrastructure, it has a specific communication channel, using Bluetooth, to interconnect with the Inspector application. Basically the Inspector application works as follows:

1. The driver orders the Driver TPV application to boot the thread of interconnection with the Inspector application. This thread is placed in waiting state.

2. The Inspector application, running on a cellular telephone, goes into a state of discovery of Driver TPV service.

3. If the Inspector application discovers a Driver TPV service, the Inspector program sends an authentication packet to the Driver TPV and, if the authentication is successful, then the Driver TPV sends a production data packet to the Inspector application, and the data about the driver service is displayed on the mobile phone screen.

4. Conclusions

This article has described a case of ubiquitous system for the world of public transport by road. It solves the traditional problem of the current onboard systems, consisting of its closed functional structure which results of the proprietary nature of its components. This system provides a flexible and scalable ubiquitous environment to run applications that provide services to all the users involved in a vehicle: drivers, control of operations and maintenance staff and travellers. As an illustration of their ability to respond to different users, to integrate mobile devices of various kinds and to use different types of communications infrastructures, two applications, called Driver TPV and Inspector, have been described. The first one, used by drivers, runs on a Table PC and it uses IEEE 802.11 as communication infrastructure. The second one, used by the control operation staff uses a mobile phone as execution platform and Bluetooth as mean of communication. As a conclusion, we can say that this system illustrates the validity of the model of ubiquitous computing to automate production processes of enterprises, providing attractive solutions, both, from a technological point of view and effective costs.

Acknowledgements

This work has been partially supported by the Transport Public Company Global Salcai-Utinsa S.A.

References

[1]   Weiser, M.: The computer for the 21st century. IEEE Pervasive computing, mobile and ubiquitous systems, Vol. 1, Num. 1 (reprinted with permission Copyright 1991 by Scientific American Inc). IEEE Computer Society pp.18-25. (2002)
[2]   Patterson, D.A.: 20th Century vs. 21st Century C&C: The SPUR Manifesto. Comm. ACM, Vol. 48, Num. 3 pp. 15-16. (2005)
[3]   Prassad, K.V., Gluli, T.J. and Watson, D.: The Case for Modelling Security, Privacy, Usability and Reliability (SPUR) in Automotive Software. Proc. Automotive Software Workshop, https://arxiv.org/pdf/cs.SE/0604019. (2006)
[4]   Saha, D., ukherjee, A.:Pervasive Computing. A paradigm for 21st Century, Computer, Vol. 36, Num. 3. IEEE Computer Society (2003)
[5]   Gluli, T.J., Watson, D. and Prassad, K.V: The Last Inch at 70 Miles Per Hour. IEEE Pervasive computing, mobile and ubiquitous systems, Vol. 5. Num. 4, IEEE Computer Society pp.20-27. (2006)

Ambient Intelligence Perspectives
P. Mikulecký et al. (Eds.)
IOS Press, 2009
© *2009 The authors and IOS Press. All rights reserved.*
doi:10.3233/978-1-58603-946-2-112

From the Home to a BlackBerry: Informatics-based Telehomecare

Anthony P. GLASCOCK[a], David M. KUTZIK[a]

[a]*Department of Culture and Communication, Drexel University, USA*
apglas@comcast.net

Abstract: Research on remote monitoring technologies has led to the development of an Informatics-based Telehomecare system that both allows data input and information display on a BlackBerry mobile device. This integrated system has the advantage over more conventional Telehomecare systems of providing caregivers with usable information as they are delivering care in the homes of their clients.

Keywords: informatics, Telehomecare, mobile interface, electronic records

Introduction

Telehomecare is generally viewed as a sensor technology that collects and transfers data on behavior, vital signs and/or environmental extremes. However, this view has actually limited the full potential of Telehomecare because it largely ignores the essential fact that the data collected must be usable and useful in a caregiving context. In other words, although receiving 95% of development effort, the sensor technology is actually only half of the total Telehomecare system. The other half is the informatics and communication technologies that translate, display, track and manipulate the sensor data so that the caregiver can actually deliver more appropriate and timely care. Without this half being fully developed, the sensor data is little more than noise that lacks meaning and usefulness.

Thus, after spending a decade developing and testing sensor technologies for the remote monitoring of behavior [1] we have shifted our attention to the informatics component of Telehomecare as we attempt to link the two halves into a fully integrated caregiving tool. This effort has resulted in a realization that the needs of the end-user—the caregiver—are paramount and in order for these needs to be met, end-users must be at the center of development, not as an after-thought. This does not mean that caregivers are to become developers or that end-users are going to collaborate on the development of algorithms. On the contrary, the ultimate goal is for the end-users to not even be aware of the informatics and communication technologies being used to provide the information that they use in the delivery of care. However, as we will argue later, for any Telehomecare based informatics "product" to be embraced by the home care market, it must take into consideration two factors: 1) caregivers already have a multitude of information on which they base their care decisions; and caregivers already have a way of "doing things". Thus, any informatics" product" must provide information that is viewed as valuable by caregivers and must deal with the fact that the provision of this information will change the way caregivers do their jobs. Thus, it's really all about implementation, that is, how the information provided by the total Telehomecare system is integrated into existing care models.

1. Background

The development of Telehomecare is a response to the current and expected growth in what is generally labeled home care. Home care includes a profusion of services provided in people's residences including, among others: 1) the delivery of personal health care, e.g., visiting nurse; 2) rehabilitation services, either delivered in person or remotely; 3) devices or special equipment or materials, e.g., bottled oxygen; 4) non-health related services—meal preparation, cleaning services; and 5) Telehomecare. This growth is fueled by the ever increasing cost of health care, especially institutionally based care, resulting in the belief that delivering services in the home will enable better care, reduce institutionalization and save money. In addition to the assumption that the delivery of care in the home will result in cost savings, the development of Telehomecare is also based on the parallel assumption that the use of technology will lead to greater efficiencies, thus reducing costs. Even though there are only a limited number of studies that support these assumptions, the development of all forms of Telehomecare continue at a rapid pace [2, 3, 4].

Although there is much debate over the definitions, [5, 6] we consider Telehomecare or Remote Monitoring to be: any application that uses technology to monitor a person in a residence, to send the data to an external location to provide appropriate and timely response in the delivery of care. Given this definition, there are four basic sub-types of Telehomecare:1) Behavioral Monitoring or Life Style Monitoring—any application that monitors task oriented activity in a residence and sends the data to an external location, e.g., meal preparation, medication; 2) Vital Signs Monitoring—any application that monitors vital signs in a residence and sends the data to an external location, e.g., blood pressure; 3) Environmental Extremes Monitoring—any application that monitors environmental conditions in a residence and sends the data to an external location, e.g., smoke alarm; and 4) Personal Emergency Response Systems (PERS)—any application that provides access to a signaling device in a residence that sends the data to an external location in case of an emergency.

Each of these applications consists of: some form of sensor technology to collect data in a residence; a base station or some other mechanism to transfer the data to an external location, usually a server; algorithms to establish thresholds and generate alerts; and the ability to send alerts to the appropriate end-user. We have discussed the way a behavioral monitoring system operates in a series of publications (see References), and the other three types of Telehomecare applications are quite similar in operation. As we discussed previously, what we just described is to most people a Telehomecare system. And that included us, at least until four years ago when we began to analyze the first findings on the actual use of the alerts generated by the system by caregiving organizations. As our research moved from one such care organization to another, for a total of eight separate organizations in three countries [7] it became clearer and clearer that what we thought was a Telehomecare system was, in fact, only half of the system.

2. Informatics

Our basic finding from this multi-site research was that, on one level Telehomecare was a success, but on another level it had not, and in all likelihood would not, fulfill its full potential. The primary reason for this apparent contradiction was that almost everyone believed that if the system generated alerts, caregivers would figure out how to use this and that once they did, new care models would emerge sui generis. The belief was that the superiority of these new care models would then be quickly recognized and there would be a wave of installations and Telehomecare would take off and fulfill the promise of better care at reduced cost. Clearly this has not happened and we believe that the reason for this is that the second half of the Telehomecare system had been largely ignored. Developers had just not given enough thought to how the sensor data is translated, displayed, tracked and manipulated so that the caregiver can use it effectively. Thus, if Telehomecare was going to be an effective and widely implemented caregiving tool and not just a clever technological gadget, the informatics and communication component had to be developed.

2.1. End-user Needs

The development of the informatics and communication technologies which would enable the second half of the integrated Telehomecare system to become operational was predicated on three basic characteristics of the home care market: mobility; timeliness; and customizability. First, by definition, home care takes place outside a central location as care/services are being delivered at an individual's residence. The reality is that the caregiver spends most of her day "on-the-road" traveling from one client's residence to another. Consequently, any informatics product would also need to be mobile in order that the caregiver could both input data and access information while sitting in her car or inside the client's residence. In addition, since time is of the essence in home care, both input and access would need to be quick and easy; taking no more than two to three minutes. Finally, the display would need to be such that the most important information would be the first displayed and navigation to other information requiring no more than one or, at most, two actions. Although several mobile devices were considered, including PDAs and laptop computers, the mobile device that provided the combination of ease of use, high speed and cost effectiveness was the BlackBerry.

The timelines of the information made available to caregivers while "on-the-road" is the second characteristic of home care that had to be taken into consideration in the development of the informatics product. The attempt to meet this challenge highlighted the difference between "real time" and "timeliness". Existing communication technology allows information to be sent at any time of the day. In other words, information can be sent to an end-user almost simultaneously to the event taking place, e.g., blood pressure rising beyond a given threshold. However, it does no good to send this information if there is no one at the other end to receive it and take appropriate action. Therefore, the key development issue was to develop protocols that took into consideration when caregivers were able to actually access information, where they were able to access it and how much information could be absorbed.

Perhaps the most challenging trait of home care that had to be taken into consideration in the development of the informatics product is its diversity. Just a short list of the individuals who would have need for such a product is daunting—visiting nurses, nutritionists, physical therapists, care coordinators, home help (meals, cleaning), social workers. Thus, to have an impact with the home care market, there either had to be a series of different products or one product that could be easily customized to meet the variable needs of a wide range of caregivers. The latter course was much more cost effective, but at the same time developing a single product meant that certain features had to be built in from the beginning. The most important feature was in many ways the most logical: the individual caregiver had to have the ability to both designate and design her own home-page and how she wanted to navigate through the other pages. However, it was not desirable to allow total design freedom and therefore definite limitations were imposed so that the caregiver was selecting from a limited number of options. The result was that, not only did the specific caregiver have a product that responded to her need, she also had participated in its "design" and thus had more ownership in the product than if it had been imposed from above.

2.2. Informatics and Communication Technologies

As discussed above, the nature of the home care market drove the design of the informatics product that was subsequently named the HomeCare Assistant (HCA). The HCA consists of two main features: the data input feature; and the information display feature[8]. The data input feature consists of a screen page displayed on the BlackBerry (See Figure 1). The individual caregiver[9] accesses her Home-Page by entering her name and password and once accessed, she then clicks the *Data Entry* button at the bottom of the page, navigating to the actual Data Entry Page which prompts data entry through both auto-populated and check-box cues. For example, Figure 2 shows the auto-populated fields of: client name; date; specific alert; and caregiver. These fields are automatically entered each time an alert is generated and the caregiver has only to confirm their accuracy through clicking the *Confirm* button. Figure 2 also shows the check-box prompts to which the caregiver responds by checking the correct box, for the type of care action taken, e.g., visited client at residence. Finally, the screen prompts the caregiver to enter a short narrative summarizing the outcome brought about by the care action, e.g., I checked her blood pressure and made an appointment for her to see her physician. By clicking the *Send Data* button, the data just recorded are sent to the server where they are automatically analyzed and updated to the particular client's home care record.

The information display feature is, once again, designed to be accessed on the BlackBerry, but of course, both it and the data entry page can be accessed on a workstation or a laptop. Once the Home-Page is accessed the end-user clicks the

---

[8] The HCA utilizes Red Hat Enterprise Linux running on an AMD 64 based system. The server receives alert information from the registered the QuietCare servers via a proprietary SSL HTTP connection. The HCA also consists of a set of PHP pages on front end with standard 128-bit SSL encryption technology. The site takes advantage of the model, view, controller architecture of CakePHP API. This allows for quickly adapting the front end to various environments, such as a BlackBerry, or Desktop PC, and end user locales, e.g., internationalization, change of languages. M The data is stored in a MySQL RDBMS using the Innodb table format for additional robustness, i.e., foreign key constraints. Nightly shell, SQL and PHP scripts run aggregate and store collected alert information. In this way, less work is done at the time users request the reports, while the server takes advantage of its least busy time. This aggregated information is then reproduced in customized reports using CSS/DHTML for print formatting. Any graphs and charts are produced using Gnuplot, with raw data fed into it from the nightly aggregated information.

[9] The alert is sent to the caregiver's BlackBerry by phone, email and/or text message. The particular type of notification is left to the individual caregiver.

Reports button to access the care report page. The Care Report Page is one of the customized features of the HCA and, therefore, there is variation in not only the look of the page, but also which of the various pages comprising the HCA is designated as the home-page by a particular end-user. Figure 4 displays the most common Care Report Page which is actually a narrative, in blog form, of all the care/services that have been delivered to a particular client.

Figure 3 shows only a single page of the total narrative for a given client. Of course, depending on the length of time and the nature of the services there will be many pages of narrative for any given client. It is possible to scroll through these pages, but there are also three navigation buttons at the bottom of the page that allow the narrative to be manipulated more efficiently. The *Sort* button is a pull-down menu

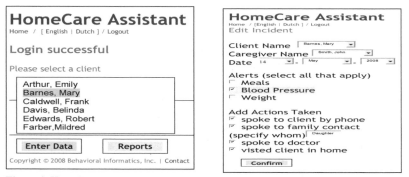

Figure 1. Home Page   **Figure 2.** Data entry.

that allows the narrative to be sorted by: caregiver, e.g., visiting nurse; date care was provided; type of care action taken, e.g., visited client at residence; nature of outcome, e.g., change in medication; and type of alert. This allows the caregiver to very quickly see patterns and trends in, for example, the type of care actions she or any other caregiver has taken over a given period of time.

In order to gain even more insight into the overall trends and patterns in any of the sorted categories, the caregiver can use the *Charts* button which is also a pull-down menu that lists a series of options. The caregiver can select: a specific category, e.g., type of alert; a particular time period, e.g., last three months; and type of chart, e.g., bar graph. Once selected, the HCA automatically generates the appropriate chart (see Figure 4).

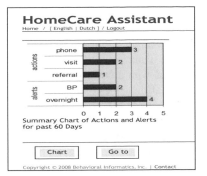

Figure 3. Narrative page.   **Figure 4.** Charts.

2.3. Challenges to Implementation

Much of the thinking about and development of the HomeCare Assistant occurred during a six month Pilot Study of an innovative Informatics-based Telehomecare service delivery model to enhance person-centered care in South Limburg, the Netherlands. The Pilot Study included 25 clients, 13 of whom lived in the community and were served by a home health care agency and 12 of whom lived in a continuum of care residential facility. The monitoring technology installed for the Pilot Study was the QuietCare® whose sensor array collected data on six conditions/activities, three that generated urgent alerts and three that generated non-urgent alerts. The urgent alerts included: 1) late wake-up, the client had not gotten out of bed within an hour of her normal wake-up time; 2) possible fall, the client had not returned to bed within an hour when getting out of bed in the middle of the night; and 3) the temperature in the residence was either higher or lower than normal. The non-urgent alerts included: 1) decline in meal preparation; 2) either a decline or increase in overnight toileting; and 3) a decline in overall activity which is a composite of all other activities [1].

Any new caregiving tool, be it MRIs, by-pass surgery or Telehomecare, requires changes in at least three different areas: 1) the systems and practices employed; 2) staff behavior; and 3) client behavior [8]. And we found that the implementation of an Informatics-based Telehomecare system did just that. First, the implementation required changes in the systems and practices employed by each of the care organizations. The organizations had to incorporate the new information into their care models, one result being bi-weekly care reviews of individual clients. Additionally, the information allowed a new level of staff accountability as assessments could be based upon precise records of care delivery and health outcomes.

Second, the use of an informatics based Telehomecare system changed the behavior of every staff member in the care organizations, regardless of level and function. At the caregiving level, staff were required to change their daily routine, e.g., respond to alerts first thing in the morning. At the managerial level, the care delivered by staff could be reviewed daily by accessing websites that contained detailed information on both actions and outcomes. Finally, the introduction of an informatics based Telehomecare system had a direct impact on the clients of the care organizations. In the first place, clients had to be persuaded that installing the technology and collecting information on their activities was worthwhile. Perhaps equally important was the need for clients to change their expectations about how the new information generated by the system affected their care. Some clients had more direct contact with care providers, others had less, and the type of care also in some instances changed, i.e., more phone calls, fewer home visits.

We found that the best way to meet and overcome these hurdles was to develop an implementation guide that included a set of mutually agreed upon protocols. The guide started with answering three basic questions: 1) what are the care needs of the client population, e.g., congestive heart failure (CHF); 2) what information is needed to meet the needs of the client population, e.g., for CHF, information on blood pressure, client weight, overnight toileting, meal preparation and medication adherence is needed; and 3) what sensor array is required to obtain this information, e.g., blood pressure cuff, scale, motion sensors in bathroom and kitchen, and medication caddy.

The next section of the implementation guide consisted of series of protocols. The first protocol explained and walked caregivers through the use of the HCA—how to enter data, how to access the client narrative, how to sort, how to update, how to access charts. The second protocol described the appropriate responses to different types of alerts—when to phone the client versus when to go to the client's residence. The third protocol outlined how managers could use the information provided in a supervisory capacity, and the final protocol summarized the process to use in the bi-weekly care reviews. Perhaps most importantly, we determined that protocols cannot just be handed to staff members with the expectation that they will just follow them. There must be training and training cannot be a one-time event; it must be on-going and take place at regular intervals.

3. Discussion

In the long run, the findings from the Pilot raised questions and provided some answers to the place of Informatics-based Telehomecare within the home care market. One conclusion that was clearly demonstrated was that this particular Informatics-based Telehomecare system produced records of the care and services that were delivered to the clients. The system was able to collect, transfer, interpret and display information in a meaningful way to caregivers. As a result, the system created an electronic record for each of the clients. Since this record was limited to the care and services provided after an alert had been generated by the sensor technology, it was not a comprehensive record of the client's care. Such a comprehensive record would include information on all care provided to the client—institutional and out-patient—as well as to that delivered in the home. However, the system did create a home care record that was permanent, automatically updated and could be customized in order to provide the most appropriate information in a timely manner to caregivers. Although not part of either the Pilot or the Demonstration, it would be possible to integrate this home care record with other electronic record systems, e.g., hospital electronic records, to produce a much more comprehensive care record for specific clients.

Secondly, the Pilot showed that the system could be incorporated into existing home care models—not without some difficulties, but not insurmountable difficulties. Clients accepted the installation of the sensor array in their homes, the emergency care center incorporated the alerts into their response protocol, staff at both care organizations took care actions based on the alerts and recorded these actions along with the health outcomes brought about by the actions and bi-weekly reviews were held to discuss the care that was delivered as a result of the alerts. There were problems, some of which were discussed earlier, but these problems were overcome and the emergency care center and the two care organizations signed on to the larger and more complex Demonstration Project, an indication of their assessment of the system.

These are all good signs, not just for the potential success of the Demonstration Project in the Netherlands, but more importantly, for the use of an Informatics-based Telehomecare system in general. The growth of the home care market will demand innovative, cost-effective means of delivering an increasingly wide range of service in the home. The ability to record and track these services, as well as eventually integrating them with care provided in other environments, appears to be an absolute necessity, if the home care is going to achieve its goal of the provision of better and less costly care. The piloted Informatics-based Telehomecare system is a first step in meeting these ambitious goals.

4. Conclusion

We started this article by arguing that the general view of Telehomecare as being principally a sensor technology limited its acceptance as a caregiving tool within the home care environment. We suggested that without the ability to translate the data produced by the sensor technology into usable and useful information, Telehomecare would remain a clever, but marginal contributor to the delivery of care in the home. Finally, we maintained that much more time and money needed to be spent developing the informatics half of Telehomecare that would translate, display, track and manipulate the sensor data than has been spent over the last decade. Our work in the Netherlands has only reinforced these views; Telehomecare only becomes an effective caregiving tool when the two halves become one. We have termed this integrated system Informatics-based Telehomecare and we are convinced that the advantages inherent in such a system will allow for the success that as yet to be achieved by more conventional Telehomecare applications. This success will come primarily because the "end-product" of the system is an electronic record: a record of all the care and services rendered in the home, regardless of the source of this care/service. The creation of such a record, not only allows for better tracking of care, but more importantly, places emphasis on health outcomes, thus allowing for the assessment of which care practices bring about more favorable results. Additionally, the ability to create home care records places Informatics-based Telehomecare solidly within the fastest growing and potentially one of the most beneficial sectors of health care—the electronic record industry. The ability to create such electronic records, whether in a hospital or community context can truly revolutionize health care in the near future and if Telehomecare does not move in this direction, it will be left behind.

For all of these reasons, we have continued to research and develop an Informatics-based Telehomecare system. The on-going Demonstration Project in the Netherlands will allow for continued refinement of the current system, as well as the development of new features, e.g., data entry through voice recognition. However, the most positive result that could be achieved in the Project would be the delivery of better and timelier care to people in their own homes.

References

[1]　A. Glascock & D. Kutzik, An evidentiary study of the uses of automated behavioral monitoring. Conference Proceedings of the 21st International Conference on Advanced Information Networking and Applications, Niagara Falls, Ontario, Canada, 2 (2007), 858–862.

[2]　M. Alwan, E.Sifferlin, B.Turner, S. Kell, P.Brower, D. Mack, S. Dalal, & R. Felder, Impact of passive health status monitoring to care providers and payers in assisted living. *Telemedicine and eHealth* 13 (2007), 279-285.

[3]　B. Celler, N. Lovell & J. Brasilakis, Using information technology to improve the management of chronic diseases. *Medical Journal of Australia* 179 (2003), 242-246.

[4]　J. Cleland, A. Louis, A. Rigby, U. Janssens & A. Balk, Noninvasive home telemonitoring for patients with heart failure at high risk of recurrent admission and death. *Journal of the American College of Cardiology,* 45 (2005), 1654-1664.

[5]　S.Hards, What is Telecare? Retrieved October 18, 2007, from http://www.telecareaware.com.

[6]　S. Soon, V. Mbarika, S. Jungoo, R.Dookhy, C. Doarn, N. Prakash & R. Merrell, What is telemedicine? A collection of 104 peer-reviewed perspectives and theoretical underpinnings. *Telemedicine and e-Health,* 13 (2007). 573-590.

[7]　A. Glascock & D. Kutzik, *A care informatics approach to telehomecare applications. Handbook of research on IT and clinical data administration in healthcare.* IGI Publishing, Hershey. PA, In press.

[8]　C. Paley & C. Slasberg, Implementing outcome-based commissioning. *Journal of Care Service Management,* 1 (2007), 353-361.

Ambient Intelligence Perspectives
P. Mikulecký et al. (Eds.)
IOS Press, 2009
121

doi:*10.3233/978-1-58603-946-2-121*

Architecture for the Internet of Things: API

Inge GRØNBÆK [a]
[a] *Telenor R&I*
inge.gronbak@telenor.com

Abstract. The architecture includes a secure API, a backbone and separate device networks with standard interface to the backbone. The API decouples innovation of services and service logic from protocols and network elements. It also enables service portability between systems, i.e. a service may be allocated to end-systems or servers, with possible relocation and replication throughout its lifecycle. Machine-to-machine services for Connected Objects (CO) could benefit the society in many areas, including environmental, health care, trade, transportation, alarms and surveillance. However, such development depends on the availability of global interoperability and powerful communications features. There are urgent actions to be taken to pave the way for this development to take place. The pivotal point is service ubiquity which depends on interoperability not only for a standard QoS controlled IP bearer, but also for cross domain security, mobility, multicast, location, routing and management, including fair compensation for utility provisioning. The proposed architecture with its API not only includes these critical elements but also caters for multi-homing, mobile networks with dynamic membership and third party persistent storage based on indirection. The API supports end-to-end service control and offers capability features as a vehicle for service development and ubiquitous deployment. The architecture is more generic than traditional hierarchical sensor and actuator networks as it supports grids and autonomous neural type of networks.

Keywords: Architecture, API, M2M, Connected Objects.

Introduction

This document describes the core of a service oriented architecture offering generic functionality for Connected Objects (CO). The architecture supports network and/or end system based services and service features. The architecture is more generic than traditional hierarchical sensor and actuator networks, as it supports grids and autonomous neural types of networks.

The functionality offered to objects via an API is either peer-to-peer (P2P) or enabled by a minor set of new generic functional entities. These include a gateway and an anchor point entity class. The gateway can be instantiated for interconnect of a rich variety of COs, including layer two proprietary COs. It can also be designed to support interoperability for native General Packet Radio Service (GPRS) devices on GPRS networks. The anchor point entity handles global mobility management and mobile M:N multicast. Additionally, these new entities support presence and location based services. Locations of COs can be identified, and the set of COs at a specified location may be found. Privacy is also handled by the same entities.

The architecture is functionally layered, with protocols and components identified for each layer of the well known OSI stack. Diverse protocol stacks and object characteristics are supported by relating the CO identity and the profile.

The two critical elements for the support of ubiquitous services are interoperability for services and bearers. Bearer interoperability requires both interoperability for the IP bearer (user plane) and for the bearer control (control plane).

The background for the strong interoperability demand is described by Metcalfe's Law, stating that the usefulness of a network increases by the square of the number of nodes (users or devices) connected to the network. Furthermore, Reed's law states that the utility of large networks, particularly social networks, can scale exponentially with the size of the network. Formation of such groups is gradually happening, e.g. the social utility Facebook which connects people with friends and others who work, study and live around them. These strong positive network externalities, where the benefits are an increasing function of the number of other users, represent a huge commercial potential which may be severely reduced by the lack of interconnect [1] and missing ubiquity in service support and provisioning.

The major area in demand for harmonization belongs to what is here termed the Internet layer (Figure 1). The Internet layer is the IP network layer, extended to include the inter-domain functionality required for end-to-end maintenance of QoS, Security, Mobility, Location, Multicast, Name resolution, Routing, Authentication Authorisation and Accounting (AAA), and Management. This functionality is required to interoperate across interconnected domains, i.e. administrative and technology domains, for the Internet of Things to support ubiquitous multifunctional services. In order for higher layer functionality and applications to get access to this functionality, there is a need for Application Programming Interfaces (API) at selected layers of the protocol stack (e.g. as depicted for the application and the Internet layer of Figure 1).

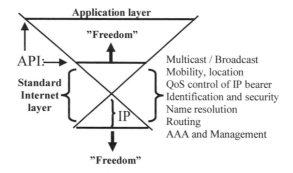

Figure 1. Internet layer with API

The rest of the paper focuses on the API part of the architecture starting with identification (chapter 1). Layering with functional aggregation, and primitive (method) design principles are described in chapter 2. Chapter 3 describes example API service elements. Network elements and functional components required for support of the API are briefly described in chapter 4.

1. Object identification

Applications benefit from objects being identifiable and/or locatable through different mechanisms. The most important ones are:

- By identifiers
- By the location (e.g. geographical confinement)
- By an objects profile or element(s) thereof, e.g. in combination with location.

The major challenge is to define and standardise a globally unique namespace supporting ubiquitous services. A solution is proposed by [2] and [3], introducing a new flat namespace based on public and private key pairs. This namespace is called the Host Identity namespace. It fills the gap between the IP and DNS namespaces. The Host Identity namespace consists of Host Identifiers (HIs), the public key of an asymmetric key-pair. Each host will have at least one Host Identity. Each Host Identity uniquely identifies a single host.

For efficiency purposes a Host Identity Tag (HIT) is defined as a 128-bit representation of a Host Identity. It is created by taking a cryptographic hash over the corresponding Host Identifier. A HIT presents the identity in a consistent format to a protocol, independent of the cryptographic algorithms used.

2. API Services and layering

The API describes capabilities and services between objects. Capabilities and services may freely be allocated to end systems (COs) or to servers. This enables functional allocations at the discretion of the developer. The same API may be used for network centric services and for P2P services. This enables services and service components to move, i.e. the architecture is agnostic to functional allocation and location.

Generic service elements may serve as building blocks for the full class of event oriented (i.e. data centric) and streaming oriented CO services.

The actual CO protocol (e.g. monitoring or remote control) is carried as payload by the user plane service elements of the API. These protocols may be proprietary, related to actual sensors or controllers, or adhere to standards. The architecture allows multiple application specific protocols to coexist, and it allows new applications and protocols to be defined without changing the basic API or its primitives (i.e. methods).

The service logically provided between COs, via the service API (Figure 2), shall be flexible in also offering subsets of the functionality. The idea, in particular applicable to device networks, is for the implementation to apply the simplest and most efficient protocol stack meeting the service requirements, with no or minimum processing and transmission overhead. It shall further be possible to increase the level of functionality by adding or including functional (sub) layers as required. Figure 2 shows aggregation of functionality from the set of service layers and protocol entities in the protocol stack. Any of the layers shown may be functionally transparent, depending on the protocol stack profile in use. Flexibility is enabled by resolution of the CO characteristics from the CO identifier.

The aggregated IP bearer service is logically provided at the top of the enhanced Network layer (i.e. to the Transport layer as shown in Figure 2). However, in an operational configuration, any of the layers may apply no protocol for communication with its protocol peer(s), i.e. the layer is empty except possibly from a inter layer service mapping.

A standardised API and protocols at the Internet layer (Figure 2) is key for support of inter operator ubiquitous services.

2.1 Service aggregation

The functionality of the API service offered to COs is aggregated from the services offered by the sub-layers shown in Figure 2. The description adheres to the well known ISO OSI model, and the approach relies on the same principles as the Platform-Based Design Methodology explained in [4]. The aggregated API functionality represents the Platform Design-Space Export.

The aggregated network service, i.e. the Aggregated IP bearer at Layer 3+, enhances the basic IP bearer service, which may be limited to offering a best effort service (IPv4 or IPv6).

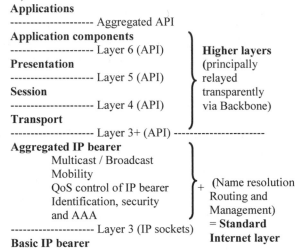

Figure 2. API and service aggregation

The layers above the Layer 3+ are the Transport, Session, Presentation and the applications. The service primitives offered by these layers are termed higher layer service primitives.

2.2 Service primitive design principle

According to the REST [5] principle, all basic service primitives shall offer a container for carrying data of a separately defined type. This creates an environment where clients and servers (i.e. objects) that encode their information the same way work together (i.e. share a common data definition). The uniform API interface can evolve over time. That is why it is built from three different parts, serving different and independent purposes:

- Identifiers (e.g. HITs),
- Methods (i.e. service primitives),
- (Document/data) types.

Each part is designed to change independently of the other parts. For example, new methods do not require the addition of new (data) types, and new (data) types do not require the addition of new methods.

3. Example service primitives

The following service elements are defined as part of the API, but not fully presented here: Storage and retrieval, Session service, Transport service, Location, Multicast, Mobility, QoS control, Data transmission, Security association creation, Basic IP bearer. A more complete overview of API services is given in [6] together with a description of how the IMS/Parlay-X service can be offered as a part of the API.

3.1 Micro-payment management

Settlement and compensation is allocated to the Management domain, as the functionality may be applicable to all layers of the protocol stack.

Fair and flexible compensation schemes between cooperating and competing parties are required to correlate resource consumption and cost, in order to avoid anomalous resource consumption and blocking of incentives for investing in infrastructure.

The proposed functionality is based on micro-payments as defined in [7] and is based on hash-chain trees.

The following service primitive initiates the acquirement of Length number of tokens (returned in Tokens), each valued Value and honoured by Vendor (e.g. via a macro transaction):

- Buy-Tokens (Broker-ID, Length, Value, Vendor-ID, P0)

The Commit-Token is used to initiate payment, and it allows the Vendor to verify the validity of the tokens via the Broker:

- Commit-Token (Vendor-ID, Broker-ID, Length, Value, P0)

Explicit micro-payment is made by invoking the primitive:

- Submit-Tokens (Vendor-ID, Length, Tokens)

Length number of tokens is transferred to the Vendor.

The Submit-Tokens functionality may be integrated in other primitives, e.g. in the Data transmission primitives for real-time payment of utilized transmission resources.

The Vendor applies the following primitive for redeeming the tokens (e.g. macro-payment):

- Redeem-Token (Broker-ID, Tokens)

3.2 Application component sub-layer

The application component sub-layer functionality may be offered as either complete services or as additional building blocks for in-house or third party services. The following represent example services.

3.2.1 Event reporting

The following primitive is used for event subscription at the event server (Registrar-CO-ID), for events at the Target-CO-ID (both could be the same CO):

- Event-Subscription-Send (Registrar-CO-ID, Target-CO-ID, Parameters)

An event subscription shall be confirmed by an event notification from the Registrar. The event notification indicates an event at the Target-CO-ID, or a subscription for events.

- Event-Notification-Send (Subscriber-CO-ID, Target-CO-ID, Parameters)

The Event-Report primitive is used for carrying reports from a CO (e.g. a simple censor) to the recipient (e.g. the Registrar event server).

- Event-Report-Send (Registrar-CO-ID, Parameters)

The Parameters may specify a distinct value or a set of values (e.g. representing upper and lower limits). Events may also be complex in that more COs and parameters may be involved.

3.2.2 CO presence

The following primitive is used for dynamic CO presence registration:

- Register-Send (Registrar-CO-ID, Parameters)

A registration shall be confirmed by an event notification to the registering party, and to all parties having subscribed on this registration event.

3.3 Presentation service

This layer defines the vocabulary for (control of) CO service applications; i.e. the data structures and commands required for COs to interoperate, e.g. for an advanced control and surveillance application.

The actual monitoring or control protocol may be proprietary, related to actual sensors or controllers, or standards may be applied. The identification or standardization of such protocols is for further study, but architecturally the vocabulary of such protocols is allocated to the Presentation layer.

3.4 Network service at the Internet layer

The Internet layer in Figure 2 is the IP network layer, extended to include the inter-domain functionality required for end-to-end maintenance of QoS control, Security, Mobility, Location, Multicast, Name resolution, Routing and Management. This functionality is required to be maintained across interconnected domains of the Internet of Things, to support ubiquitous multifunctional services. This functionality is therefore critical for end-to-end service provisioning, since network elements in interconnected domains need to contribute to the functionality on a hop-by-hop basis. These services are crucial to the architecture, however their description can not be included here due to space limitations.

4. The topology and network elements

The Internet of Things comprises two logically distinct, but closely coupled, network domains (Figure 3), i.e. the backbone and the device network domains. Both domains may be serving COs directly.

The backbone network offers ubiquitous interconnect for services at the Internet layer (Figure 2), while connected objects interconnect at the Application layer, i.e. the higher layer protocols are transparent to the Internet layer.

Device networks connecting clusters of objects must be flexible in technology and topology. A limited set of interfaces need to be standardised for interconnect with and via the backbone network. There is a need to integrate simple low-end devices, e.g. with limitations in functionality and power supply.

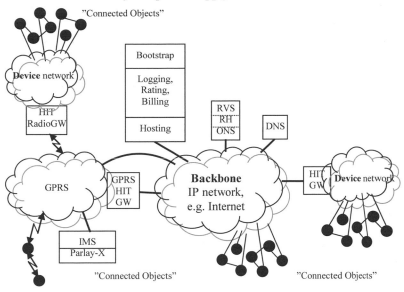

Figure 3. Components and their relation

The naming reflects the use of the Host Identity Protocol (HIP) [2] for e.g. obtaining name/address separation, security and mobility for objects.

The Host Identity Tag (HIT) gateway (Figure 3) is based on HIP and allows global addressing of COs while maintaining the use of IPv4 addresses. The HIT gateway shall keep track of the location of all COs under its control. Each gateway shall be allocated a coverage area, allowing identification of objects within that area. Each gateway shall furthermore keep track of all its physical gateway neighbours, to allow extended area search for COs.

The basic functionality of the Rendezvous Server (RVS) is to offer mobility anchoring, i.e. maintenance of the HIT to address bindings. It may also be engaged in traffic forwarding in cases where privacy is required. Event reporting shall also be handled by the RVS serving the target CO, i.e. the CO at which events are monitored for reporting. This implies that the registrar and notification functionality shall be implemented at the RVS as well.

The Resolution Handler (RH) is an RVS extension offering generic name resolution from a flat namespace (e.g. HIT to address resolution). Retrieval of CO characteristics is part of the functionality, e.g. identification of protocol stack and other capabilities.

The Object Naming Service (ONS) is part of the EPC Global Network [9]. The ONS may be integrated with the RVS entity, or can be implemented as a self-contained entity. The ONS offers name resolution for Electronic Product Codes (EPC)

A detailed description of the topology and network elements required to support the functionality of the API is given in [8].

5. Conclusions

The API of the architecture shields applications from the underlying technologies, and reduces efforts involved in service development. At the same time, services and technology platforms are allowed to evolve independently. The architecture will support ubiquitous services on an end-to-end basis. This will provide efficiency in scale and scope in service infrastructures, service production and service development.

The architecture may serve as a vehicle for migration to the true all-IP Internet of Things. However, this presupposes avoiding the mistakes made by ISPs for the Internet [1], i.e. by not cooperating and coordinating between operators in order to allow service and transport level interoperability at the Internet layer. This is required for service ubiquity, in order to enlarge the total global market, thereby benefiting the whole ICT industry.

Acknowledgement

The author is grateful for enlightening discussions, comments and contributions from Jan Audestad, Terje Jensen, and Anne-Grethe Kåråsen, all with Telenor.

References

[1]   P. Faratin, D. Clark, P. Gilmore, S. Bauer, A. Berger and W. Lehr, Complexity of Internet Interconnections: Technology, Incentives and Implications for Policy, 2007.
[2]   Host Identity Protocol (HIP) Architecture, IETF RFC 4423, May 2006.
[3]   T. Koponen, et al., A Data-Oriented (and Beyond) Network Architecture, SIGCOMM'07, August 27–31, 2007, Kyoto, Japan.
[4]   Alberto L. Sangiovanni-Vincentelli. Quo Vadis SLD: Reasoning about Trends and Challenges of System-Level Design. Proceedings of the IEEE, 95(3):467-506, March 2007.
[5]   REST: http://rest.blueoxen.net/cgi-bin/wiki.pl?RestInPlainEnglish.
[6]   Inge Grønbæk, et al., Abstract Service API for Connected Objects, Telenor R&I Research Report 18/2007, June 2007.
[7]   Hitesh Tewari, Donal O'Mahony, Real-Time Payments for Mobile IP, IEEE communications-magazine, february2003, pp 126-136.
[8]   Inge Grønbæk, Sune Jakobsson, High level architecture for support of CO services, Telenor R&I Research Report 37/2007, November 2007.
[9]   Electronic Product Code, http://www.epcglobalinc.org/standards/architecture/architecture_1_2-framework-20070910.pdf.

Ambient Intelligence Perspectives
P. Mikulecký et al. (Eds.)
IOS Press, 2009
© 2009 The authors and IOS Press. All rights reserved.
doi:10.3233/978-1-58603-946-2-129

Towards Empowering Design Practises

Veikko IKONEN
VTT, Finland
veikko.ikonen@vtt.fi

Abstract. Design of future smart environments (and services and products included in these environments) requires agile and stakeholder involved methodologies for the greater success among targeted user populations. Furthermore the factors affecting to the design decisions in the future are sundry and in many cases frequently in conflict. Currently user and usability studies are conducted in order to get better effectiveness, efficiency, and user satisfaction and user acceptance for new products and services. Even though the design approach is called human-centred or user-centred the design of new products and services has been quite technology or market driven in Information and Communication Technology (ICT) business. Instead of putting technology or market to the core of design process and product development the human needs and values should form the fundamental basis of design. Human Driven Design (HDD) refers to the design approach which broadens the perspective from focused product or service development process model to the more holistic design perspective. Stakeholder Based Design approach (SBD) furthermore broadens the scope and role of involved participant groups in the actual design process. Integrating HDD and SBD includes inevitably ethical assessment of design process and artifacts while trade offs in design have to be well justified. Hence HDD and SBD call for new Empowering Design (ED) practices which could accomplish more deliberative but still agile approach to design of future smart environments.

1. Introduction

Information and communication technologies are supposed to have even more vital role in future society. Future smart environments are imagined to be intelligent, adaptive, intuitive and interactive. The combination of mobile computing and technologically embedded environments brings new challenges to the design, implementation and introduction of novel applications. New solutions for various fields of work and leisure also challenge the potential users and inhabitants of, or visitors to, these smart environments. Extensive (all stakeholders included) and democratic participation for future smart environment design is essential but challenging when designing solutions that may be unfamiliar in their appearance, functionality and impressiveness compared to the people's current everyday life. New approaches are needed for design and evaluation of smart environments to build systems and solutions that naturally support users in their daily life and give them seamless and enjoyable experience of the solution. Furthermore the implemented designs should not bear overwhelming encumbrance of conflicts between different relevant stakeholders. The Human Driven Design (HDD) approach strives to tackle challenges and problems confronted in current design approaches. We should not just study applications and their usability but to take into account more holistic perspective when designing and evaluating applications and environments that follow philosophy of Ambient Intelligence (AmI). Ethical issues (including e.g. privacy and security) are naturally always present and covered in Human Driven Design approach

2. Towards Transparent Design Processes

Design principles for smart environments have been published but in these statements the technological issues are emphasized to a greater extent. (e.g. Coen 1998, Remagnino et al. 2005, Cook and Das 2005) More profound co-operation between designers, developers, researchers and potential users is needed to be able to put forward new theories and methodologies that will help to develop solutions that naturally support humans in their living environment and take into account both the complexity of the systems and technological aspects as well as social, ethical and cultural issues.

Hence we kindly accept the Information and Communication Technologies as best solutions and answers to all problems and questions. We tend to keep development and utilistion of ICT as natural law like positive. This kind of technology belief is very close to traditional conception of religion where there are articles of faith (from programming practises and languages to high-level statements of omnipotence of ICT technologies), presenters of these articles (evangelists, leaders of companies and organisations) and even rituals for ICT adoration (different kinds of meetings, happenings and exhibitions). Furthermore as we handle technology as a religion we believe that complexity and uncertainty are most valuable features of these novel ICT systems. Complexity is praised as a cornerstone for future smart environments. Complexity with enormously massive infrastructures and architectures make these systems incomprehensible all the others but people who are deeply involved to the system development; people who know secrets of the system and can configure these systems for the uncomprehending.

To be able to handle development and design of future smart environments in a more objective manner we need to have also critical perspective towards current technological development. Melvin Kranzberg's (1986) first law of technology states, that"Technology is neither good nor bad; nor is it neutral". This is something we should always remember in our developmental work. We are always as designers in position that bears some fundamental cultural values and beliefs. Weather we are and want to be aware of our current design framework is relevant because this framework determines our relationship to the design process and to the actual designs themselves. Through emerging empowering design practises we as designers and developers of our future smart environments can have genuine possibility to be active and influential partners in design process. Through extensive stakeholder involvement throughout design process we can offer this possibility to all the other relevant stakeholders and expose transparent design process for the public discussion.

3. Human Driven Design of New Everyday

The human world has always been technologically embedded. One of the main arguments behind the human culture is the definition of a technologically enhanced living environment. The human relationship with technology has always been goal-oriented. Our basic needs have been fulfilled with the help of technological inventions. Furthermore, we have also used technology to satisfy our secondary needs (e.g. need for communication in distance and self-expression). (Maslow 1943)

In the very beginning the design of human technology has been quite near to the actual usage situation and the need for design has been also rather self-evident. Often the designer, manufacturer and user have been the same person. In more complex societies the skills and professions have been differentiated: the user, or in a more general terms the human, is no longer the same person as a designer or maker. In our times the computers and programs are tools which are assumed to satisfy almost all of our needs for everyday living. The design and development of computer-based applications and services has long been separated from the actual users. Human-Centred Design (HCD) of technologies has tried to narrow the gap between developers and actual users or those who utilise the technology. Participatory design (also called co-design) and standardised HCD processes were introduced more than two decades ago, but mainly for task-oriented desktop computing. The world, and especially the computing world, has changed since and new methods and theories for design have also been introduced.

Brand and Schwittay (2006) bring out four dimensions that should be taken into account in developing information technologies for developing regions: local practises, participatory design processes, socio-cultural contexts and political conditions. Furthermore they emphasise that so called rapid ethnography is not the right answer in these research contexts but what is needed is long-term participant observation. However in our context (developing smart environments) of Human Driven Design we believe that there is place for both kinds of approaches: rapid ethnography for inspiring totally new design and long-term living laboratory type of studies for validating the adaptation of technology in particular situation. HDD studies and develops e.g. interactive and intuitive user interfaces and services, as well as methods for human-centred design. When studying for example intuitive user interfaces, people and their natural behaviour is the starting point in the research Extensive user requirements gathering (interviews, observations, focus groups or group interviews) should be interlocked seamlessly to the technological work of defining system requirements and e.g. reference architecture. There should be special emphasis for integrating social and technical requirements by enabling authentic dialogue between different stakeholders during the early developmental phase. The objective of the early phase of development (i.e. requirements gathering) is to build a common vision and starting point for the developmental work, where all partners and other stakeholders (including potential users) take part in order to define the detailed scope for the work and detailed requirements (user, social, ethical, technical, economical, system) for the developmental work of applications and services. When defining the user requirements, the end-users are often not the only actors whose requirements should be taken into account. In addition to the actual end-users it is important to take into account the points of view of the user organisation, the service providers and society as a whole. There will also be business and technical requirements for the system, which will be identified and developed in parallel with the user and organisational requirements.

As a result of a recent joint effort (Kaasinen and Norros 2007), a theoretical basis for a new design framework for smart systems was presented. The framework was labeled *ecological approach to design of smart environments*. The approach states that the traditional product design approach needs to be extended to two new design, immediate design and remote design levels, due the current design tensions and demands. According the framework immediate design focuses on local and immediate user needs and experiences, and emphasises the increasing role of users in the design. Design alone or technology by itself cannot create practices but they offer possibilities that users utilise and shape into their practices. Remote design is more distant or strategic in a sense that it aims at abstracting from the immediate and creating more general solutions (eg. physical or technical architecture, standard, platform, political decisions) that provide possibilities and prerequisites for the future.

As a part of the immediate design it is necessary to develop co-design methodology that allows different stakeholders to take part to the design as equal partners. Changing the shift from research objects to research partners or stakeholders (research subjects) could be called an Empowering Design practice for potential end-users of a product or a service. In addition empowering design should focus also to other design levels and to the all stakeholder perspectives and not just to the end-users. Empowering design practice should give an opportunity to influence to the design in all levels and by different actors so that the dialogue built in design process could be open and mindful between different levels and between different kinds of stakeholders. Part of the empowering design practice is to perform an ethical assessment for the whole design. Ethical issues should be studied throughout the design process: from the requirements gathering phase to the testing including all stakeholders perspectives for the design and implementation of the system.

4. Case Study: Example of Scenario Assessment in Minami Project as Empowering Design Practice

4.1 The scenario: Mrs. Bates

Mrs. Bates is a 73 year old lady. She lives on her own with her cat named Norman. Her daughter Sarah lives nearby and lately she feels a little bit worried because she can't visit her as much as she would like. Sarah convinces her mother to install a new home security and comfort system. After gathering information from several companies, they choose "ACME Home Security" services. The salesman informs then about the very latest advancements in home comfort and security, in particular about a vision detection sensor table to discriminate between pets and persons. Mrs. Bates and Sarah decide that this is a good idea to keep track of Norman outside the garden and to detect intruders. The salesman argues that this is also a good sensor to confirm a person's fall in a room and assures that this sensor does not retransmit any image outside, only performs detections. However Mrs. Bates doesn't feel comfortable with cameras inside the house.

After several days, the technician comes to Mrs. Bates' house. He installs the vision sensor in the backyard's garden, open door sensors in doors and windows, infrared motion detectors in every room. He also asks her some questions regarding her lifestyle. During the day, all the sensors in every room will work in "comfort mode" offering friendly reminders about open doors in empty rooms. At night, the sensor network will operate in security mode, notifying the homecare/security company of alarms and making audible alarm tones. He also gives her a simple two-button remote control to activate/deactivate functions and a medallion – with an accelerometer embedded – to detect falls.

A few days later, Mrs. Bates has been used to her new system. She has just received a remainder that the garage door is open She walks downstairs to the basement of her house to check it. The staircase lights up automatically when she walks down: falling down may happen so quickly…

Mrs. Bates goes up and sits down comfortably in her armchair. As there have been several burglaries in the neighborhood, she uses her "friendly-home remote control"® to turn on the anti-intrusion alarm system in the basement.

The movie is now beginning. When the suspense reaches its peak, Mrs. Bates' mobile phone rings and indicates that a pet was detected in the backyard. She remembers that Norman followed her when she went downstairs a while ago. She stands up to open the staircase door and lets the cat in. Mrs. Bates can now enjoy the end of the movie with Norman, happily purring on her lap. She falls asleep.

Not long after, a burglar breaks into the basement through the back door, which is not protected. The friendly-home system detects the intruder and activates the siren with a pre-alarm ringing. Having heard this unexpected noise, the burglar runs away. Mrs. Bates wakes up in a start, rushes up and trips over Norman. She heavily falls down and cannot rise to her feet again.

Fortunately, the accelerometer the event and detects an emergency. The friendly-home system quickly sends a message to her daughter Sarah and ACMES' monitoring service which organizes an intervention at Mrs. Bates' house as quickly as possible.

It just took a few days before Mrs. Bates got over this accident and resumed a normal life.

4.2 Scenario analysis from life cycle point of view

Scenario analysis is based on identified Minami ethical principles (Ikonen et al. 2008), principles of value sensitive design (Friedman and Freier 2005) and to the more focused approach of product lifecycle (Topo et al. 2004).

Identified design concept of Home surveillance scenario
Home surveillance system / home security system

Identified stakeholders of Home surveillance scenario:
Mrs Bates, 73 years, Norman (cat), Sarah (Daughter), Home Security Company, Installer, Intruder

Analysis
In the *early phase of design* of Home surveillance System (HSS) different stakeholders related to the usage of a system should be recognised. In *identifying user needs and further defining user requirements* the relevant question is who are considered as the users of a product or service. In addition to this it is important to consider how the information regarding the users is gathered. Assessment of user needs and defining user requirements should take into account and emphasise the end user aspects while also considering other involved stakeholders. All Minami ethical principles are relevant to go through in this phase as well as in the next phases: concept creation/design and product/services testing/piloting.

In the HSS *concept design and product/service testing phase* the ethical issues (problems, challenges and threats) are confronted in the level of empirical and technical analysis. The HSS developers should be aware of ask advice from ethical and social accountability specialist and legal specialists who should be integrated in project to ensure timely assessment of ethical and legal issues.

The *marketing* of HSS should be respectful and honest. The features and functionalities of a system should be clearly explained and e.g. reliability of the system or sensitiveness to malfunctions should be reported. The overall costs of the system (e.g. procurement, installation alarm service, maintenance) should be clearly informed. In *implementation* the overall system functionalities should be explained when needed or if the customer is just willing to know for example about technical details. Functionality of the system should be tested right after installation and it should be repeated regularly either in the actual space of surveillance or by the reliable remote testing system. In the marketing and implementation of the system it is worth of noticing that there are also other stakeholders (here: family members, public authorities of health and social affairs) that might affect to the procurement and usage of the system.

From the point of view of the *use of a system* it is important that the information needed for the use of the equipment is easily available for the user and that (s)he has been sufficiently instructed in its use. From the point of view of the user, it is also relevant that (s)he is aware of the costs of use. From the point of view of the service provider it is appropriate that the user pays for the use according to an agreement. If the system collects some information of the people it should be explained and justified. In the use of the HSS system one should consider carefully again the issues of privacy, dignity and autonomy. If the *maintenance* of the service is needed then it should arranged so that the respect of users privacy, dignity and autonomy are taken into account carefully. If the system is not working due the undone maintenance the actual end user (Mrs. Bates) and other involved (Daughter) may trust in the false feeling of safety and security.

According to the product lifecycle described here *abandoning (or replacing)* of use of HSS is the last phase of the cycle. From the ethical point of view it is relevant how a user can delete information of him/herself from the service and whether (s)he knows how to abandon the use of the service. It is also worth of noticing how the whole product cycle and especially the discarding of the service and product is designed to be as ecological as possible.

Some issues for the re-thinking

If the HSS systems would be widespread would it restrain intruders or would it change the nature of intruding actions?

Is this kind of HSS system giving a wrong kind of feeling of safety and security?

Is HSS system reducing contacts between Mrs. Bates and her daughter (or e.g. between neighbours) while there is no need to do so called check calls or visits anymore?

Conclusions

Ethical assessment is required throughout the product life cycle. A remarkable challenge is how to get the attention of the designers and increase the awareness of ethical issues with different stakeholders throughout the design process. Possible negative consequences or threats noticed in any of the design phases should be brought out clearly. Hiding negative effects could also be damaging in business sense in the long run. A holistic view to the design is needed (Figure1): extending the view of users in the design from individual users to other people involved has already taken into account in many cases. Still we need to look these questions also on higher levels (organisations, society) to be able to assure that the best possible design decisions are chosen in the case of conflicts between different stakeholders. It is also important to understand the forthcoming nature of the future designs: it is assumed that in the future Ambient Intelligence environments people are not just mere objects for the design but active participants and subjects in all phases of design.

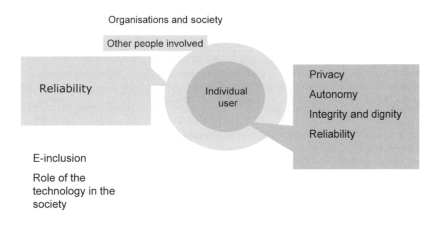

Figure 1. MINAmI ethical principles on different levels of the society

Human Driven Design refers to the new design approach which tries to broaden the perspective from focused product development process model to the more holistic design perspective. Human Driven Design approach emphasises user involved design which should be integrated to the all parts and levels of design. In HDD both the laboratory and field studies are seen equally important but contextually depending on the actual developmental situation. HDD furthermore aims to develop the design approach both for the emergent and flexible and formalised and validated design practises. As modelled and structured design approaches aim to achieve more effective and routine like a way of building good smart environments at the same time we need agile and impugned design practises for testing new ideas. The basic idea is to observe and study human behaviour: to see, hear, listen and learn from how people have done things before and how are they doing things at the moment and what could be their preference for the next generation of services. Then involving all stakeholders to the innovation process enables us to imagine new solutions that could solve emerging problems or make everybody's' life little bit more comfortable.

The notice that the traditional product design approach needs to be extended to two new design levels is included to the Empowering Design practice. The remote design or strategic design, which is kind of enabling framework for actual design work and the immediate design, which focuses on local and immediate user needs and experiences, and emphasises the increasing role of users in the design, form a holistic perspective to the design practices in any context. But empowering design should also focus to other design levels and to the all stakeholder perspectives and not just to the end-users.

Empowering design practice should give an opportunity to influence to the design in all levels and by different actors so that the dialogue built in design process could be open and mindful between different levels and between different kinds of stakeholders. Part of the empowering design practice is to perform an ethical assessment for the whole design.

References

Brand, P. and Schwittay, A. (2006) The Missing Piece: Human Driven Design and Research in ICT and Development. In *Proceedings of the International Conference on Information and Communications Technologies and Development*, May 2006.

Coen. M.H. (1998) Design principles for intelligent environments. In Proceedings of the Fifteenth National Conference on Artificial Intelligence (AAAI'98).. 547-554.

Cook, D.J. and Das, S.K. (2005) Overview. In Cook and Das (Eds.). Smart Environments. Technology, Protocols and Applications. Hoboken. John Wiley & Sons, Inc. 3-10.

Friedman, B. & Freier, N. G. (2005) Value Sensitive Design. In K. E. Fisher, S. Erdelez, & E. F. McKechnie (Eds.). *Theories of information behavior: A researcher's guide* (pp. 368-372).Medford, NJ: Information Today

Ikonen, V. et al. (2008) MINAmI deliverable D1.4 Ethical guidelines for mobile-centric ambient intelligence. Available
http://www.fp6-minami.org/fileadmin/user/pdf/WS/MINAmI_D14_EthicalguidelinesforAmI.pdf

Kaasinen, E. & Norros, L. (eds.). (2007) Älykkäiden ympäristöjen suunnittelu – Kohti ekologista systeemiajattelua [Design of Smart Environments – Towards Ecological System Approach]. Teknologiateollisuuden julkaisuja nro 6/2007. Teknologiainfo Teknova, Helsinki [in Finnish]. ISBN 978-951-817-944-6

Kranzberg, Melvin (1986) *Technology* and History: "*Kranzberg's Laws*", *Technology* and Culture, Vol. 27, No. 3, pp. 544-560.

Maslow A. H. (1943). A Theory of Human Motivation. Originally Published in *Psychological Review*, 50, 370-396. Available at http://psychclassics.yorku.ca/Maslow/motivation.htm

Remagnino, P., Foresti, G.L. and Ellis, T. (Eds.), (2005) Ambient Intelligence.A Novel Paradigm. Springer.

Topo, P., Rauhala, M., Sotamaa, O., Saarikalle, K. and Vainio, T. (2004). Ethical Issues in Personal Navigation. Deliverable 4 of the project Key Usability and Ethical Issues in NAVI-programme (KEN).

Ambient Intelligence Perspectives
P. Mikulecký et al. (Eds.)
IOS Press, 2009
© 2009 The authors and IOS Press. All rights reserved.
doi:10.3233/978-1-58603-946-2-137

Semantic Interactions for Context-aware and Service-oriented Architecture

Mehdi KHOUJA [a], Carlos JUIZ [a], Ramon PUIGJANER [a] and Farouk KAMOUN[b]

[a] *Universitat de les Illes Balears, Palma de Mallorca, Spain*
[b] *Université de La Manouba, Ecole Nationale des Sciences de l'Informatique, La Manouba, Tunisia*
mehdi.khouja@uib.es

Abstract. Designing an architecture that supports pervasive computing usually addresses two issues: the context within interact the system components and the services which are available in the environment. This paper proposes a semantic approach to design an architecture for pervasive systems focusing on these two issues. The ambient is viewed as a set of context elements named CoxEl. Physically a CoxEl is a (mobile) device presents in the environment. The core of a CoxEl is an ontology that represents the context, the services, the resources and the neighbourhood of every CoxEl. This ontology is also used for semantic interaction between the CoxEls. This paper illustrates the different semantic interactions that may occurs among the CoxEls. It also describes the roles that play the CoxEls within the ambient.

Keywords. Context-awarness, ontology, service-oriented

Introduction

Context-aware systems are heterogeneous systems due to the diversity of devices they incorporate. Due to this, it's necessary to build a system architecture that can deal with all the components. Designing such an architecture has to take into consideration the main characteristics of context-aware systems: the context definition, the services offered and the restrictions of resources. The design process of such a system has to focus on two level of multiplicity: individual level and group level. The first level consists on establishing the structure of one element of the context named CoxEl. This can be done by modelling the context within the CoxEl. In previous work [5], we have chosen an ontology-based model for the CoxEl. The second level of design is to consider the group of CoxEls. The concept of group organises the ambient following certain criteria. In fact, the CoxEls may form groups according to common parameters such as sensoring data. Simularity of the service offered within the ambient is also considered a criterion to constitute groups. The CoxEls act like users in virtual social network. Besides, the group concept implies the definition of interactions among the CoxEls. In this paper we present the concept of context group. We also specify a set of interactions related to CoxEl group formation and services. These interactions aim to establish an architecture that is service-oriented for a context-aware system.

    The paper is organised as follows: In section 1, the related work about semantic contextaware freameworks is briefly depicted. Section 2 devotes to the CoxEl-based environment. In this section, we introduce the concept of group and decribe the CoxEl core ontology. Finally, section 3 deals with the semantic interactions that may happen among the CoxEls.

1. RelatedWorks

Various context aware systems have been developed following different architectures. Baldauf et al. [1] made a survey on context-aware systems. The Context Broker Agent (CoBrA) system [2] uses a broker-centric agent architecture to provide services for context-aware systems in smart spaces. It uses an ontology-based context model. Due to its architecture, the CoBrA approach is specific to agent systems. In [4], Gu et al. propose a service oriented context-aware middleware (SOCAM) architecture for the building of context-aware services. They define two-level ontologies for context modeling. The first one is a generalized ontology which defines the basic concept of person, location, computational entity and activity. The second is a domain specific one that defines the details of general concept for a specific application such as a smart home domain. This approach focuses on characterizing user situation with a set of user-defined first order logic rules. In [6], an ontology-based modelling is used for the context. The ontology is person centric. In fact, it describes the context component: devices, tasks, resources, role and preference as related to the person within the context.

The architectures studied above use the ontology to describe the entire system and do not focus on the components of the ambient. In our approach, we propose to define the context according to a single element of the context. Then, the union of all the elements will define the system ontology. Since the studied approaches focus on the system before the components, they do not deal with the interactions among the elements. We will focus, in this paper, on decribing the set of interactions that may occur among the context elements.

2. Context Element Based Environment

In this section, we describe the context-aware environment. First, a general view of the ambient is described by defining the context. We also introduce the concept of group of CoxEl. Finally, the core ontology of the CoxEl is explained

2.1. Environment Overview

To have a good representation of a context-aware environment, it is necessary to define the context. We adopted the definition of context proposed by Dey et al. [3]: "*Context is any information that can be used to characterise the situation of an entity. An entity is a person, place, or object that is considered relevant to the interaction between a user and an application, including the user and applications themselves.*"

This definition represents the context as a set of entities. We call them context elements (CoxEls). As shown in figure 1, the CoxEl within the ambient have the capabilities to

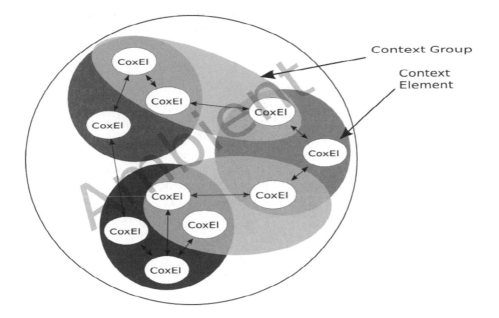

Figure 1. CoxEl-based Environment Showing Context Groups

interact and to form groups according to shared criterion. The group concept is a way to organise the ambient. In fact, CoxEls may form groups depending on their location, type (Sensor, PDA,..), resource restriction and services provided. Like social networks, CoxEls create group based on a common interest. The Group management among CoxEl will be detailed in section 3.1.

2.2. Context Element Core Ontology

In previous work [5], we adopted the ontology-based model for context modeling. This is because we have not only to describe the context but also relate the different elements composing the ambient, in order to facilitate the interactions between them. Our ontology-based model is based on the concept of the context element (CoxEl). The CoxEl is the atomic component of pervasive environment that has awareness and uses resources to perform specified tasks. From this definition, three concepts arise: awareness, task and resource. The awareness concept corresponds to the CoxEl knowledge about itself (self-awareness) and concerning to the ambient around it (surrounding awareness). Since the tasks to be performed are proper to the context element, they are part of the selfawareness. The CoxEl tasks can be of two types: dedicated or acquired tasks. The first type consists on tasks that are integrated in the CoxEl for specific purposes. The second one are tasks learned from other CoxEls. Performing tasks requires various types of resources: memory, computing and communication resources. The CoxEl has to adapt itself to the available resources. As the CoxEl can perform tasks, it may need also to access to other tasks from other CoxEls. This is can be fulfilled through the "need" concept. It includes functionalities for searching services on others CoxEls. Thus, the CoxEl has to be aware of other

CoxEls in the same context. This is represented by the neighbourhood concept. In fact, CoxEls that share the same interest or characteristics may form groups. Figure 2 presents the main concepts and relationships of the CoxEl ontology.We present only the concepts proper to our model.

Since the final goal of our research is to design a service oriented semantic architecture, The model described previously integrates in its concepts, the SOA core components. In fact, the "need" concept corresponds to the service requester. Moreover, the "task" concept is the service provider in the SOA. The CoxEl neighbourhood contains the service registry for discovering context services.

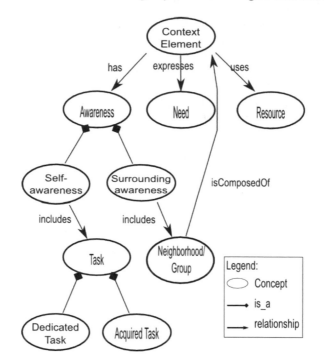

Figure 2. CoxEl Core Ontology

3. Semantic Interactions

The interactions that may happen among the CoxEls are related to the concepts of the core ontology. In fact, we can found group, resource or task related interactions. In this section, group and tasks interactions are described through sequence diagrams.

3.1. Group/Neighbourhood Interactions

The sequence of creating a new group or joining an existing one is shown in Figure 3. The group creation is based on certain criterion such as location, CoxEl type (sensor type), resources or task. The decision of creating or joining a group can be taken automatically by the CoxEl or initiated by the system supervisor. In the first case, the CoxEl has the task to discover periodically its ambient and hence joins to or creates groups. In the second one, the system administrator may change the CoxEl group structure for performance purpose. Within a group, one CoxEl plays a specific role: the group moderator. The main task of the moderator is to maintain the list of CoxEls that share a common criterion. Since, ambient element have limited resources, they do not have reference to the entire list of CoxEl of the same group. They have only to pinpoint the moderator. The sequence diagram of Figure 3 shows the case where a CoxEl (CoxEl1) starts the group creation process. First, a CoxEl checks whether a group exists according to certain criterion (criterion1). The CoxEl (CoxEl2), receiver of the checking message, searches in its core ontology for the adequate group. If the group exists, CoxEl2 notifies CoxEl1 of the result. It initiates at the same time a join message to the group moderator on behalf of CoxEl2. The Group moderator adds CoxEl1 to group list and notifies it. CoxEl1 creates a new group into its core ontology referencing the group moderator. In the case where the group does not exist, CoxEl1 creates a new group only if CoxEl2 shares the same criterion as CoxEl1. Then, the group creator attributes itself the role of moderator unless

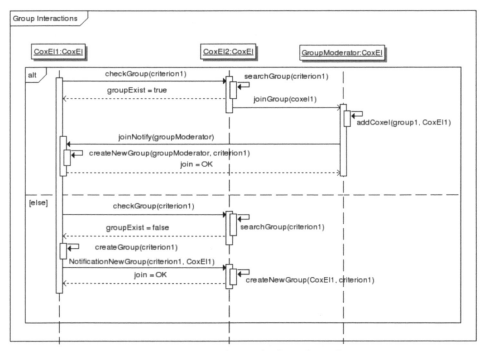

Figure 3. Sequence Diagram for Group Interactions

resource restrictions. It notifies CoxEl2 of the new group. The later CoxEl update its core ontology by adding a new group.

3.2. Task Interactions

The sequence diagram depicted in Figure 4 shows the interactions for task invoking. First, CoxEl1 invokes a specific service to CoxEl2 by passing the corresponding parameters. Then, CoxEl2 checks the resources needed to perform this service. A resource failure forces CoxEl2 to contact with the group moderator corresponding to the service criterion in order to look for another CoxEl. The Moderator looks for a CoxEl that can perform the service invoked by CoxEl1. Once it is found, it sends a message to the invoker with the new end point information. At this moment, CoxEl1 has to re-invoke the desired service to the new CoxEl (CoxEl3). Before performing the task, CoxEl3 has to check its resources. Once the service executed, the results are send back to CoxEl1.

4. Conclusion and Future Works

In this paper we presented a set of semantic interactions within a context-aware system. The Context elements (CoxEls) use a core ontology to perform interactions. These interactions permit to the CoxEls establishing groups within the context and offering tasks. The concept of group is a way to organise the context information within the ambient. In fact, the CoxEls form groups depending on criterion such as sensing information,

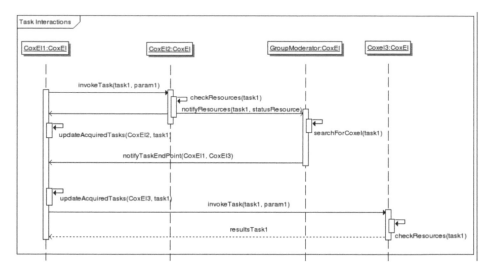

Figure 4. Sequence Diagram for Task Interactions

resource availability or common tasks. The task interactions give the system architecture a service-oriented characteristic. The panoply of interaction can be extended to the resources. Designing resource-related interactions is one of our future work. Since, we described the interaction via an UML unformal approach (sequence diagram), we will consider a design with an interaction specific language such as ISDL (Interaction System Design Language). We have also to determine whether ISDL supports semantic interactions. An implementation of the designed interaction through a real case of study will be done in the future.

Acknowledgement

This work is partially supported by the project TIN2007-60440 Arquitectura Semántica Orientada a Servicios (SOSA) under Programa Nacional de Tecnologías Informáticas of Ministerio de Ciencia e Innovación, Spain.

References

[1]   Matthias Baldauf, Schahram Dustdar, and Florian Rosenberg. A survey on context-aware systems. Int. J. Ad Hoc Ubiquitous Comput., 2(4):263–277, 2007.
[2]   Harry Chen, Tim Finin, and Anupam Joshi. An intelligent broker for context-aware systems. Adjunkt Proceedings of Ubicomp 2003, pages 183–184, October 2003.
[3]   Anind K. Dey. Understanding and Using Context. Personal Ubiquitous Comput., 5(1):4–7, 2001.
[4]   Tao Gu, Hung Keng Pung, and Da Qing Zhang. A service-oriented middleware for building context-aware services. Journal of Network and Computer Applications, 28(1):1–18, January 2005.
[5]   Mehdi Khouja, Carlos Juiz, Isaac Lera, Ramon Puigjaner, and Farouk Kamoun. An ontology-based model for a context-aware service oriented architecture. In SERP'07, volume 2, pages 608–612. CSREA Press, June 2007.
[6]   Philip Moore, Bin Hu, and Jizheng Wan. Smart-Context: A Context Ontology for Pervasive Mobile Computing. The Computer Journal, page bxm104, 2008.

Ambient Intelligence Perspectives
P. Mikulecký et al. (Eds.)
IOS Press, 2009
doi:10.3233/978-1-58603-946-2-144

User Interfaces for the Digital Home on the basis of Open Industrial Standards

Martin KLIMA [a], Miroslav MACIK [a], Elena URDANETA [b], Cristina BUIZA [b],
Eduardo CARRASCO [c], Gorka EPELDE [c] and Jan ALEXANDERSSON [d]
[a] *CTU, Czech Republic*
[b] *Fundación INGEMA, Spain*
[c] *VICOMTech, Spain*
[d] *DFKI GmbH, Germany*
xklima@fel.cvut.cz

Abstract. In this paper we describe the design, development and evaluation of user interfaces for a modern digital home based on the ISO/IEC 24752 standard: Universal Remote Console—URC. Two target groups were addressed: seniors aged 65years and above and people suffering from Alzheimer's disease. Our goal is to de-sign user interfaces (UI) for our target groups that make use of all available modalities, such as, graphics, voice, and video. We provide a set of recommendations and design patterns for developing UIs for seniors and Alzheimer's disease patients. We present the results of tests of user interfaces designed for smart home environment.

Keywords. i2home, intuitive interaction, user-centered design, eInclusion, URC

1. Introduction

In the last couple of years, we could see an increase in the number of networked digital devices in our homes which is why we talk about digital homes. These systems are quickly becoming ambient and thus become a natural part of our life. For young people who are experienced in using computer-based technologies, it is easy to smoothly adapt to these ambient systems. The situation is different for seniors however, who rarely have any experience with computers and who have difficulties to adapt to new technologies. While young people currently drive the economy, seniors are only of small interest to main stream manufactures. However, as the population in Europe is getting older, we expect a growing interest in senior users; the elderly will have a larger purchasing power and attending to the needs of this overlooked group will be a must for the main stream manufactures.

In the EU-funded project i2home, we are focusing on two areas: development of a standards-based technical infrastructure for the digital home and on the implementation of user interfaces for this system for people with special needs. In this paper we report on the results of our efforts in developing user interfaces specially developed for seniors and people with moderate Alzheimer's disease.

Our technical infrastructure provides an integrated environment based on a central hub (Universal Control Hub—UCH) connected to a number of household devices and services along with some user interfaces, see section 2. The integration makes it possible to control household devices using a number of different controllers or their combinations.

Our development methodology follows the User-Centered Design (UCD), e.g., [6], i.e. it is essentially the users themselves who are driving the technological development and hence the final user interfaces are tailored to their needs. We understand the UCD methodology as the iteration of a four-phase process. This process will be outlined it what follows. In the **Requirements** phase, personas are developed (see section 3), a STAR for technology established, and appropriate scenarios including a selection of controlled devices (targets) are defined [1,7,5]. In the **Implementation** phase, the basic techno- logical infrastructure as well as the targets get implemented/refined (see section 2), and prototypes of user interfaces are designed and developed in three steps (see section 4): from paper prototypes we move to mockup prototypes and, finally, to fully functional controllers. In the **Testing** phase, the individual prototypes and later the complete integrated environment are tested. Finally, in the **Evaluation** following the testing we use a common evaluation plan, initially using a *qualitative* evaluation to evaluate the different systems, see section 5. The results from one phase serve as the input for the following phase. The project is scheduled for three complete iterations.

2. System Architecture

We base our technical infrastructure on an open international standard ISO/IEC 24752 1–5, the *Universal Remote Console—URC* standard, e.g., [8]. The standard allows for a coherent and standardized low-level interaction with—in principle—arbitrary appliances, devices or services, called *targets*. A *controller* is a device or user interface that is used by a human to interact with the targets via the hub, see figure 1. The standard provides a precise description for how the functions of a target may be described by a *socket description* and a *target adaptor*. The user interface designers/programmers can thus author a UI without the need of implementing low-level interaction, such as power- line, Zigbee or Instabus etc. but can concentrate on conceptual issues. There are several advantages with this architecture: it is *easy to replace a user interface* with another one since the standard allows for *pluggable user interfaces*. It is possible to share arbitrary resources, such as, socket descriptions, user interfaces, target adaptors, et cetera through one or more resource servers.

For this first UCD cycle, we have integrated the following targets: TV with EPG, a calendar and an HVAC from the serve@home series.

3. Personas

In the first phase of the UCD we have analyzed the target users of the i2home system using Alan Cooper's methodology [4]. We made a number of interviews with the potential users and transformed the results of these interviews into definition of *personas*. Each of these personas represents one target group with a typical set of requirements and properties. Below, we provide excerpts of three personas derived from these interviews:

Blanka (passive persona) is a 73 years old woman who lives alone in a small flat. She has recently moved there so that her daughter Jirina can take better care of her.

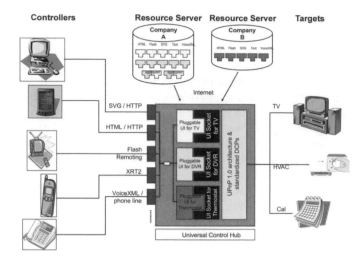

Figure 1. A depiction of the Universal Control Hub. To the right are the targets, in this case a Home Movie Center, HVAC, and a calendar. Possible controllers are on the left side. Note that a TV can act both as a controller and as a target. Above the hub, two resource servers providing, for instance, target adaptors and/or user interfaces are depicted.

Blanka has no experience with computers. Her performance with regard to memory, vision and hearing is in decline but is nevertheless self-sufficient in her everyday life. TV has become the major interactive point in Blanka's household. She has major problems with new devices like state-of-the-art TV remote control, DVD or digital radio. Moreover, she is afraid to touch unfamiliar devices: as she might be unable to reset it to it's initial state. Blanka feels inferior when she has to ask her daughter for help. More complicated operations will always be done by her caregivers or relatives.

Arnost (active persona) is a 68 years old man who recently retired but still maintains his hobbies and keeps in touch with his colleagues from work. He has gathered some experience with computers during his time at work. He wears glasses, can operate a cell phone and a PDA but has minor problems with small fonts.

Manuela (passive persona) is 73 years old woman who has been diagnosed with Alzheimer'S Disease (AD) three years ago and who now attends a Daily Care Center. Manuela does not take her daily medication but she is still able to perform simple tasks under supervision. She will become progressively more dependent. Manuela can answer the phone when she hears it but as dialing causes her problems she tends to avoid it or wait for somebody to help her. Despite her anxiousness to fall, Manuela still goes out alone to make small shopping. However, she usually goes out with her daughter or grandson.

In addition to the personas above we have defined additional personas that represent care givers and other seniors, who are also potential users of the i2home system but are not the primary users of it. During the recruitment for the evaluation we match the person to be tested to one of our personas in order to get results that are relevant.

4. User Interface Design

For each of the defined personas a customized user interface was developed. For Blanka and Arnost, the selected set of controllers was a graphical user interface implemented on a touch-screen enabled PDA or a TV. For Manuela, we have designed a speaking avatar running on the TV in combination with simplified remote control. The main re- quirement from all personas is simplicity. This requirement was especially emphasized by the Blanka and Manuela persona. While Arnost requires a larger number of functions, Blanka needs only a very basic set, see Figure 2 for comparison of the HVAC GUI for Blanka and Arnost. The first version of Manuela's UI is based on the interaction with the calendar only.

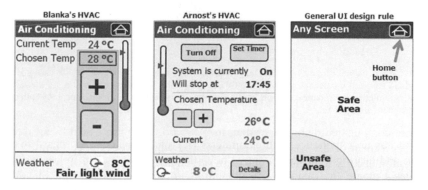

Figure 2. UI design for HVAC for Blanka to the left, for Arnost in the middle. The general UI design to theright.

4.1. UI for Arnost and Blanka

For the first prototype we have designed a graphical user interface (GUI) running on the PDA which should be controlled with the finger. With this GUI, Blanka and Arnost can, for example, browse the EPG (Electronic Program Guide) or control the HVAC on their PDA while watching the TV. Although the PDA with a touch screen is not a perfect controller for neither Blanka nor Arnost, we have selected this for it's availability and capability to easily make functional prototypes for the first phase of the project. When designing the UI we have considered the following rules as a result of the user interviews. **Depth of UI structure**. The depth of the UI structure should be restricted, that is, any screen in the UI should be reachable through a limited number of preceding screens, see Figure 3. In Blanka's case the limit is set to two since she will not remember more than one step back. In Arnost's case the limit is not given but it is recommended to be set to three.

Safe and unsafe areas are defined on the GUI. The GUI is controlled by the fingers and not the stylus. When holding the PDA by left hand and touching it by right hand fingers, there is a danger of accidently touching the screen by the left hand. Therefore, an unsafe area was defined where no active UI elements should be placed, see Figure 2.

Home buttons are always leading to the main screen. For both Arnost and Blanka there is a home button in the upper right corner of each screen (except, of course, for the home screen itself), see Figure 2. Blanka expects an immediate reaction from the system, as she is used to from other hardware devices like white goods, and so the number of con- firmation dialogues is kept to a minimum. This also reduces the depth of the UI struc- ture. The confirmation dialogues are a design pattern overtaken from computer UI and it is not understandable to Blanka. In case Blanka needs to go through

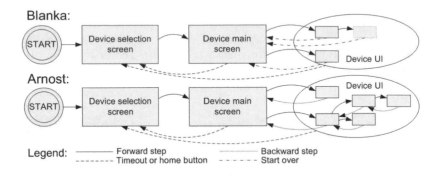

Figure 3. Example of User Interface structure for Blanka (top) and Arnost (bottom).

a more complicated dialogue, leading to a wizard, there must be a "Start over" button on each screen of the wizard which resets the whole process, see Figure 3. The GUI will automatically transmit into the main screen after a given time of inactivity.

Size of all touchable elements on the screen must be big enough to be easily accessible for elderly people. The size of the elements limits their number on the screen. All text, labels and symbols must be big enough to be easily readable for people with vision impairment— remember that both Blanka and Arnost wear glasses.

Affordance each UI screen must be self-explanatory, making both its purpose and its functions obvious. Blanka suffers from short-term memory problems and should be able to operate the GUI despite the fact that she might have forgotten how she got to the particular screen.

4.2. UI for Manuela

Manuela interacts with the targets via the TV, where a speaking avatar announces differ- ent reminders and notifications. The interaction with the system is purely system initiated and Manuela reacts on yes/no queries by pushing a particular button on the remote control, see figure 4. The avatar has been chosen because it is an interface that Manuela can easily interact with, see [2] for more details. Based on the results of the user interviews we have taken the following points into consideration when designing the UI.

Personification Since it is very unnatural for users represented by Manuela to communicate with any kind of electronic device, we have decided to use 3D-modeled avatar which looks, behaves and speaks like a human.

Speech synthesis of a high quality in combination with lip synchronization should make the user experience as realistic as possible, see [3].

Figure 4. Manuelat's user interface - speaking avatar on the TV and a simple remote control.

Simplified remote control enables Manuela answer question asked by the avatar quickly and easily. She can answer simple yes/no question by pressing the appropriate buttons. In order to change the settings on some devices, i.e. the HVAC, she can press +/- buttons. The range of values is however still limited to for example +/- 2 °C. More advanced settings of the i2home system are dedicated to Manuela's caregiver.

5. Evaluation

The goal for the current study is to perform an evaluation on the feasibility, accessibility and usability of the first prototypes. A data analysis from both a quantitative and a qual- itative perspective has been performed. From a quantitative point of view, frequencies of right-wrong answers and response time have been measured. The qualitative analysis helped to determine why the participant answered in a wrong way, record his/her feel- ings with regard to the presented UI, gather whether or not he/she has understood the meaning, etc. Prior to the evaluation, the participants agreed to take part in this evalua- tion by signing a consent form and the test supervisor filled out a questionnaire in order to record factors like age, gender, education, and previous experience with information, and communication technologies.

Blanka and Arnost: The purpose of this study was to determine the usability and accessibility of the user interfaces previously described. 14 participants conforming mostly to Arnost persona were hired at the University of the Third Age. The tests took place at the usability lab at the Czech Technical University. 14 participants mostly conforming to the Blanka persona, were tested at the Recovery Center in Motol, Prague. Several iterations of tests were performed starting with the initial interview, moving on to the paper prototype and the mockup prototype, and ending with a functional prototype.

Manuela: The purpose of this study was to access whether the interaction of a person with Alzheimer's disease and an avatar on TV is possible via the use of a remote control. 20 participants with mild to moderate Alzheimer's disease (GDS 3-5) conforming to the Manuela persona participated in the evalution which took place at the INGEMA residen- tial home in San Sebastain. The participants were evaluated with a neuropsychological screening evaluation, according to UMA (Memory and Alzheimer Unit) procedures pro- viding measures for perception, language and memory capacities, and task performance time

6. Results

Below we provide a subset of the result of the qualitative usability tests of UI proto-types designed according to the design patterns introduced in section 4 followed by a discussion and when possible also by proposed solutions.

6.1. Arnost and Blanka

The design of the UI based on interaction with PDA touch screen in combination with the TV screen was very well accepted by most users. As a positive aspect we consider the fact that almost all users were able to fufill all given tasks without the need to be trained in advance. All users experienced a steep learning curve and most of them reported an intention to use the technology in their home environment. We are now focusing on aspects causing problems that can be generalized to other controllers, not just the PDA used

Multitasking – Four users conforming to Blanka and two confirming to Arnost were confused by the fact that it is possible to interact with other targets, say the HVAC, while the TV is still running. Consequently, as soon as these users were instructed to switch to the HVAC, they switched off the TV and then navigated to the HVAC GUI. Our recommendation in this situation is to synchronize the two devices as much as possible: the GUI shown on the PDA should also be shown on the TV.

Distribution of UI across multiple devices – Four users conforming to Blanka and three to Arnost were confused in situations where different devices displayed different information content at the same time. For example the user switched to EPG on the PDA and expected the information to appear on the TV screen which did not happen. This problem is similar to the multitasking problem and can by solved in the same way.

Status and action areas – Users often confuse areas that are displaying the current status of the system with areas that may change the current status. An example of this problem can be seen in Figure 2 where both users conforming to Blanka and Arnost tend to click on the status (28 °C resp. 26 °C) rather than on the + and - buttons. There are several possible strategies to avoid this. First of all the action areas—in this case the buttons—should be displayed in a more plastic way including shades and having dedicated coloring. Second, the usage of touch screens should be kept low since most users are not generally used to handling them. Instead, we recommend to use devices with physical buttons.

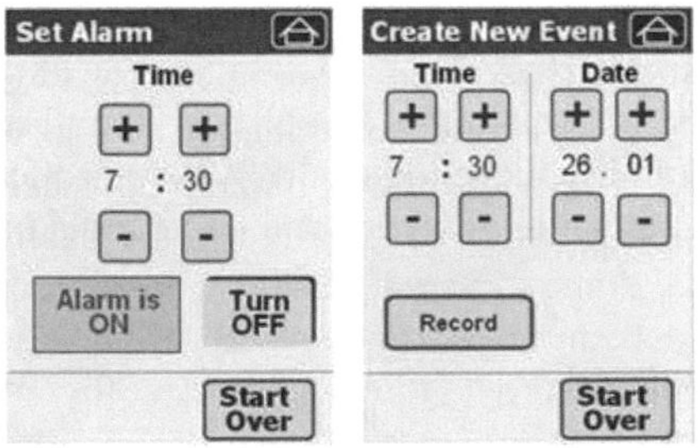

Figure 5. Blanka's UI for setting the alarm and for creating new event

Immediate and confirmed operations – Especially Blanka expects all settings to be accepted as soon as they are modified. For example, in the alarm UI, users conforming to Blanka expected the alarm to be set after modifying the time see Figure 5. The button actually setting the alarm to ON or OFF (functioning as a confirmation button) was mostly overseen. The recommendation is to omit the confirmation buttons whenever possible. Arnosts in contrast understood the confirmation metaphor very well thanks to their experience with PCs.

6.2. Manuela

The user interface based on a speaking avatar was very well accepted. 100% of the test persons completed the tests. The following findings will be taken into account while preparing the next version of the UI:

Timing issues – The black screen before the appearance of the avatar caused user reactions ranging from indifference to insecurity (wondering if the TV set is broken). In order to maintain the users' attention, the presence of the black screen should be reduced to a minimum. Also, the time interval between the avatar's appearance and 'her' speech should be reduced.

Explicit instructions – If the avatar does not explicitly say "press yes on the remote control", some users do not know where they have to press.

Speech input – Almost 80% of the users answered the avatar by speech although the user can only interact with the remote. This suggests that future versions of the user interface should include this modality.

7. Conclusions and Future Work

We have designed and implemented a set of customized user interfaces for two groups of users with special needs: elderly people and people suffering from Alzheimer's disease. By following the user-centered design methodology, we made it possible for these user groups to interact with a modern digital home equipped with main stream technology. We provided basic design rules for different types of interactions based on a qualita- tive investigation of user tests. Our users have shown a steep learning curve and a fast acceptance of the introduced UIs.

7.1. Future work

In the next round of the UCD cycle, we will improve our personas, include more targets, extend our scenarios and improve our user interfaces accordingly. We will investigate in greater detail the inclusion of the WII controller as a possible extension of user interfaces, social networking, speech and multimodal interaction.

Acknowledgement

This project has been funded by the European Commission under the grant 033502 (i2home).

References

[1]   C. Buiza, J. Franc, J. Görlich, J. Kunnari, M. Klíma, O. Langr, M. Macík, I. Maly, A. Rylén, A. J. Sporka, and E. Urdaneta. User Requirements Report (both). Technical Report D1.1, INGEMA, CTU, HI, SBS, 2007. i2home Deliverable D1.1.

[2]   Eduardo Carrasco, Gorka Epelde, Aitor Moreno, Amalia Ortiz, Igor Garcia, Cristina Buiza, Elena Urdaneta, Aitziber Etxaniz, Mari Feli González, and Andoni Arruti. Natural Interaction between Virtual Characters and Persons with Alzheimer´s Disease. In Proceedings of the 11th International Conference on Computers Helping People with Special Needs, University of Linz, Austria, July 2008.

[3]   Eduardo Carrasco, Carlo Moritz Göllner, Amalia Ortiz, Igor García, Cristina Buiza, Elena Urdaneta, Aitziber Etxaniz, Mari Feli González, and Iker Laskibar. Enhanced tv for the promotion of active ageing. In Gorka Eizmendi, José Miguel Azkoitia, and Gerald Craddock, editors, Challenges for Assistive Technology AAATE 2007, volume 20 of Assistive Technology Research, pages 159–163, Amsterdam, Netherlands, October 2007. IOS Press.

[4]   Alan Cooper.   The Inmates Are Running the Asylum. Macmillan Publishing Co., Inc., Indianapolis, IN, USA, 1999. Foreword By-Paul Saffo.

[5]   M. Klíma, A. J. Sporka, M. Macík, I. Maly, O. Langr C. Buiza, E. Urdaneta, M. Dubielzig, J. Goerlich, K. P. Wegge, J. Kunnari, and A. Rylén. Scenario Description Report. Technical report, ATG, VICOMTEC, SBS, DFKI, ZGDV, CTU, Meticube, 2007. i2home Deliverable D1.3.

[6]   Debbie Stone, Caroline Jarrett, Mark Woodroffe, and Shailey Minocha. User Interface Design and Evaluation (The Morgan Kaufmann Series in Interactive Technologies) (The Morgan Kaufmann Series in Interactive Technologies). Morgan Kaufmann, March 2005.

[7]   G. Zimmermann, E. Carrasco, C. M. Göllner, J. Görlich, M. Lindemann, J. Besser, N. Pfleger, D. Weber, T. Gehrmann, R. Lauer, M. Macík, J. Bund, and H. Felgar. STAR and Technical Requirement Report. Technical report, ATG, VICOMTec, SBS, DFKI, ZGDV, CTU, Meticube, 2007. i2home Deliverable D1.2.

[8]   Gottfried Zimmermann and Gregg Vanderheiden. The universal control hub: An open platform for remote user interfaces in the digital home. In Julie A. Jacko, editor, Human-Computer Interaction, volume 4551 of LNCS, pages 1040–1049. Springer, 2007.

Ambient Intelligence Perspectives
P. Mikulecký et al. (Eds.)
IOS Press, 2009
doi:10.3233/978-1-58603-946-2-153

Simplifying Human to Environment Interaction through Touch Computing

Diego LÓPEZ-de-IPIÑA, Juan Ignacio VAZQUEZ
University of Deusto, Spain
dipina@eside.deusto.es

Abstract. This work analyses the use of NFC technology to simplify the interactions of users with context-aware services offered by intelligent environments. Touch Computing is a novel explicit user interaction mechanism in which users accompanied by their NFC-enabled mobile devices request services from the environment by touching tags or other NFC-enabled devices. This paper describes the deployment of three NFC-aware services within SmartLab, our AmIdedicated lab, and the user experience derived from them. Moreover, it analyses the possibilities offered by the current state of the art on NFC and suggests some future lines of work, which may revert into its more widespread deployment in the near future.

Keywords. AmI, human-environment interaction, NFC, Internet-of-Thing.

1. Introduction

The promotion of natural user interaction to access surrounding intelligent services is one of the main goals of Ambient Intelligence. Using the current context of a user (location, identity or current action) as implicit input and voice commands or movement (i.e. natural interaction) as explicit input, an AmI environment adapts to the user preferences and habits. As a result of these implicit or explicit inputs, the environment reconfigures and changes its behaviour by triggering and activating services which aid users in their daily activities. Besides, AmI environments undertake these adaptations without the users being aware of the underlying sensing and computing infrastructure which makes it possible.

An interesting technology which has emerged in the last year and which seems as an ideal candidate to help on providing a more natural way of interaction between the user and the environment is Near-Field-Communication (NFC). This technology is a combination of contact-less identification and interconnection technologies that enables wireless short-range communication between mobile devices, consumer electronics, PCs and smart objects. NFC offers a simple, touch-based solution that allows consumers to exchange information and to access content and services in an intuitive way.

Thus, the emergence of NFC should simplify human to environment interaction, giving place to the Touch Computing paradigm, where users have only to wave their representing mobile devices in front of everyday objects augmented with RFID tags and visual markers or other NFC-aware devices in order to trigger the inteligent services offered by them. In fact, the combination of RFID and visual tagging of everyday physical objects and NFC-enabled devices will foster the Internet-of-Things [1][6] where every resource that surrounds us and its associated services are available through some kind of networking (Bluetooh, Wi-Fi, GPRS/UMTS) and programming infrastructure (web service, semantic web service, RSS feed and so forth). In order to progress towards the upcoming Internet-of-Things and the realisation of AmI is important to start experiencing with the application of NFC technology in the provision of the intelligent services within our environment that they provide. Undoubtedly, the consumption and triggering of such services will be improved by the Touch Computing provision enabled through NFC.

In order to study the interest of applying NFC technology and its associated Touch Computing paradigm to AmI, three NFC-aware services have been developed and deployed within SmartLab (www.smarlab.deusto.es), our research laboratory dedicated to AmI. The selection of these three services has been based on the current NFC application domain taxonomy published by the NFC Forum [5] and summarised in the following three types: a) service initiation and configuration, b) P2P data sharing and communication and c) payment and ticketing. Three services corresponding to the first and second application domain, less commercially oriented than the third one, but more suitable for the interaction with environment services through Touch Computing, have been chosen. In the service initiation and configuration domain, the following two services are analysed:

- *Touch2Open*, an NFC-aware service to enable a user to open the door of his office by simply approaching a mobile device to an RFID tag on the door.
- *Touch2Launch*, a service which complements our Internet-of-Things enabling platform, namely Sentient Graffiti (www.smartlab.deusto.es/dsg), by enabling the automatic activation and configuration of its mobile client by pointing an NFC device to an RFID tag. On the other hand, belonging to the P2P category the following service is proposed:
- *Touch2Print*, a service to enable users to print files by simply approaching an NFC-enabled mobile device bound to a PC to a printer.

The structure of this paper is as follows. Section 2 offers an overview of work developed by other researchers on human to environment interaction through mobile phones, NFC and middleware for the Internet-of-Things. Section 3 describes the Touch2Open service and discusses some user experience issues with it. Section 4 does the same with the Touch2Launch service, whilst section 5 describes our most innovative service Touch2Print, which attempts to put in practice the pairing of two devices in a simple manner through an NFC mobile. Finally, section 6 draws some conclusions and discusses some further work.

2. Related Work

Several researchers [8][10][12][13] have studied the prominent role that mobiles devices which accompany their owners everywhere at anytime are going to play as intermediaries between them and their environment. Those devices equipped with the latest communication (Bluetooth, Wi-Fi, GPRS/UMTS), sensing (GPS, RFID readers, NFC [4] or cameras) and computation (Java ME, Compact .NET, Symbian) infrastructure are most suitable than ever to act on behalf of the user and discover, negotiate, activate or offer intelligent services to them. In essence, if the web browser has been the agent that has fostered Internet usage, the mobile phone with its accompanying sensing and computation facilities will be the main interaction agent in the upcoming Internet-of-Things [6].

NFC [3][9] is a short-range wireless connectivity standard that has evolved from a combination of contactless, identification, and networking technologies. The NFC range extends to approximately 20 cm and it is complementary to existing longer range wireless technologies, such as Bluetooth and Wi-Fi. NFC operates in the unregulated radio-frequency band of 13.56 MHz and is interoperable with existing contactless smartcard and RFID standards. A typical exchange using NFC involves an initiator device that initiates and controls the exchange of data and a target device that answers the request from the initiator. The data acquired is usually very precise and structured. It is an open interface platform that allows fast and automatic set-up of wireless networks, which also works as a virtual connector for existing cellular, Bluetooth and wireless 802.11 devices.

NFC is compatible with Sony's FeliCa card and the broadly established contactless smart card infrastructure based on ISO 14443 A, which is used in Philips' MIFARE technology. To drive development and adoption of NFC, Philips, Sony and Nokia established the NFC Forum, a non-profit industry association which promotes implementation and standardization of NFC technology to ensure interoperability between devices and services. The NFC Forum [9] has currently more than 70 members around the globe including MasterCard International, Panasonic, Microsoft, Motorola, NEC Corporation, Nokia, Samsung, Sony, Philips, Texas Instruments and Visa International. The following three categories of services may be available according to a NFC Forum whitepaper [5]:

a) *Service initiation and configuration* – The user touches an NFC-enabled device, e.g. a mobile phone, against a specially located NFC tag on everyday objects, such as posters, bus stop signs, street signs, medicines, certificates, and food packaging, which then typically provides a small amount of information to the device. This could be some lines of text, a web address (URL), phone number or other simple piece of data, which the user can then use to obtain information about such object or connect to its representing computing service. This application type is based on existing tag and card technologies, thus minimizing start-up costs, and being the most adopted application form.

b) *P2P (peer to peer) data sharing and communication* – NFC is used to enable communication between two devices so that data can be transmitted locally between the two. If the amount of information is relatively small (up to one kilobyte), it is possible to use NFC to transmit the data itself. However, a more common peer-to-peer scenario is likely to be when NFC is used to establish another wireless connection method (such as Bluetooth or WiFi) to carry the information to be shared. This type of application is together with the previous form the best candidate for being applied to Ubiquitous Computing scenarios.

c) *Payment and ticketing* – NFC enables smartcard payment and smart ticketing scenarios to be developed further by enabling any NFC-enabled device to be used as a payment and ticketing device – i.e. as an 'electronic wallet'. Ultimately this would replace the myriad credit, debit, loyalty, pre-paid and other cards that people carry around in their wallets today. NFC phones also offer enhanced security, enabling the user to protect the secure applications through the phone's user interface features. Contactless-payment and contactless-ticketing infrastructures through NFC has an important business push behind and several organisations such as VISA, MasterCard or mobile operators are very keen their widely adoption. There are already some commercial deployments such as the payment of public transport in the German city of Hanau through NFC mobiles.

The Nokia 6131 NFC SDK [4] allows developers to create and emulate Java applications (MIDlets) for the Nokia 6131 NFC mobile phone. The SDK includes the Contactless Communication API (JSR 257), which enables the use of the Near Field Communication (NFC) features of the Nokia 6131 NFC phone. In addition to the standard JSR 257 API, the SDK includes extensions for several tag technologies, peerto- peer connections, and branding configuration. The Nokia 6131 NFC SDK contains a Nokia 6131 NFC phone emulator, Java APIs, example MIDlets, and documentation. This is the tool that we have used to implement the three NFC-aware services described in this work.

There have been already some earlier research experiences analysing the role NFC will play in AmI. Broll et al. [1] have applied NFC and Semantic Web technology to automatically generate mobile user interfaces from objects tagged with RFID or visual markers. Their goal is to offer a middleware platform to enable the Internet-of-Things. Bravo et al. [2] have used RFID and RFID-readers to extract activity identification context with mobile phones and so activate services by touching or proximity in classroom and conference sites. Krisnamurthy et al. [7] have used near-fieldcommunication to automatically adapt the profile mode (silent, meeting, normal) of mobile phones based on their current context, so that the disturbances associated to mobile phones in sensible settings such as hospitals, conference halls or lectures, are avoided. The Touch Project [14] aims to promote the Touch Computing interaction paradigm as a mechanism to link mobile phones and physical things. Their interdisciplinary team is developing applications and services that enable people to interact with everyday objects and situations through their mobile devices. Their main goal is to achieve real deployments of NFC technology and analyse the social effects that such technology can have in our everyday life.

3. Touch2Open Service

As has been reviewed, NFC-enabled devices are meant to turn a mobile device into an electronic wallet and why not also into an electronic key that gives us access to our work premises, car or home. In order to assess the usability of such scenario, the Touch2Open service has been developed and deployed within SmartLab. So far we could enter into our research lab by swapping an RFID identification card in front of an RFID reader by the door. Unfortunately, every time a user forgot the card, they had to ring the bell of the lab so that another member inside could open the door or instead use a standard key to open the door.

The Touch2Open service aims to solve this problem by allowing users equipped with an NFC-enabled mobile phone (in our case Nokia NFC 6131 mobiles) to enter the lab when they simply place their phone in front of an RFID tag attached to the frontdoor. In order to prevent misuses of this service and to enhance security the user is required to enter once a day, the first time in the day when he tries to open the door, his user password which is memorised for the following interactions of the day in the Touch2Open Mobile Client application. This password is transmitted by the NFC enabled device to a door opening service in order to be granted permission to enter the office. The architecture of the Touch2Open service consists of two main components: •

- *Door Controller Web and Bluetooth Service* – this service hosted in a Bluetoothenabled machine next to the front-door offers both a web and a Bluetooth interface front-end and has been implemented on top of the API supplied by the provider of our lab access front-door (www.dorlet.es). The web service provided offers an open() method to which the userName and password of a previously authorized user must be supplied as parameters. •

- *Touch2Open Mobile Client* – this application is launched automatically every time the user places his mobile nearby the front-door RFID tag. This is possible thanks to the MIDP 2.0 Push Registry [11] specification which in the Nokia NFC 6131 enables the activation of a MIDlet (programmed with the Nokia NFC 6131 SDK), in this case the Touch2Open Mobile Client, whenever an RFID is read. The contents of the card read are processed by the MIDlet, which extracts from it the connection details to communicate the mobile device with the Door Controller Bluetooth server. Once the server connection details are processed, the Touch2Open mobile client sends the user login and password to the server that checks with the Dorlet web service whether the user has access to the office or not. If so the door is opened, otherwise it ignores the command.

Figure 1. Touch2Open Service in Operation.

Figure 1 shows how a user equipped with a Nokia NFC 6131 where the Touch2Open Mobile Client has been previously installed accesses our lab by simply approaching his mobile device to an RFID tag. Note that the screen that requests the password details of the user only appears the first time in the day that the user utilises the mobile to enter the lab. Thereafter it is remembered, as if a web session key was considered.

In essence, the Touch2Open service simplifies the access of people to their work or living environments by simply requiring them to carry a device which is always with them, i.e. their mobile phone. Moreover, the NFC technology, assisted by the Push

Registry MIDP 2.0 technology, simplifies enormously the required user interaction with their mobile in order to activate an environment service. In this occasion, a touching gesture is enough to, under the hook, establish a Bluetooth connection between the mobile and a Bluetooth service and issue a door opening passwordauthorised request.

4. Touch2Launch Service

A second service initiation and configuration NFC-aware service has been developed, namely Touch2Launch. In this case, the goal has been to simplify the way that our Internet-of-Things platform, Sentient Graffiti (http://www.smartlab.deusto.es/dsg) [8], enables a user to retrieve public and private virtual graffitis associated to surrounding resources, i.e. smart objects, in their environments. In Sentient Graffiti, a virtual graffiti is defined as a virtual post-it note in the form of an XML document which combines some content (multimedia presentation or web service front-end) with some keywords summarising the content, and some contextual attributes (profile of creator, location, time interval and so on) which restrict who, when and where can those annotations be seen.

Sentient Graffiti is a Web 2.0-based platform designed to make the development and deployment of AmI scenarios in global (both indoor and outdoor) environments much simpler. Both mobile and web-based clients enable a user to publish, browse, search and discover based on their current context and topics interest (keywords) virtual post-it notes published by other users in the Sentient Graffiti back-end. The most interesting contribution of Sentient Graffiti is that enables augmenting everyday objects (posters, doors, locations, sculptures and so on) with software services by simply placing them in a specific geodesic location range, nearby a Bluetooth server or sticking to them visual or RFID tags. The Sentient Graffiti Mobile Client enhances user to environment interaction by enabling the following interaction mechanisms: •

- *Pointing* – the user can point his camera phone to a bi-dimensional visual marker and obtain as result all the graffitis associated to such marker which are relevant and can be seen by him.
- *Touching* – the user can use a mobile RFID reader bound to a mobile through Bluetooth to touch an RFID tag and obtain all the relevant graffitis associated to that tag.
- *Location-aware* – mobiles equipped with a GPS in outdoor environments can obtain all the relevant nearby graffitis in a certain location range which are relevant to the user.
- *Proximity-aware* – the Sentient Graffiti mobile client can retrieve all the graffitis published in nearby accessible Bluetooth servers when the device is in Bluetooth range from the server.

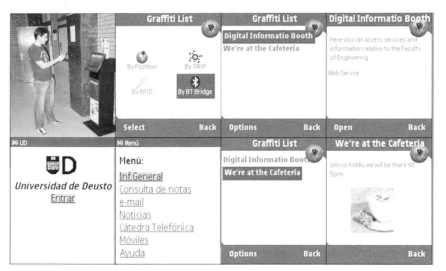

Figure 2. Sentient Graffiti project.

Figure 2 shows a scenario where a user by means of proximity interaction scans for nearby Sentient Graffiti Bluetooth servers, finds one installed in a near digital information booth and browses through the private and public notes available for him in that kontext

Our previous incarnation of Sentient Graffiti had been implemented on the following non NFC-aware Nokia series 60 devices: 6330, N90, N91 and N95. The adoption of NFC technology and the incorporation of the Touch2Launch service in our latest implementation, available for the Nokia NFC 6131 device through its NFC SDK, has provided the following improvements for the touching and proximity aware interaction modes:

- *Touching interaction through NFC.* So far, enabling touching interaction required the complicated scenario of pairing a Bluetooth RFID reader such as the ID Blue (http://www.cathexis.com/) with a mobile device, and then force the user to carry both the mobile and the RFID reader, to be able of touching the RFID tags identifying intelligent service enhanced surrounding objects. This cumbersome scenario is now simplified for users with a Nokia NFC 6131, since the device itself is able of reading smart object identifying RFID tags. Again, the combination of Push Registry MIDP 2.0 and NFC technology prevents a user from even having to have the Sentient Graffiti mobile client started in their device. As soon as the user approaches his device to an RFID tag, the Sentient Graffiti Mobile Client is started and configured to retrieve all the virtual graffitis associated to the read RFID tag.

- *Proximity-aware interaction through NFC.* An important drawback of the scenario described in Figure 2, is that the user had to wait until the Bluetooth discovery process concluded (about 10 seconds) to figure out whether that information point contained a SG server providing virtual graffitis of his interest. The use of NFCtecnology has simplified this scenario considerably. Now, the binding between an NFC-enabled device (Nokia NFC 6131) and the Bluetooth server is carried out by simply touching with the mobile an RFID tag attached to the information point. Such tags offer Bluetooth connection details such as the Bluetooth MAC address of the server and the port where a service is waiting for mobile client requests. Moreover, thanks again to the combination of the Push

Registry capacity of MIDP 2.0 and NFC, it is not even necessary that the user has the mobile Sentient Graffiti application started. By pointing his device to the information point tag, the application is automatically initiated, and most importantly, correctly configured so that it automatically retrieves virtual graffitis for the user from the nearest Bluetooth Sentient Graffiti Server.

In conclusion, the Touch2Lounch service incorporated into the Sentient Graffiti Mobile Client has enhanced the capacities of this platform to enable both touch and proximity-aware interaction with nearby smart objects providing services. Thus, NFC makes Sentient Graffiti even more suitable as a platform to enable the discovery and consumption of services within the Internet-of-Things.

5. Touch2Print Service

The third NFC-aware service developed and deployed in SmartLab is termed Touch2Print. This service aims to make more natural the way people print their documents within an organisation. Traditionally, whenever a user wants to use a printer, he needs to configure a driver for such new printer in their system. Moreover, oftentimes, consultants and customers visiting our offices require printing some documents. Normally, due to access rights and the need for login details such guest users are not allowed to use our printers. Finally, we often have in our systems access configuration for only the printer closest to our location and not necessarily that one which is in the meeting room where we meet with customers. As we can see, all these facts demand for a more natural way of pairing with and accessing nearby printers. For printers available in public spaces such as meetings rooms, it would be very convenient that the user could "print his documents in that printer next to him", without having to know the domain name, IP address or login details required for accessing it. In order to address this issue, the "Touch2Print" service has been devised.

The Touch2Print service enables a user to obtain a printout of his selected documents by simply approaching his laptop to the printer where those documents want to be printed. In order to use the current implementation of the system the following software installation requirements are needed:

1. *Users must install in their laptops the Touch2Print PC Client.* This service makes available to the user a print queue where new documents can be imported or removed whenever they want to be printed. Figure 3 shows the user interface of such client. As can be seen, the user can easily add, remove and order the documents he wants to print out whenever a printer is made available. Note that this service does not only offer a user friendly interface, but it is also composed of a Bluetooth server which enables nearby Bluetooth devices to connect and browse the list of files in the queue and command which specific files should be sent to the printer.

2. *Users must be equipped with an NFC-aware device where the Touch2Print Mobile Client is installed.* This mobile application enables the user to bind his mobile to his laptop though a Bluetooth channel, select the files to be printed, recognise the RFID tag attached to a printer where its connection details are encoded, and command the Touch2Print PC Client through the Bluetooth channel to connect to the printer and print the selected files. The mobile user interface which allows the user to bind his mobile to a Touch2Print PC Client,

browse through the available files and select them for printing is shown in Figure 4. This binding process between the mobile and the laptop can be carried out in two forms: a) using Bluetooth service discovery, or b) the user places the mobile on an RFID tag on the laptop providing the Bluetooth connection details of the Touch2Print PC Client.

3. *The organisation offering the Touch2Print service needs to install the Touch2Print Printer Client in a Bluetooth-enabled server attached to the printer where the documents will be printed.* This application makes use of the attached printer HTTP interface or SDK (in our case a Ricoh Aficio MP C2500 has been used) to print the documents. This client is also a Bluetooth service which is used by the laptop when the files to print out are sent.

File Name	Extension	Size	Absolute Path	State
Creator.pdf	pdf	35 KB	C:\Documents and Settings\Administrador\Escritorio\Cr...	Sent
Dibujo.pdf	pdf	17 KB	C:\Documents and Settings\Administrador\Escritorio\Di...	Printing...
Screenshot0042.png	png	8 KB	C:\Documents and Settings\Administrador\Escritorio\Sc...	Waiting...
icon.png	png	8 KB	C:\Documents and Settings\Administrador\Escritorio\ic...	Waiting...
Dibujo.JPG	jpg	7 KB	C:\Documents and Settings\Administrador\Escritorio\Di...	Waiting...
NoteSorry.png	png	18 KB	C:\Documents and Settings\Administrador\Escritorio\N...	Waiting...
Information Expert.pdf	pdf	40 KB	C:\Documents and Settings\Administrador\Escritorio\Inf...	Waiting...
Binder1.pdf	pdf	5 MB	C:\Documents and Settings\Administrador\Escritorio\Bi...	Waiting...
NFC_Forum_14Feb07_Press_and_Analy...	pdf	1 MB	C:\Documents and Settings\Administrador\Escritorio\N...	Waiting...
Screenshot0043.png	png	8 KB	C:\Documents and Settings\Administrador\Escritorio\Sc...	Waiting...
Map (Java 2 Platform SE 5.pdf	pdf	36 KB	C:\Documents and Settings\Administrador\Escritorio\M...	Waiting...
Screenshot0044.png	png	8 KB	C:\Documents and Settings\Administrador\Escritorio\Sc...	Waiting...
Technology_Roadmap_News_Conferenc...	pdf	359 KB	C:\Documents and Settings\Administrador\Escritorio\Te...	Waiting...
trip.JPG	jpg	99 KB	C:\Documents and Settings\Administrador\Escritorio\tri...	Waiting...

Figure 3. Touch2Print PC Client.

The system architecture of the current implementation of the Touch2Print service is shown in Figure 5. Currently only mobile devices such as the Nokia NFC 6131 or the Samsung SGH-X700 are available which enable us to profit from the advantages brought forward by the NFC technology to the human environment interaction domain. Therefore, although the most natural would be to simply approach a laptop to a printer and thus immediately initiate a required printing, as shown in Figure 6, we still need to make use of an NFC-enable device as intermediary between the printer and the laptop. In fact, most of the currently available printers neither they are NFC-aware nor they provide a Bluetooth interface. Consequently, a second level of indirection is still required in the architecture of Figure 5, including a Bluetooth-enabled PC server attached to the target printer. In conclusion, the actions a user must undertake to be able of printing his documents in the nearest printer are as follows:

1. The user starts-up the Touch2Print PC Client in her Bluetooth-enabled laptop and places in the queue those files she wants to print out.

2. The user starts-up the Touch2Print Mobile Client in her Bluetooth-enabled NFC-aware mobile device and binds it to her laptop through a Bluetooth link or even better points his device to a tag attached to the laptop which launches the mobile client and established a Bluetooth link between the mobile device and the laptop. This binding process is required only every time the user decides to connect her device to a different machine providing the Touch2Print PC Client. Otherwise, the connection details of the last laptop/PC with which the Touch2Print Mobile Client communicated are remembered through Java 2 ME RMS.
3. The user selects the files to be printed through the mobile's user interface.
4. The user approaches her NFC mobile phone to an RFID tag attached to the printer, from which the Bluetooth MAC address and service port of the Bluetooth-enabled server attached to the printer can be obtained. Such connection details are transferred by the mobile device to the bound laptop running the Touch2Print PC Client.
5. The Touch2Print PC Client sends through a Bluetooth channel the files to print to the Touch2Print Printer Client running in the PC attached to the printer. Such client makes use of the Ricoh Java SDK to print out the documents in the printer.

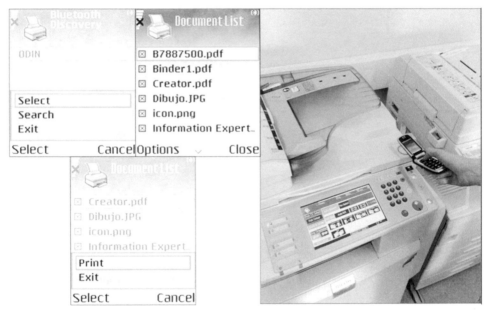

Figure 4. Touch2Print Service in Operation.

The current incarnation of the Touch2Print service, although providing a more natural way of printing documents, is still rather cumbersome due to the fact that 3 pieces of software need to be installed. Every user needs to install the PC and Mobile clients in their respective devices. An organisation offering this service needs to deploy the Printer Client in a PC attached to the printer in question. Ideally a situation like the one depicted in Figure 6 would be much more convenient, where a user would carry out the following simpler process:

1. The user equipped with an NFC-aware laptop opens a document he wants to print out and selects as printer the Touch2Print Virtual Printer. This printer appears in the user's system once the Touch2Print PC Client has been installed in a system.

2. The user approaches his laptop to an NFC-aware printer that automatically exchanges the file to be printed using either NFC, default behaviour, or any other communication channel available with higher bandwidth, such as Wi-Fi or Bluetooth.

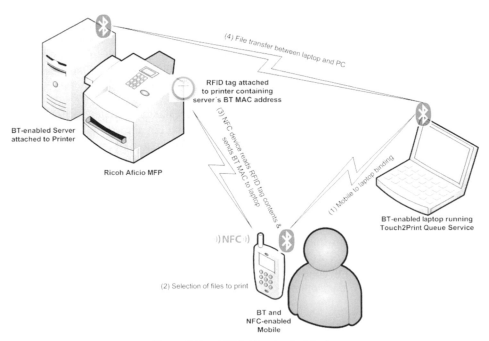

Figure 5. Touch2Print Service Architecture.

Although mobile devices are the ideal devices to incorporate NFC technology, it is foreseeable to expect that other customer electronic devices follow suit soon, such as digital cameras, PDAs, printers and laptops. Thus, Touch Computing scenarios between those types of devices will be soon possible, without the complicated arrangements currently required and shown in Figure 5, if compared with the truly more natural pairing mechanism shown in Figure 6.

Figure 6. Touch2Print Future Ideal Configuration.

6. Conclusions and Further Work

This paper has described three interesting NFC services deployed within SmartLab which enable us to approach to the Internet-of-Things vision through a more natural interaction mechanism, i.e. Touch Computing. The services described have allowed us to draw the following conclusions about NFC technology:

- NFC-enabled mobile devices not only will serve as our electronic wallets but also as our electronic keys in a near future. We will not have to carry a plethora of keys to open our office, home or car doors any longer, but one single NFC-enabled device to reach the same purpose.
- The adoption of NFC technology through touch interaction, assisted in Java platforms with the MIDP 2.0 Push Registry, will simplify the activation and automatic configuration of sessions with surrounding services. This has been proved by the adoption of the Touch Computing paradigm within our Internet-of-Things enabling platform, namely Sentient Graffiti.
- Pairing devices through NFC, in other words the NFC application domain "P2P sharing and communication", is still in its infancy. However, the development of services such as Touch2Print should motivate manufacturers of electronic devices to cooperate through the NFC Forum to enable seamless pairing of functionalities and data exchanges among their different devices.

In future work we will carry out a user study analysing the experiences of a community of users (about 20) during two months using the three NFC-aware services described, together with our Internet-of-Things enabling platform, Sentient Graffiti, at the University of Deusto. This study should enable us to draw some scientific and social conclusions about the actual value of NFC technology and its application to the Internet-of-Things, in order to enhance user to environment interactions in AmI environments.

Acknowledgements

We want to thank José Bravo of Castilla-La Mancha University for encouraging us to study and use NFC technology. We also thank to Raúl de Benito and Rubén Abuín for undertaking most of the implementation of this work.

Reference

[1]   Broll, G.; Siorpaes, S.; Rukzio, E.; Paolucci ,M.; Hamard, J.; Wagner M.; Schmidt A. (2007). Supporting Mobile Service Usage through Physical Mobile Interaction, 5th Annual IEEE International Conference on Pervasive Computing and Communications, White Plains, NY, USA
[2]   Bravo, J.; Hervás, R.; Chavira, G.; Nava, S. (2006). Modelling Contexts by RFID-Sensor Fusion. Workshop on Context Modelling and Reasoning (CoMoRea 2006) at the 4th IEEE International Conference on Pervasive Computing and Communication (PerCom'06), Pisa, Italy.
[3]   Forum Nokia. (2007). Near Field Communication Home Page. Forum Nokia, http://www.forum.nokia.com/main/resources/technologies/nfc/
[4]   Forum Nokia. (2007). Nokia 6131 NFC SDK: User's Guide v1.1. Forum Nokia, http://sw.nokia.com/id/77d9e449-6368-4fde-8453-189ab771928a/Nokia_6131_NFC_SDK_Users_Guide_v1_1_en.pdf

[5] Innovision Research & Technology plc (2007), Near Field Communication in the real world – Turbiny the   NFC   promise   into   profitable,   everyday   applications,   NFC   Forum, http://www.nfcforum.org/resources/white_papers/Innovision_whitePaper1.pdf
[6] Kindberg, T.; Barton J.; Morgan et al. (2002). People, Places, Things: Web Presence for the Real World, Proc. WMCSA2000, in MONET vol. 7, no. 5.
[7] Krishnamurthy, S.; Chakraborty, D. (2006) Context-Based Adaptation of Mobile Phones Using Near-Field, Proceedings of Mobiquituos 2006
[8] López-de-Ipiña, D.; Vazquez, J.I.; Abaitua, J. (2007) A Web 2.0 Platform to Enable Context-Aware Mobile Mash-ups, To appear in Proceedings of European Conference on Ambient Intelligence (AmI-07), Lecture Notes on Computer Science, Springer-Verlang.
[9] NFC Forum (2007). http://www.nfc-forum.org/aboutnfc/.

Ambient Intelligence Perspectives
P. Mikulecký et al. (Eds.)
IOS Press, 2009
© *2009 The authors and IOS Press. All rights reserved.*
doi:10.3233/978-1-58603-946-2-166

Some Approaches to Make the Internet Searching Easier

Kristína MACHOVÁ[a], Jozef VRANA[a] and Martin DZBOR[b]

[a] *Technical University of Košice, Slovakia*

[b] *Open University, United Kingdom*

kristina.machova@tuke.sk

Abstract. This paper presents two various approaches to decreasing effort of Internet users during searching the Internet. The focus is on a particular mapping of a web sub-graph of the nearest surroundings of an actual web page for better orientation and on interpretation of web pages content through the explanation of the meaning of concepts with the aid of the Magpie system. Particularly, we tried to generate the lexicon for Magpie from the ontology of a domain.

Keywords. semantic web, ontology, web graph, particular mapping

Introduction

There exist many approaches to the problem of searching such extensive network as the Internet is. Anyway, it is very difficult to orientate in it and find some concrete information there. The problems are caused by web structure and various quality and formal representation of web pages. Some of solving strategies are: brute force (increase of power of working stations), data mining in web setting and semantic web. Our work focuses on the last one. We want to be helpful for Internet users through two ways: a particular mapping of a web sub-graph and transformation of some ontology into the form, which can be used for explanation of meaning of a concept from a web page.

The first approach is connected with the structure of the Internet, particularly with existing hypertext references. The technology of the hypertext references makes the basis of the web structure. The references and their use allow the mutual interconnection of pages. The result is the formation of a net in which any orientation is very difficult. During searching the Internet, a user often visits a web page, which does not contain the required information. Therefore he/she must backtrack to some previously visited page but he/she does not remember the way back to the actual page. Therefore, we have tried to help the user with solving this situation with the aid of a particular mapping of the web graph. This particular mapping represents a map of the nearest surroundings of the actual page. This map can help the user to orientate while searching.

The second approach is connected with a content of the web page user is looking at, because it forms explanations of the meaning of those concepts, which can be found on this web page. These explanations are generated through the Magpie system (Dzbor-Motta-Domingue, 2004). Accessibility of these explanations is depended on the accessibility of the ontology for the given source. This ontology must be transformed into the form of a lexicon in order to be usable for the system Magpie. The ontology lexicon is a specialized version of the actual ontology. Our focus is on generating the lexicon.

1. Particular Mapping of the Web Graph

Our work deals with acquiring relevant hyperlinks of a base web site, generation of adjacency matrix, distance matrix and matrix of converted distances of hyperlinks, detection of compactness of web representation and visualization of its graphical representation using the visualization software Graph Visualization Software (Low, 2007) and Prefuse Visualization Toolkit (Spencer, 2007). Some other aproaches are known as well, for example Tulip Software and TouchGraph, which are used by search engines like Amazon, Google or LiveJournal (Volavka-Sajal-Svatek, 2003).

The visualized graph representation can help users of the Internet to orientate in the nearest particular surrounding of an actual web page. Our approach is based on identification of the URL addresses containing on the actual web page to obtain information about next pages - the nearest neighbours of the actual one. This process represents the first level of nesting (direct access). On the second level of nesting (indirect access), there are more neighbours and therefore the particular web graph is larger and more complicated. It is possible to continue to such nesting level on which the corresponding web graph will be so complicated that it will not help user with orientation any more.

The first thing we have to do is pre-processing of data, which contain HTML code. Figure 1 illustrates the data after pre-processing.

```
0 http://www.kukfuk.sk/
1 http://www.kukfuk.sk/o_firme.html
2 http://www.astudio.sk
3 http://www.kukfuk.sk/certifikat.html
4 http://www.kukfuk.sk/produkty.html
5 http://www.kukfuk.sk/foto_firmy.html
6 http://www.kukfuk.sk/kontakt.html
7 http://www.kukfuk.sk/obrat.html
8 http://www.kukfuk.sk/ochranna_znamka.html
9 http://www.astudio.sk/index.sk.html
10 http://www.astudio.sk/index.en.html
```

Figure 1. Output file corresponding the web page at *http://www.kukfuk.sk*

The particular graph of the web can be constructed from the output file after pre-processing. We have generated several tables during the pre-processing phase. The most important is the table, which represents the shortest paths. This is illustrated in Table 1 where "ID"s identify unique URLs and "Inf" represents an infinite indirect access. For example, the cell (1,6) contains number 2, which means, that from page 1 we can access page 6 within 2 steps along the graph's path.

Table 1. Matrix of the shortest paths

ID	URL	1	2	3	4	5	6
1	http://www.cmiinsulation.com/	0	1	1	1	1	2
2	http://www.cmiinsulation.com/service/service.htm	inf	0	1	1	1	1
3	http://www.cmiinsulation.com/products/products.htm	inf	1	0	1	1	1
4	http://www.cmiinsulation.com/eeo/eeo.htm	inf	1	1	0	1	1
5	http://www.cmiinsulation.com/company/company.htm	inf	1	1	1	0	1
6	http://www.cmiinsulation.com/index.htm	inf	inf	inf	inf	inf	0

There are many possibilities to visualize the particular web graph. We tried to do it utilizing two tools: Graphviz (Low, 2007) and Prefuse Visualization Toolkit (Spencer, 2007). Figure 2 illustrates such graph in the Prefuse Visualization Toolkit with the first level of nesting and Figure 3 illustrates the same graph in Graphviz.

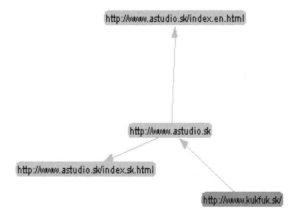

Figure 2. The graph in the Prefuse Visualization Toolkit using the first level of nesting

For illustration, the graph in the Prefuse Visualization Toolkit with the second level of nesting follows. This graph is quite complicated, as it can be seen in Figure 4. The question is if it can help user in the orientation within the web graph.

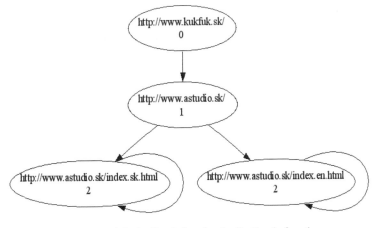

Figure 3. The graph in the Graphviz using the first level of nesting

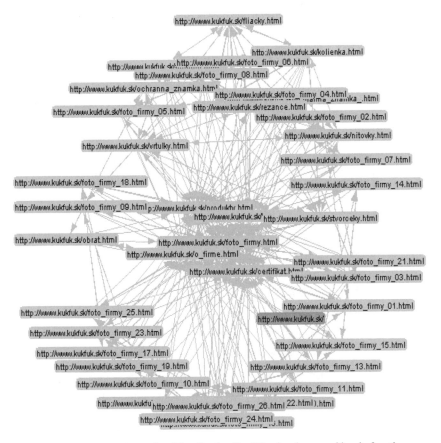

Figure 4. The graph in the Prefuse Visualization Toolkit using the second level of nesting

2. Ontology and the Semantic Web

Searching the Internet is sometimes a quite difficult task. Searching engines are based usually on key word searching. The recall of this kind of information retrieval is low. This fact is one of the reasons, why many alternative approaches were evaluated in last few years (Machova, 2005). Currently much attention is being devoted to the semantic web (Antoniou-VanHarmelen, 2004). One of the fundamental problems in the semantic web is that one and the same term can be labeled by different codes. In such case, a semantic agent must have a possibility to differentiate what meaning is for the given data source it can get in touch with. It is just ontology that was designed for solving this problem. Such ontology increases the functionality of the web. In this way it allows to specify the web retrieval. It could lead to the complete automatic retrieval of all the relevant references.

3. Explanation of Concept Meaning

3.1 Working with Magpie Component

Nowadays, the semantic web is predominantly in the stadium of development. This has also its real outcomes for example the tool named Magpie (Domingue-Dzbor-Motta, 2004). Magpie was proposed as the component of an Internet browser, which serves for the interpretation of the content of web pages. Magpie connects Internet source with its semantic content. Accessibility of this layer is depended on the accessibility of ontology for the given source, transformed into so called magpie lexicon.

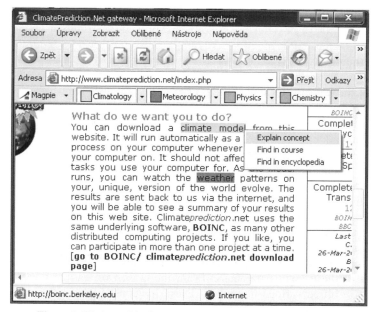

Figure 5. Window of the Internet Explorer with running Magpie

After installation, Magpie is displayed in the panel of browser tools. At first it is necessary to choose a concrete Magpie lexicon. It is set in the file with the suffix "*.

Onto". After the opening of Magpie lexicon, buttons of different colours are displayed in the panel of the component. Their content and number depends on the selected lexicon. Magpie differentiates individual words by the help of coloured blocks. If we choose lexicon "climate-glossary.onto" and push the button "Climatology", words from Figure 5 (for example climate model, climate change…) will be chosen.

Buttons like Climatology, Meteorology, Physics and Chemistry stand for the designation of so called top categories. To each of these Top categories it is possible to assign a group of words or phrases which logically belong to it. And for each such a group relevant services are defined. After the click on an individual term the context menu is displayed. For example if you click on the service "Explain" the window opens and includes the explanation of this collocation.

3.2 Lexicon Generator

It was said that the Magpie component is not able to read the ontology directly, but only a relevant Magpie lexicon. The Magpie lexicon is a snapshot of ontology for selected classes in the given moment. Unlike ontology it is a file that cannot be modified (in case of changes a new lexicon will be generated). We have created the Lexicon Generator program for an easy generation of Magpie lexicons from ontologies. It is an application that generates corresponding "*.onto" file on the basis of assigned inputs. The file including ontology in the format OWL is the first and the most important input to the generation process. "Top_class" and "Actual_class" are other inputs. The "Actual_class" is the category from OWL file and we are interested in it. The "Top-class" (a button on the Magpie panel) is the category covering the relevant "Actual_class". The file with "*.menu" suffix is necessary to be created manually. Because of the fact that it contains the list of services it is not possible to generate it from ontology. Such a kind of information does not occur in ontology (Domingue-Dzbor-Motta, 2003). Lexicon Generator is an application written in Java. It is a console application therefore it is able to be started by a distant server, without the necessity of graphical output export.

We decided to aim our effort at this aspect to elevate the contribution of Magpie lexicon at the increase of lexical richness. We had the file "kmi-basics-portal-kb.owl" at our disposal from Knowledge Media Institute. The ontology originated from the project Advanced Knowledge Technologies. This project is aimed at the development of new technologies for the knowledge management and it is supported by many universities. One of these technologies is also the Magpie component. Thus, the ontology contains the names of research workers, conferences, students participated in the projects, and so on.

We have suggested heuristic algorithms, that are also the part of the Lexicon Generator program and that are designed for working with names. From this reason we have adapted the choice of "Actual_Class". We aimed at these three categories: "kmi-research-staff-member", "kmi-phd-student" and "kmi-academic-staff-member". These categories are covered by a top category "Community". "Kmi-basic-portal-kb.onto" is the result of these input parameters. From the reason of testing, three lexicons were generated by three various heuristics. These lexicons differ in the degree of lexical richness. All other attributes as "Actual_classes" stayed identical for all the versions of the lexicon. We have chosen KMI and AKT pages for testing; ontology "kmi-basic-portal-kb.owl" was created for them. Table 2 presents the numbers of found entities on each from the test pages and for each test lexicon. Table 3 presents the recall of found entities for individual versions of the lexicon.

Where:

KMi-people are from page *http://kmi.open.ac.uk/people/index.cfm*,

Magpie is from *http://kmi.open.ac.uk/projects/magpie/main.html*,

AKT-people are from *http://kmi.open.ac.uk/projects/akt/people.cfm*,

AKT-publications are from http://kmi.open.ac.uk/projects/akt/publications.cfm)

Table 2. Numbers of found entities on the chosen test pages for the individual versions of the lexicon

	KMi	Magpie	AKT – people	AKT - Publication
kmi-basic-portal-kb_ver1	26	5	14	13
kmi-basic-portal-kb_ver2	26	6	14	28
kmi-basic-portal-kb_ver3	26	20	15	58

Table 3. Recall of found entities on the chosen test pages for the individual versions of the lexicon

	KMi	Magpie	AKT – people	AKT - Publication
kmi-basic-portal-kb_ver1	1	0.25	0.933	0.224
kmi-basic-portal-kb_ver2	1	0.3	0.933	0.483
kmi-basic-portal-kb_ver3	1	1	1	1

The first heuristics generates a lexicon "kmi-basic-portal-kb_ver1". The second one – the modified heuristics generates a lexicon "kmi-basic-portal-kb_ver2" and gives better results. The best results were achieved by the last heuristics applied on given training data. It leads to a lexicon "kmi-basic-portal-kb_ver3". The significance of used heuristics for the increase of lexical richness clearly follows from the values in the Table 2. Their usage has bigger meaning for those pages where the names are a part of more extensive text chunks (e.g. the list of literature). It is the case of Magpie pages and AKT-publications.

4. Conclusion

Our work focused on two different ways of decreasing the cognitive load of Internet users. The first one is a particular mapping of the web graph, which can help users of the Internet not to lose their way in the labyrinth of the web pages. It can be extended by drawing the history in the particular graph of the journey, which user executed through the searching the Internet.

The second one is the ontology transformation into a Magpie lexicon for using in explanation of concepts meaning for the interpretation of web page contents. Magpie is the first attempt on the semantic web browser. Although it is not any breakpoint theory, the ideas used during the development have big potential for further utilization.

The work presented in this paper was supported by the Slovak Grant Agency of Ministry of Education and Academy of Science of the Slovak Republic within the 1/4074/07 project "Methods for annotation, search, creation, and accessing knowledge employing metadata for semantic description of knowledge.

References

[1] Antoniou, G., VanHarmelen, F.: Semantic Web Primer, MIT Press, 2004, 258p., ISBN 0262012103A .

[2] Domingue, J.B., Dzbor, M., Motta, E.: Collaborative Semantic Web Browsing with Magpie, In Proc. of the 1st European Semantic Web Symposium (ESWS), May 2004, Greece.

[3] Domingue, J., Dzbor, M., Motta, E., Semantic Layering with Magpie, In Handbook on Ontologies in Information Systems, Staab, S. and Studer, R. (Eds.) 2003, Springer Verlag.

[4] Dzbor, M., Motta, E., Domingue, J.B.: Opening Up Magpie via Semantic Services, In Proc. of the 3rd Intl. Semantic Web Conference, November 2004, Japan.

[5] Low, G.: Graphviz – Graph Visualization Software. http://www.graphviz.org/ (accessed on 21/11/2007)

[6] Machová, K.: An Application of Machine Learning for Internet Users. In. Emerging Solution for Future Manufacturing Systems. Springer Science+Business Media, New York, USA, 2005, 459-466, ISBN (HB) 0-387-22828-4 / e-ISBN 0-387-22829-2

[7] Spencer, S., Heer, J.: Prefuse Visualization Toolkit http://prefuse.sourceforge.net/ (accessed on 21/11/2007)

[8] Volavka F., Sajal M., Svátek V. Topology–based discovery of navigation structure within websites. In: Popelínský L. (ed.) DATAKON 2003. Brno, Masarykova univerzita, 2003, s. 295–300. ISBN 80-210-3215-4.

Ambient Intelligence Perspectives
P. Mikulecký et al. (Eds.)
IOS Press, 2009
© 2009 The authors and IOS Press. All rights reserved.
doi:10.3233/978-1-58603-946-2-174

The Role of Multi-disciplinary B2(B2B) Networks in the "Future Enterprise"

Peter MIHÓK [a], Markus RABE [b]
[a] *Technical University of Košice, Faculty of economics, Slovakia*
[b] *Heiko Weinaug, Fraunhofer IPK, Germany*
peter.mihok@tuke.sk

Abstract: The "ERA Coordination Initiative in the field of Networked Enterprise" is a study, launched by DG INFSO, D4: Networked Enterprise & RFID Unit. One of the major inputs of the study is the interest towards an ERA-NET that would focus on "the Future Enterprise", a cross-thematic, cross-disciplinary and cross-sectoral research area of horizontal nature. In this paper the authors consider the challenges and the role of multi-disciplinary B2(B2B) networks in this research area. Some relations to the "Advanced ICT for the Product Lifecycle" (AITPL) - a broader research area - are presented.

Key words: ERA Co-ordination Initiative, B2(B2B) Network, Product Lifecycle

Introduction

The "ERA Coordination Initiative in the field of Networked Enterprise" is an ERA Coordination Study, launched by DG INFSO, D4: Networked Enterprise & RFID Unit. The Study focuses on the field of Networked Enterprise and is facilitating the networking among the EC, national and regional policy makers and key stakeholders and improving the coordination of the related research policies, programmes and joint activities. The Study covers all the EU Member States (EU-27) and Turkey.

The web portal of the project: "http://www.networked-enterprise-era.eu "contains valuable information and reports. A comparative analysis with a set of "prominent research areas for coordination actions in the ICT field of Networked Enterprise", a "Coordination Action Plan" to improve ERA Coordination in the field and a "Compendium of European, national, regional policies / initiatives in the field of Networked Enterprise (EU27 + Turkey)" are presented. The compendium includes a European and 28 national reports and it is accompanied by 28 summary tables which provide the relevant national / regional ICT policies / research programs along with their technologies / research areas of focus. Moreover, the "Compendium of ERA coordination actions in the Networked Enterprise & RFID Unit" presents and analyses the policy-related ERA activities of the unit's ongoing 53 FP6 projects and the ERA related activities of the respective four projects clusters. Furthermore a "Compendium of effective knowledge hubs examining the existing inter-organizational networks in the Networked Enterprise field" was prepared.

The "Ambient Intelligence Technologies for the Product Lifecycle" (AITPL) cluster of European projects has been established by the EC under the 6th framework program in the domain of Enterprise Networking. Following the AITPL mission statement, the strength of the European economy is substantially based on relationships among many enterprises, which together form agile networks, able to react to market demands in shortest time. These networks are competing successfully on a worldwide scale with enterprises from distant countries, which offer wages in completely different dimensions. This success can only be maintained if the networks establish and maintain smooth communication and collaboration, as well as integration of enterprise infrastructures and resources, which cover the complete lifecycle of a product. The goals and challenges considered by the AITPL cluster are available e.g. at: http://www.ve-forum.org/ [10].

Our paper is based on the research which is a part of the IST Project FLUID-WIN: "Finance, logistics and production integration domain by web-based interaction network" (No. IST-FP6-27083). The FLUID-WIN project targets business-to-business (B2B) manufacturing networks and their interactions with the logistics and financial service providers. The FLUID-WIN platform ensures the seamless integration of 3rd party service providers with their manufacturing networks, based on easy-to-use electronic services, with the innovative B2(B2B) approach. It aims to develop and implement a multi-disciplinary B2(B2B) Network, which can seamlessly integrate and transfer data among all the various partners. More on the FLUID-WIN project can be found at www.fluid-win.de and in the papers [1] – [7].

In this paper we summarize the ERA Study Comparative Analysis key findings, present some output of the AITPL cluster work and share our experiences in building a multi-disciplinary B2(B2B) Network.

1. The "Future Enterprise"

The "ERA Coordination Initiative in the field of Networked Enterprise" Study's coordination activities have already started on November 2007. These include the organization of the on-line consultation (Nov.-Dec. 2007) and four ERA coordination workshops. Key national and regional representatives / policy makers from the public sector (i.e. from ministries, research agencies, etc) and representatives of the research and industrial communities actively participated in the above activities. Finally, in the 4th Workshop in Brussels (June 2008), based on the outcomes of the ERA study workshop in Paris (April, 2008), an interest by Member States representatives towards an ERA-NET that would focus on the *"Future Enterprise"*, a cross-thematic, cross-disciplinary and cross-sectoral research area of horizontal nature was presented, discussed and proposed. The "Future Enterprise" will combine research on key ICT enabling technologies for enterprise and business networks with research on the respective business and socio-economic aspects and disciplines.

During the Paris discussions, the "Future Enterprise" was selected by the participating member states' representatives as an important cross-disciplinary domain of common interest that combines research on key enabling technologies for enterprises (i.e. mostly ICT / Networked Enterprise research) and on the respective interrelated business and socio-economic aspects and disciplines that evolve around their potential cross-sectoral application areas. The existing call for ERA-NETs provides a good opportunity towards a concrete coordination initiative in the area of the "Future Enterprise", more details can be found in [9].

The field of Networked Enterprise includes research on ICT and on novel processes, organisational models and strategies which can radically improve the way future business are networked and interoperate and future products and services are created and managed. Research in the field of Networked Enterprise aims to facilitate the emergence of future business forms designed to exploit the opportunities offered by the technological and socio-economic revolutions of the 21st century in order to make future organizations more competitive, innovative, agile and value creating.

The ERA Study Comparative Analysis key findings are summarized into the 6 prominent research areas and selected topics:

1. **Business Networks and Services** - reference models, engineering frameworks and technologies for new business collaborative forms, ICT architectures and platforms for the intra-inter enterprise collaboration in supply (value chains) business networks;

2. **AITPL-RFID** - Internet of Things, ubiquitous computing or ambient intelligence, RFID enabled ICT architectures and platforms supporting innovative applications for the product lifecycle (e.g. in a variety of business sectors), highly distributed RFID/sensor based systems;

3. **Interoperability in business networks and services** - interoperability reference architecture and associated methodologies, guidelines and best practices, service oriented architecture, service discovery and composition, business models for Enterprise Interoperability (in web 2.0 era)

4. **Interoperability and Semantic Web** – ontologies and semantics, web technologies for Enterprise Interoperability, semantic web technologies, semantic systems and applications, registries and repositories;

5. **Trust, contract and security management in ICT systems and business networks** - trust, contract and security management enabling secure collaborative business processes, next generation e-business tools enabling secure and trusted collaboration between partners in real time, trust in IT Systems and Business Networks

6. **Digital Business Ecosystems** – 4 broad research areas (e.g. interdisciplinary research on new value systems, standards, distributed decentralised dynamic P2P architectures, natural and formal languages to connect business knowledge and requirements) of special interests on Digital Business Ecosystems.

As a conclusion it was stated, that there is a common base for coordination actions in the field of "Future Enterprise" and the ERA-NET are the most suitable scheme for coordination. The final results of the Study will be available soon [9].

2. AITPL - The "Ambient Intelligence Technologies for the Product Lifecycle"

Ambient intelligence (AmI) is a concept (ISTAG 2003, ISTAG 2001) representing a vision where humans are surrounded by various computing and networking devices, unobtrusively embedded in human environments. This vision emphasises user friendliness and participation, efficient and distributed services support, intelligent interfaces and support for human interactions. The realisation of this vision requires development of numerous new technologies like: unobtrusive miniaturised hardware, seamless communication infrastructures, massively distributed device networks (often referred to as an Internet of things), intelligent interfaces, security and dependability.

Product lifecycle management (PLM) is the process of managing the entire lifecycle of a product from its conception and design, production, support, and upgrade, to the product recycling. During a product's lifecycle an enormous diversity of workers' competencies, working styles and environments, as well as tools may be required. Often workers and their tools are distributed over numerous enterprises that also can be geographically dispersed. Even a basic analysis of benefits of the use of AmI technologies in PLM reveals a great potential for improvements of numerous characteristics of a product, like customisation, configuration by users, easiness of maintenance and upgrade of product services, self diagnostics, as well as reduction in material waste and increased recycling.

Ambient Intelligence in the 6th Framework Programme of the European Union has been focussed on human centred environments, like home, workplace or healthcare. Although this approach still has the prime concern, new AmI technologies address also manufacturing and thus in fact the whole product lifecycle. The visions and conclusions presented in the book [8] are the result of two workshops, the "Workshop on Ambient Intelligence Technologies to Enhance the Product Lifecycle (February 27, 2006, Brussels) and the AITPL Forum (June 28, 2006, Milan). The primary intention of both events was to identify and discuss within the broad cluster community the research agenda of the AITPL domain for the next decade. The output of these workshops will also be used for the identification of potential activities in the context of the ERA.

The key research areas were determined at the beginning of the AITPL Cluster work:

- Frameworks, new business- and service models
- Distributed semi-structured data management
- Smart objects identification
- Secure and trusted communication
- Wireless radio frequency based technologies
- Real time monitoring of flows
- Middleware interfacing with legacy databases
- Agent based systems
- Knowledge discovery in distributed semantic networks
- Self-configuring networks
- Community memories
- Operations research

"The AITPL cluster's mission was to bring these topics forward and to identify potential new strategies for further research. This included the development of new disrupting methods and IT support as well as the promotion of new stabile networks. This will substantially include field studies, which investigate the real business needs, as well as the constraints, depending on companies' product categories, enterprise structures and size, in order to ensure that the project results will lead to substantial improvements in the immediate future" [10]. Some presentations of the cluster's projects results may be found in the book: New Technologies for the Intelligent Design and Operation of Manufacturing Networks, Results and Perspectives from the European AITPL Project Cluster [8].

This approach requires novel collaboration procedures, which especially exploit the research promoted by the European Community in the area of networked enterprises. Recent research was guided by a process perspective, where product information is shared, for example, as part of the ordering process, the product-design process etc. between enterprise systems and services. However, the need for product lifecycle management empowered by unique instance identification calls for an object perspective in the retrieval, sharing and management of information, representing a paradigm shift for enterprise systems. Each object should be interchangeable in these heterogeneous worlds, leading to the notion of an Internet of Objects, where the information can be online or bound to physical entities, synchronous or asynchronous (potentially leading to different states of the same object at the same point of time). The challenge ahead is to integrate these two perspectives and ensure a seamless interaction between **the Internet of Objects and the Internet of Services**. This will open up new horizons for interoperability and collaboration in a networked environment.

3. Multidisciplinary B2(B2B) Networks

As already mentioned, the term "Future Enterprise" covers, amongst others, business networks with their respective business and socio-economic aspects and disciplines, seamless communication, ICT, etc. In this context, a multidisciplinary B2(B2B) network is one special kind of a "Future Enterprise". But what stands behind the idiom B2(B2B) network?

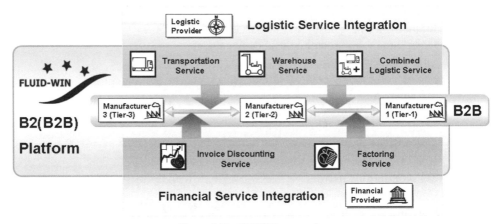

Figure 1 The B2(B2B) approach

European enterprises have increased the degree of outsourcing, steadily, in the last decade leading to many more partners along the supply chain. In combination with smaller batch sizes and delivery requests on shorter notice, the coordination requirements are tremendous for all the companies involved. The number of processes to be synchronised has increased, significantly. Nevertheless, investigations demonstrate that up to 30% of the administrative effort can be saved by establishing electronic interchange mechanisms in the supply chain. A very efficient additional effect could be achieved by connecting the B2B network with service providers. This approach has been described by Rabe and Mussini and introduced as the business-to-B2B or shorter B2(B2B) mechanism (**Figure** 1) [2,4,5].

Obviously, financial services providers can offer services based on the electronic invoices circulating in the B2B network. Also, logistic service providers can provide services based on the electronic transportation documents available through the B2B network, taking into account current order information that includes announced or expected delays as well as forecast information. However, there is a need for a systematic approach and easily applicable instrument as a prerequisite to establish multi-disciplinary B2(B2B) services and to develop supporting tools for multi-enterprise B2B networks. Especially, the approach has to handle the large set of enterprises included in B2B manufacturing networks, whereas each has its own wishes, constraints and might be embedded in various other B2B networks. Moreover, the processes of the services providers have to be synchronized and integrated with the network processes.

For that purpose, the FLUID-WIN consortium has developed novel processes which support the cross-enterprise, cross-discipline workflow of business services, and strategies which radically improve the way of future business service integration into networked and interoperate environment (**Figure** 2).

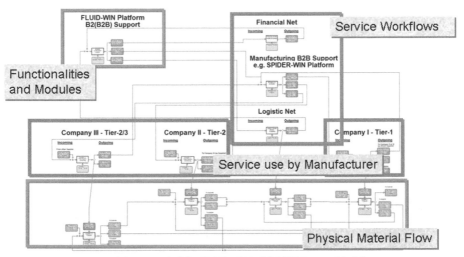

Figure 2 Highest Level of the FLUID-WIN B2(B2B) Process Model

The new processes in combination with the support of an intelligent and context-sensitive information conditioning by the FLUID-WIN software platform enable the complete and smooth integration of the *business service* workflow (B2) into an existing manufacturing B2B-structure which can initiate significant potentials for both sides, for the business service providers as well as for their business partners within the manufacturing networks. For example, the service providers can profit on up-to-date information from their B2B partners, such as manufacturing forecasts and status information as base for the logistical planning at the LSP, or, the manufacturing clients within the B2B has a seamless integration of their service providers in their own IT environment.

With that future organization the network as whole can act more competitive, agile and values creating, which are essential advantages in the global market, especially, when the most partners of the network is located in the EU27 and have to compete with other global players. In this context the FLUID-WIN project consortium leads the AITPL cluster and shares there its experiences coming from the development of new disrupting methods and IT support for new stabile and service-embedded networks.

4. Conclusions

Considering the ERA Study Comparative Analysis key findings we can conclude that the role of multidisciplinary B2(B2B) Networks in the "Future Enterprise" is very important. Some results in this direction have been published (see [1]-[8]), some other are defined as research challenges in ERA for the near future.

Acknowledgements

This work has been partly funded by the European Commission through IST Project FLUID-WIN: Finance, logistics and production integration domain by web-based interaction network (No. IST-FP6-27083). We wish to acknowledge our gratitude and appreciation to all the FLUID-WIN project partners for their contribution during the development of research presented in this paper.

References

[1]   MIHÓK, P. – BUCKO, J. – DELINA, R. – PAĽOVÁ, D.: Trust and Security in Collaborative
       Environments. In: Martins K., Popplewell K., Rugaber R., Xu. X (eds.): Enterprise
       Interoperability III, New Challenges and Industrial Approaches, , Springer – Verlag London
       Limited, 2008, pp. 135-143.
[2]   WEINAUG, H. - RABE, M.: Models and Methods for Web-support of a multi-disciplinary
       B2(B2B) Network. In: Enterprise Interoperability III: New Challenges and Industrial Approaches.
       K. Martins, K. Popplewell, R. Rugaber, X. Xu (eds.), Springer – Verlag London Limited, 2008,
       pp. 113-123.
[3]   DELINA, R. - MIHÓK, P.: Trust building processes on Web-based information-sharing platforms.
       In: Pawar, K.S.; Thoeben, K.-D.; Pallot, M. (eds.): Proc. of the 13th International Conference on
       Concurrent Enterprising (ICE), 4.-6. June 2007, Sophia Antipolis (France), pp. 179 - 186.
[4]   RABE, M. - MUSINI, B. - WEINAUG, H.: New, Web-based Integrated Services for
       Manufacturing Networks. In: Rabe M., Mihók P. (eds.): New Technologies for the Intelligent
       Design and Operation of Manufacturing Networks, Results and Perspectives from the European
       AITPL Project Cluster Fraunhofer IRB Verlag, Stuttgart (2007), 129-148.
[5]   RABE, M. - WEINAUG, H.: Distributed Analysis of Financial and Logistic Services for
       Manufacturing Supply Chains. In: Pawar, K.S.; Thoeben, K.-D.; Pallot, M. (eds.): Proc. of the
       13th International Conference on Concurrent Enterprising (ICE), 4.–6. June 2007, Sophia
       Antipolis (France), pp 245 - 252.
[6]   FRANK, T. G., MIHÓK, P.: Trust within the Established Inter-Organizational Information
       Sharing System. In: Managing Worldwide Operations and Communications with Information
       Technology, Proc. IRMA Conference Vancouver (Canada), ed. Koshrow M. (2007) 132–135
[7]   GIULIANO, A., AZZOPARDI, J., MIHÓK, P., BUCKO, J., RAMKE, Ch.: Integration of
       financial services into multidisciplinary Web platforms. To appear in: Ambient Intelligence
       Technologies for the Product Lifecycle: Results and Perspectives from European Research, IRB
       Stuttgart (2007)
[8]   Rabe M., Mihók P. (eds.): New Technologies for the Intelligent Design and Operation of
       Manufacturing Networks, Results and Perspectives from the European AITPL Project Cluster
       Fraunhofer IRB Verlag, Stuttgart , 2007, ISBN 978-3-8167-7520-1

[9] NETWORKED ENTERPRISE ERA, European RTD policies, Available at: http://www.networked-enterprise-era.eu

[10] AITPL - The Ambient Intelligence Technologies for the Product Lifecycle Cluster, Available at: http://www.ve-forum.org/apps/pub.asp?Q=1271

[11] FLUID-WIN Finance, logistics and production integration domain by web-based interaction network. FP6 IST STREP 27083 funded by European Commission. Available at: www.fluid-win.de

Ambient Intelligence Perspectives
P. Mikulecký et al. (Eds.)
IOS Press, 2009
© *2009 The authors and IOS Press. All rights reserved.*
doi:10.3233/978-1-58603-946-2-182

Model Cheking Ambient Intelligence with AVISPA

Antonio MUÑOZ, Antonio MAÑA, Daniel SERRANO
University of Malaga - E.T.S.I.Informatica, Spain
amunoz@lcc.uma.es

Abstract. Current number of Ambient Intelligent systems is growning steadlily in last years. Moreover, several fields such as domotic and remote teaching are practical applications of AmI. These are some systems that interact with different ones, that is the reason of "AmI Ecosystem" term is used. An AmI Ecosystem is defined as the environment in which users interact transparently with a number of inter-connected devices to the Internet through different telematic networks.

Security in conventional systems is a currently unsolved challenge and new attacks and vulnerabilities of systems arise everyday. In AmI paradigm the problem is even more complex. Although several technical solutions have been proposed for concrete security components in AmI systems, the problem to solve the security of the whole system is still open. Among the more critical features to specify and guarantee the security in AmI ecosystems we found; dynamic configuration of AmI is translated into a static security analysis; AmI security poses a high number of controversial goals to achieve; ubiquity and conectivity make difficult to ensure the confidentiality in these poor defined systems. Ambient Intelligence (AmI) refers to an environment that is sensitive, responsive, interconnected, contextualized, transparent, intelligent, and acting on behalf of humans. This environment is coupled with ubiquity of computing devices that enables it to transparently sense context changes, to react accordingly, and even to take the initiative towards fulfilling human needs. Security challenges are hard in homogeneous solutions, but escalate when moving to highly dynamic and heterogeneous systems. In this paper we present an approach to model dynamic changes in ambient intelligence scenarios using the Avispa model-checking tools. The main goal of our approach consists on providing a starting point in the use of Formal Description Techniques (FDM) for AmI scenarios. The paper studies and assesses the suitability of the Avispa (Automated Validation of Internet Security Protocols and Applications) tool for security validation in Ambient Intelligent environments and proposes mechanisms to capture the dynamic changes that occur in these environments.

1. Introduction

Ambient Intelligent systems have attracted researchers in different fields in recent years. Fields such as health care, domotics and remote teaching are examples of the practical applications of AmI. AmI systems interact with a large number of significantly different ones, which is why the "AmI Ecosystem" term was coined. AmI environments are coupled with ubiquity of computing devices that enables them to transparently sense context changes, to react accordingly, and even to take the initiative towards fulfilling human needs. An AmI Ecosystem is defined as the environment in which users interact transparently with a number of devices inter-connected through different telematic networks. A remarkable characteristic of these systems is that they all share a double goal: comfort and simplicity of final users. Security, privacy, and trust challenges are amplified with AmI computing model and need to be carefully engineered. Security is often a neglected area as AmI developers tend to ignore its importance, fascinated by many other challenges that are present in these environments. Indeed, in most cases it is considered in add-on which can be implemented later, if it all. On the other hand, it is common practice when developing and implementing communication protocols we use Formal Description Methods (FDM). A FDM is a specification method based on a description language that uses strict and unequivocal rules for the expressions of this language (formal sintax), as well as the interpretation of these rules (formal semantic). Specifying communication protocols with security features is even more critical and the protocol validation by means of this kind of techniques becomes essential, in order to provide a higher level of confidence to final users. Taking into account the high relation between AmI systems and human beings and the typical applications of AmI the use of FDM applied to the analysis of security properties Fh in design and analysis of AmI ecosystems is essential, and it will have a great impact in society in mid term. Among the more important characteristics of AmI to be considered when dealing with the formal specification we highlight; dynamic configuration of AmI is translated into a static security analysis; AmI security poses a high number of sometimes contradictory goals, ubiquity and connectivity make difficult to ensure the confidentiality in these loosely coupled systems. In the following sections we will present a bird's eye view of our research experience within the AVISPA tool in Ambient Intelligent scenarios.

2. A Model-Checking tool for AmI:AVISPA

The main goal of this section is to briefly describe a model-checking tool called AVISPA and assess its suitability for security verification in Ambient Intelligent environments. AVISPA has already proven successful in modelling and verifying a large number of widespread security protocols. In our work we have concentrated in probably the most relevant aspect of Ambient Intelligent systems: context awareness. Our study has lead us to the development of a generic mechanism to model AmI protocols in AVISPA, including the most common networks and devices involved in typical AmI scenarios. Furthermore, traditional security protocols could later be embedded in our scheme. AmI ecosystems feature a high level of mobility and diversity. This fact makes it difficult to specify and validate these systems by means of conventional security analysis tools because it is required that specifications include all details about the solution to verify. In order to study the pros and cons of using formal security specification and validation tools in AmI ecosystems we have selected AVISPA [4] because of the indecency of the underlying verification engines(back-ends).

2.1 AVISPA description and characteristics

AVISPA is an automatic push-button formal validation tool for Internet security protocols. It encompasses all security protocols in the first five OSI layers for more than twenty security services and mechanisms. Furthermore this tool covers (that is verifiable by it) more than 85 of IETF security specifications. AVISPA library vailable on-line has in it verified with code about hundred problems derived from more than two dozen security protocols. AVISPA uses a High Level Protocol Specification Language (HLPSL) to feed a protocol in it; HLPSL is an extremely expressive and intuitive language to model a protocol for AVISPA. Its operational semantic is based on the work of Lamport on Temporal logic of Actions. Communication using HLPSL is always synchronous. Once a protocol is fed in AVISPA and modeled in HLPSL, it is translated into Intermediate Format (IF). IF is an intermediate step where re-write rules are applied in order to further process a given protocol by back-end analyzer tools. A protocol, written in IF, is executed over a finite number of iterations, or entirely if no loop is involved. Eventually, either an attack is found, or the protocol is considered safe over the given number of sessions. System behavior in HLPSL is modeled as a 'state'. Each state has variables which are responsible for the state transitions; that is, when variables change, a state takes a new form. The communicating entities are called 'roles' which own variables. These variables can be local or global. Apart from initiator and receiver, environment and session of protocol execution are also roles in HLPSL. Roles can be basic or composed depending on if they are constituent of one agent or more. Each honest participant or principal has one role. It can be parallel, sequential or composite. All communication between roles and the intruder are synchronous. Communication channels are also represented by the variables carrying different properties of a particular environment.

2.2 AVISPA Back-Ends

AVISPA has following four back end tools for mathematical processing. These are On-the-fly Model-Checker (OFMC), T he Constraint-Logic-based Attack Searcher (CL-AtSe), SAT-based Model-Checker (SATMC) and Tree Automate based on Automatic Approximations for the Analysis of Security Protocols (TA4SP). The back-end analytical tool OFMC is used for a protocol where algebraic properties of the cryptographic functions are important. After the intermediate processing (IF), several transition states are explored on-demand. CL-AtSe is constraint based system. Its strategy is to simplify the original protocols and eliminate redundancy states using heuristics. It is built in a modular way so that new specifications for cryptographic functions can easily be integrated. SATMC takes a transitional state from IF and looks for any security property violation. It generates a formula depicting the violation and translates it into an attack. TA4SP shows vulnerability of a protocol or predicts its soundness by a careful estimation of the intruder's capabilities. The use of CL-ATSE is preferable in an environment where there is need to take into account the algebraic properties of the algorithms. The language used in AVISPA is very expressive allowing great flexibility to express fine details. This makes it a bit more complex than Hermes to convert a protocol into HLPSL. Further, defining implementation environment of the protocol and user-defined intrusion model may increase the complexity. Results in AVISPA are detailed and explicitly given with reachable number of states. Therefore regarding result interpretation, AVISPA requires no expertise or skills in mathematics contrary to other tools like HERMES[9] where a great deal of experience is at least necessary to get meaningful conclusions. Of the four available AVISPA Back-Ends we selected the SAT-based Model-Checker (SATMC), which builds a propositional formula encoding all the possible attacks (of bounded length) on a protocol and feeds the result to a SAT solver. The advantage of this analysis component is that automatic SAT-based model checking techniques are based on a reduction of protocol (in)security problems to a sequence of propositional satisfability problems that can be used to effectively find attacks on protocols, which is the objective of a security protocol validation.

2.3 First steps facing the validation of AmI protocols

Once we have described AVISPA tools and justified its use we are ready to describe the main contributions of this paper. Concretely, our research aims to study and analyze the use of AVISPA to model and validate protocols in AmI environments. For this purpose, the most characteristics of relevant AmI systems have been identified. Thus, both device and connection heterogeneity, as well as context awareness are the most important ones. In order to model AmI systems we approach them from three different and complementary points of view, as mentioned before: networks, devices and context changes. Concerning networks, we considered the most widespread ones: GSM, Wifi, Ethernet and Bluetooth. We then identified and modelled the different devices involved in the common AmI scenarios, building a list of those devices together with their most relevant properties, in particular the ones of interest when modelling a full AmI environment. Some of those devices were mobile phones, pdas, laptops, pcs, tpms (Trusted Platform Modules) and smartcards. Most of them are portable: that means that the location of the devices varies and so does the set of reachable networks, possibly leading to a context change when that happens. Plus, being portable also means having batteries that, of course, can run out and hence when modelling these electronic items and their behaviours. Finally, we have assumed that each device uses a unique (symmetric) session Key whose length is different from one device to another, in order to reflect a possible difference between types and lengths of keys. Then we briefly list more common devices and their properties in AmI scenarios:

- Mobile phone. Portable: Yes. Networks: GSM.
- PDA Portable: Yes. Networks: GSM and Wifi.
- Laptop Portable: Yes. Networks: Ethernet, Bluetooth and Wifi.
- PC. Portable: No. Networks: Ethernet, Bluetooth and Wifi.
- TPM (trusted platform modules) and smartcards. Their properties are inherited from the devices they are attached to or embedded in. We modelled them though their own symmetric keys to somehow reflect an improvement in the degree of security they provide.

Context awareness [2][3] is an essential feature that AmI systems have to tackle in order to act in an adaptive and intelligent way. This context, that might be spatial, temporal, environmented, personal, social, and so on, needs to be modeled, captured, analysed and reasoned about [1]. Reasoning about context needs a model and formalization acts as a knowledge base, and enables inferring more high level knowledge. For example blood pressure and body temperature combined with user current activity and location might reveal user current mood. This mood can then be provided implicitly as an input, so AmI might take some actions as a response. The third pillar in Ambient Intelligent environments is context awareness. As aforementioned this feature can come about due to a change in the current network used for communication, the change of service due to low battery power, but also because of the arrival of a "new session" event motivated by a session timeout.

Next section provides an example that shows how to model devices, networks and context changes in AVISPA. It is generic enough so any instance of a communication protocol in an AmI system could be integrated. Providing the infrastructure to model and validate more complex protocols in AmI.

3. Example: THE BASIC MODEL

This section provides an example modeling the more relevant elements of AmI systems in AVISPA. Therefore, this example is selected to show the system mechanisms developed to help in modeling complex AmI protocols. Agent A has a mobile phone that is connected to a GSM network. She will establish a communication with agent B connected to a remote Ethernet network with a PC. Agent A's side will trigger a context change when, for instance, the mobile phone runs out of battery and she will switch to her PDA to continue the communication with B using one of the two available Wifi networks, Wifi 1 and Wifi 2 (the full list of context changes will be detailed later in the model description). It would be of special interest to be able to model the process that begins in the moment that the come to action.

Five roles have been modelled in the HLSPL language:

– The two most obvious ones are agents A and B that take part in each back end of a communication process. Their bodies include all the possible (device, network) state machines.
– Two network roles, one representing the specific network that agent A is currently connected to and the other one representing the Ethernet network on B's side, which we assume in this example does not change. Neither of them features any special properties (there are no network down situations, package losses, etc.). However our proposed scheme can be extended to include those additional network behaviours and characteristics inside the body of the role definition, which is one of the reasons why we use roles to model networks (we will show later, the HLPSL supposes by default a single network that is used to send and receive messages without the need to add roles, although it has some flaws). It could actually be possible to include as many network roles as networks agent A can connect to with his mobile phone and PDA (Wifi 1, Wifi 2 and GSM), although, for the sake of simplicity in this example, we have decided to use just one network for both devices.
– Finally a gateway role has been incorporated, which represents an intermediate framework entity or system that allows the transmission of information from one network to the other. It basically takes data from one network and sends them through the other network after making the required encryption adaptations, featuring additional functionality to support the creation and maintenance of sessions. Note that the state machine defined inside this role comprises all the (device,network) scenarios.

We have not modelled the intruder as a role itself, since in that case we would have to model all possible attack traces, task that is performed by AVISPA instead. AVISPA's HLPSL language includes an intruder model whose knowledge can be input by means of the intruder knowledge instruction, which is powerful enough for our goals. When performing a security validation AVISPA will consider the intruder intelligent enough to use information retrieved from messages exchanged between the actors in a protocol.

One problem with HLPSL modelling is that when a message is sent through one channel all listening communication channels will receive it. That means that if agent A sends a message through the Wifi 1 network using the SND (send) channel, both Wifi 1 and Ethernet networks will receive it in their respective RCV (receive) channels. To model the fact that the Ethernet network cannot directly receive such message, we used couple of fictitious (public/private) keys for each physical network. For instance, for the GSM network, information encrypted with the key of the specific device used is additionally encrypted with the GSM network's fictitious public key.

The following diagram depicts an end to end interaction according to our model. Agent A wants to send a certain message encrypted with the mobile's key through the GSM network. Before being transmitted the message is encrypted with the GSM network's public key in AVISPA-HLPSL (X Y means that X is encrypted with key Y). The outcome will be called Msg send mobile gsm (step 1). Then the network decrypts the message and its content is encrypted with the network's private key (Msg send mobile gsm 2, step 2; inv applied to a public key is the corresponding private key). The gateway receives the message and, using GSM's public key reads its content. It then retransmits the message content through the Ethernet network B is connected to, using that Ethernet network's public key (step 3). This message is called Msg send ethernet and will be finally read by B after going through the Ethernet network (Msg send ethernet 2, step 4).

The response process on B's side would be analogous to the diagram, starting with B sending a Msg receive ethernet to the gateway. Gateway would receive and decrypt Msg receive ethernet 2 and build Msg receive gsm mobile, which would be forwarded to A's mobile through the GSM network. Finally Msg receive gsm mobile 2 would arrive to the mobile phone.

In our case the intruder knows both the Ethernet and Wifi network's fictitious public key, so it can send/read messages from these networks in the same way as A, B and the gateway. It also knows the agents involved in the communication. Knowledge of the Ethernet network's public key could be removed from that set to model that that network is physically safe (something unlikely to happen in practice).

SECTION 0: Assign state machine, based on initial network value and initial device.

```
INIT_MOBILE_GSM . (State = initial) /\ (Current_device = mobile) /\
(Current_network = gsm) =|> (State' := request_session_mobile_gsm)

INIT_PDA_GSM . (State = initial) /\ (Current_device = pda) /\
(Current_network = gsm) =|> (State' := request_session_pda_gsm)

INIT_PDA_WIFI_1 . (State = initial) /\ (Current_device = pda) /\
(Current_network = wifi_1) =|> (State' := request_session_pda_wifi_1)

INIT_PDA_WIFI_2 . (State = initial) /\ (Current_device = pda) /\
(Current_network = wifi_2) =|> (State' := request_session_pda_wifi_2)
```

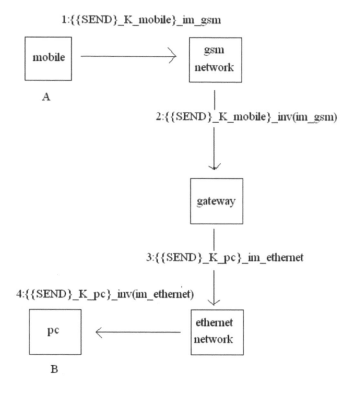

Figure 1. Example

SECTION 1: Every (device, network) pair carries out a simple interaction with the gateway. This interaction starts when A's device sends a session request message (for instance Msg request session mobile gsm), to which the gateway will reply with a corresponding new session message (Msg new session mobile gsm 2) in the case that a new session has been created (including a new session key for the device, in this example a mobile phone) or a reuse previous session message (Msg reuse session mobile gsm 2).

This two-step session request might indeed be more complex in actual implementations, involving a whole protocol with several message exchanges, but since the aim of this document is not to provide specific protocols the (device,network)- gateway interaction has been kept simple; consequently the types of these messages are defined as TBD (to be determined) in the local variables definition. However it is clear that the Msg new session mobile gsm 2 message should consist of, among other elements, the new session key for the mobile phone conveniently encrypted. The different Update Session tags would deal with retrieving the new session key and making the required updates so that each device can properly resume the communication with the end-point agent. In all cases after this direct interaction with the gateway has finished the regular communication with B can begin.

```
REQUEST_SESSION_MOBILE_GSM. (State = request_session_mobile_gsm) = |>
SND(Msg_request_session_mobile_gs) /\ (State' := wait_session_mobile_gsm)
```

```
REUSE_SESSION_MOBILE_GSM. (State = wait_session_mobile_gsm) /\
RCV(Msg_reuse_session_mobile_gsm_2) =|> (State' := mobile_gsm)
```

SECTION 2: Regular communication (send and receive) after the session to use has been resolved. The Last action variable records, as its name suggests, the last action performed by the device (send or receive). This is useful after a context change has happened: A's device can then normally resume the message interaction from where it was before the change event, being the process transparent to agent B. Once again the protocol boils down to a simple send-receive process, with the highlighted messages being formed in the way described in the diagram prior to these sections (to send, first encrypt with the device's symmetric session key and then encrypt with the network's imaginary public key, to receive proceed decrypting in an analogous way).

```
MOBILE_GSM_1. (State = mobile_gsm) /\
(Last_action = receive) =|> SND(Msg_send_mobile_gsm)
/\ (Last_action' := send)

MOBILE_GSM_2. (State = mobile_gsm) /\ (Last_action = send)
/\ RCV(Msg_receive_mobile_gsm_2) =|> (Last_action' := receive)
```

SECTION 3: Context changes are modelled here. There is no state control on the left side of the implication, so a context change only depends on the current (device-network) couple. This means that when analyzing a protocol's security properties if A has engaged in a Section 2-like message exchange AVISPA will take into account both the regular path and the case where a context change has just happened. We are therefore taking advantage of indeterminism: from one point two conditions happen to be true and hence two paths must be validated. Moreover, there might be two context changes that share the same condition but perform different actions:

T1.Condition1 ∧ Condition2 ⇒ Action1 T2.Condition1 ∧ Condition2 ⇒ Action2

This would increase the number of paths to three. The context changes detailed are the following (they are just a subset of all the possible context changes in our scenario):

1. The mobile phone runs out of battery and Wifi 1 network is reachable: then the PDA is activated in Wifi 1 network.
2. The mobile phone runs out of battery and wifi 2 network is reachable: then the PDA is activated in Wifi 2 network.
3. The PDA runs out of battery and is connected to Wifi 1. We have the posibility to use the mobile phone in GSM.
4. The PDA runs out of battery and is connected to Wifi 2: The same as the case above.
5. The PDA is connected to Wifi 1 and user moves away so his location changes to a new location where Wifi 1 is not covered but Wifi 2 is reachable. Then the PDA connects to Wifi 2.
6. The PDA is connected to Wifi 2 and user moves to a new location where Wifi 1 is reachable and Wifi 2 is not covered: Then the PDA connects toWifi 1.
7. The mobile phone is connected to a GSM network and a new session has been created by the gateway for the user due to a spontaneous timeout. Session information stored in the device must be updated (including the new value of K mobile).

The right side of these implications simply redirects to section 4 where the context change really takes place.

```
CONTEXT_CHANGE_MOBILE_GSM_BATTERY : (Current_device = mobile) /\
(Current_network = gsm) =|>
(State' : = transition_mobile_gsm_battery_1)

CONTEXT_CHANGE_MOBILE_GSM_BATTERY : (Current_device = mobile) /\
(Current_network = gsm) =|>
(State' : = transition_mobile_gsm_battery_2)
```

SECTION 4: Essentially, here the current network and device are updated, depending on the nature of the context change, and a session request from Section 1 is started. Before that further unspecified actions could be made, probably dealing with context change recovery-related procedures.

```
TRANSITION_MOBILE_GSM_BATTERY_1: (State =
transition_mobile_gsm_battery_1) =|>
ACTIONS /\ (Current_device' := pda) /\ (Current_network' := wifi_1) /\
(State' := request_session_pda_wifi_1)

TRANSITION_MOBILE_GSM_BATTERY_2: (State =
transition_mobile_gsm_battery_2) =|>
ACTIONS /\ (Current_device' := pda) /\ (Current_network' := wifi_2) /\
(State' := request_session_pda_wifi_2)
```

```
role rolenet(Net:agent,SND,RCV:channel(dy)) played_by Net
...
GSM.RCV({M'}_im_gsm)=|> SND({M'}_inv(im_gsm))
WIFI_1.RCV({M'}_im_wifi_1 =|> SND({M'}_inv(im_wifi_1))
WIFI_1.RCV({M'}_im_wifi_2 =|> SND({M'}_inv(im_wifi_2))
end role
```

The gateway role can be divided into two sections: a section for the sessions, symmetric to role A's section 1, dealing with session requests by agent A and generating spontaneous new sessions (this one would be a context change triggered by the gateway), and the regular message section, where normal messages from A are forwarded to B and vice versa. See how to model the creating a new key (a fresh value) we use the X' := new() assignment.

```
role rolegateway(Gateway,A,B:agent,SND,RCV:channel(dy)) played_by Gateway
...
REUSE_SESSION_MOBILE_GSM: Previous_session = true /\
RCV(Msg_request_session_mobile_gsm_2) =|>
Current_device' := mobile /\ Current_network' : = gsm /\
SND(Msg_reuse_session_mobile_gsm)
NEW_SESSION_MOBILE_GSM: RCV(Msg_request_session_mobile_gsm_2) =|>
K_mobile' := new() /\ Current_device' := mobile /\ Current_network' : =
gsm /\
ADDITONAL ACTIONS /\ Previous_session' := true /\
SND(Msg_new_session_mobile_gsm)
SPONTANEOUS_SESSION_MOBILE_GSM: Current_device = mobile /\
Current_network = gsm =|>
K_mobile' := new() /\ ADDITONAL ACTIONS /\ Previous_session' := true /\
SND(Msg_new_session_mobile_gsm)
```

```
...
SEND_MOBILE_GSM. RCV(Msg_send_mobile_gsm_2) =|> SND(Msg_send_ethernet)
RECEIVE_MOBILE_GSM. Current_device = mobile /\ Current_network = gsm /\
RCV(Msg_receive_ethernet_2) =|> SND(Msg_receive_mobile_gsm)
...
end role
```

On B's side we only show the regular message reception and answer section. Regarding context changes, we only contemplate for B the new session context change that has its origins in a gateway's timeout.

```
role rolenet2(Net2:agent,SND,RCV:channel(dy)) played_by Net2
...
ETHERNET.RCV({M'}_im_ethernet)=|>SND({M'}_inv(im_ethernet))
end role

role roleB(A,B,Gateway:agent,SND,RCV:channel(dy)) played_by B
...
RECEIVE_ETHERNET. RCV(Msg_send_ethernet_2) =|> SND(Msg_receive_ethernet)
...
end role

role session(A,B,Net ,Net2,Gateway,Start_device : agent, Start_network :
protocol_id)
...
composition
roleA(A,B,Gateway,Start_network,Start_device,SND1,RCV1)/\roleB(A,B,Gatewa
y,SND2,RCV2)
/\rolenet(Net,SND3,RCV3)/\rolenet2(Net2,SND4,RCV4)/\rolegateway(Gateway,A
,B,SND5,RCV5)
end role


role environment()
...
intruder_knowledge={a,b,gateway,net,net2,im_wifi_1,im_wifi_2,im_ethernet}
....
session(a,b,net,net2,gateway,mobile,gsm)
end role

environment()
```

The HLSPL code shown above simply models the scenario represented in the diagram at the beginning of this document. For this model to be suitable for AVISPA validation, security specific predicates and blocks must be included in the code. Briefly, every time a message is sent then at the end of that sentence a witness instruction should be written to impose that authentication (strong o weak one) is required; similarly a request/wrequest instruction should be written on the receiver's side. The secret instruction would indicate that some value must be a secret among a set of specified agents.We could apply this one to our model, as we are concerned about the secrecy of the different session keys (K mobile, K pda, etc.). We would have the following line in Section 2 of roleA:

```
MOBILE GSM 1.(State = mobile gsm) ∧⇒ (Last action = receive) ⇒SND(Msg
send mobile gsm) ∧ (Last action' := send) ∧ secret(K mobile,secret
1,A,Gateway)
```

The last action predicate means that the session key K mobile used by the mobile phone in encrypting the message Msg send mobile gsm should only be known by the mobile phone itself and the gateway (the latter is indicated in the form of a set as third parameter); secret 1 would be the identifier of this secrecy condition and is needed because at the end of the whole model description a goals section will state which of the goals must be validated, referencing the identifiers of all secret/authentication predicates specified in the code. In our case this section would simply be: secrecy_of_secret_1

A final actual specification would include a secret(A,B,C) predicate after every message sent by agent A. Although it is not implemented yet, it is expected that future versions of AVISPA will support validation of more complex goals, taking into account time aspects (always in the future, some time in the future, etc). In fact there is already a syntax for time-related goals which is successfully parsed and translated by AVISPA, although it is not functional in reality and cannot be used. Properties derived of indeterminist network or context change behaviours could be validated if such goals were supported. Unfortunately other properties such as the probability of an event happening do not seem that could be possible to model in the near future.

4 Conclusions

We showed new approach for modelling AmI system with AVISPA. This approach is based on the point of view of devices, networks and especially, context changes. These context changes are the real innovation in these ecosystems. Then we conclude this section with some considerations in the use of AVISPA tool, as well as a discussion about improve this tool.

AVISPA provides functionality to validate protocols in circumstances where context changes can happen. Then a plan of an attack when a context change is produced can be provided, such as in last last example shown.

We identify certain desirable features among these available in AVISPA. We must highlight the role parametrization, as a useful mechanism. This facilitates the modeling process of AmI protocols in AVISPA.

One aspect to improve is the fact that channels are defined to work in broadcasting mode. This obliges us to use symmetric fictitious keys to indicate the destination, which complicates the final code and does not provide an elegant and natural way to represent this situation. Concerning the functionality provided, we believe that a mechanism to provide protocol bisimulation is missing. Protocols in real world may interfere when they are executed simultaneously. Also some mechanism to model temporal generic predicates, such as "..if A sends to B then do.." is lacking. However, it is foreseen that the next version of this tool provides this functionality. Avispa protocol simulation tests if any intruder is sniffing in a concrete channel, then a plan where this situation is possible is found. However the analyst does not have the possibility to obtain statistics nor probabilities of the likehood of some situation occurring.

Despite of these limitations, Avispa has proven to be very useful tool. One of the more relevant advantages to work with Avispa is that we do not need to model intruders, as an additional role. The tool provides mechanisms to generate plans automatically. Then all state spaces are generated from a knowledge that we provided.

Acknowledgement

Work partially supported by E.U. through projects SERENITY (IST-027587) and OKKAM (IST-215032)

References

[1]   Krogstie, J., et al., Research Areas and Challenges for Mobile Information Systems. International Journal of Mobile Communication, 2004. 2(3).
[2]   Anind K. Dey and Gregory D. Abowd.Towards a Better Understanding of Context and Context-Awareness. In the Proceedings of the CHI 2000 Workshop on The What, Who, Where, When, and How of Context-Awareness, The Hague, Netherlands, April 1-6, 2000.
[3]   Jolle Coutaz , James L. Crowley , Simon Dobson , David Garlan, Context is key, Communications of the ACM, v.48 n.3, March 2005
[4]   Avispa Project Consortium: The HLPSL Tutorial A Beginner's Guide to Modelling and Analysing Internet Security Protocols. Available from http://www.avispaproject.org/.
[5]   C. Kaufman, Ed. Internet Key Exchange (IKEv2) Protocol. RFC 4306, Internet Engineering Task Force, December 2005.
[6]   A. Project. AVISPA Automated Validation of Internet Security Protocols and Applications. At http://www.avispa-project.org.
[7]   AVISPA Project. AVISPA Web Tool. At http://www.avispa-project.org/webinterface/.
[8]   Sebastian Modersheim and Luca Vigano and David von Oheimb. Automated Validation of Security Protocols (AVASP). Lecture slides, April 2005.
[9]   Liana Bozga, Yassine Lakhnech and Michael Perin. Hermes,a tool verifying secrecy properties of unbounded security protocols. In 15th international conferenceon Computer-Aided Verification (CAV'03), Lecture Notes in Computer Science, Springer Verlag, July 2003.

Ambient Intelligence Perspectives
P. Mikulecký et al. (Eds.)
IOS Press, 2009
doi:10.3233/978-1-58603-946-2-194

Systematic Approach to Evaluate a B2(B2B) platform

Dana Palová[1], Heiko Weinaug[2]

[1] *Technical University Košice, Faculty of Economics, Košice, Slovakia*
dana.palova@tuke.sk
[2]*Fraunhofer IPK, Division Corporate Management, Berlin, Germany*
heiko.weinaug@ipk.fraunhofer.de

Abstract: The term B2(B2B) is used by the authors to characterize the seamless integration of business services, offered by logistic and financial service providers, into existing, already IT-supported, manufacturing B2B networks. The European project FLUID-WIN has developed methods, procedures and a platform to support such business-to-network relationships. The paper shortly presents the FLUID-WIN platform itself and the significant potentials for the service providers as well as for all companies involved in the B2B network. The evaluation of the FLUID-WIN outcomes by the end users is an essential step to guarantee the quality and usability. For that purpose both the software and also the business processes influenced by the FLUID-WIN platform are evaluated. Anyway, especially the workflow oriented B2(B2B)-approach and its cross-enterprise dimension induces some specifics. The description of the challenges and experiences of the evaluation shell give an impression of that ambitious task.

Introduction

The Internet and its' services have initiated and influenced a huge number of tools for providing and searching information not only for ordinary people but also for enterprises in the way of more dynamic sharing of important information. These tools and services aim to support a more seamless cooperation and faster reaction on market changes. The impact of the Internet is visible in all enterprises at least at the management level and in the way of the cooperation among an enterprise and all its' business partners.

In the past, a number of tools have shown the benefits of IT-supported business-to-business cooperation. Most of those tools provide functionalities for manufacturing supply chains (or better networks) e.g. for the order data negotiation and exchange, status monitoring, etc.. Partially, they also offer limited capabilities to support the information exchange with service providers, for example payment instructions with financial service providers (FSP) and transportation status information with logistic service providers (LSP). However, an integration of a *complete business service workflow (B2)* into an existing manufacturing B2B-structure never occurred, even if the significant potentials for both sides - for the business service providers as well as for their business partners within the network – is obviously. The European project FLUID-WIN [4] has tackled that issue. The project consortium has developed a revolutionary new B2(B2B) business concept and the related FLUID-WIN platform (Figure 1). The FLUID-WIN platform provides an innovative way of how service providers can cooperate with the entire B2B manufacturing networks instead of to communicate to each enterprise of that network, separately, to manage business services, such as warehousing, transportation, invoice discounting and factoring service (see chapter 1). Thereby, the platform is interacting directly with already established local financial IT and logistic legacy systems, and intelligent link them with B2B-tools (such as products from i2, Oracle, Manugistics, GXS, Atomos, Tecnest, Tesi Group, TXT E-solutions, Joinet, etc.).

Based on that support, both business sides have benefits and a win-win situation. For example, the service providers can profit on up-to-date information from their B2B partners, such as manufacturing forecasts and status information as base for the logistical planning at the LSP, or, the manufacturing clients within the B2B has a seamless integration of their service providers in their own IT environment. However, such a B2(B2B) platform strongly influences a) the various local software applications, b) the cross-enterprise document and information workflows and c) the work of a many actors, even at the same company. This, of course, requires a well-planed and well-scheduled evaluation scheme to investigate the majority and quality of software and related business processes from every interoperability perspective.

The evaluation is supported by various, already established standards for measuring or guidance of different aspects of software engineering. Partially, the standards focus on the software engineering process, partially they concentrate on the software product as outcome of the engineering (see chapter 2). In any case, the evaluation of system and processes before its implementation in practice shall ensure that the end users get a safe and reliable system that matches their requirements. Nevertheless, the evaluation of a B2(B2B) platform within a B2(B2B) environment sets specific constraints and challenges, which are explained in chapter 3 and outlined on a practical example in chapter 4.

1. The FLUID-WIN Platform - Aims and Structure

In today's business it is a frequent situation that a manufacturing company has already established a common supply network IT-support for the daily B2B collaboration with its suppliers and customers. However, the logistic services and trade financial services, which are used by either one company or a set of companies of that supply network, are not seamlessly integrated. At that circumstance, the FLUID-WIN European project [4] consortium members exemplary asked themselves:

- Is it feasible to reuse the already available invoices from the B2B system, which occur daily in the business life between a supplier and its customer, for trade financial services like invoice discounting or factoring? This would reduce effort at the supplier and the bank, and raises the level data consistency.
- Is it possible to collect up-to-date status and quality information about the manufacturing process and provide it to the banks to reduce their risk and opens the chance for better conditions in the trade financial service?
- How is it possible to get manufacturing order and status information and send it as forecast to the logistic service provider for a more precise and earlier planning?

- How to avoid the number of media breaks during the whole service workflow, and how to get impartial service indicators for the provider and its business partners as base for more transparency (e.g. service quality, fulfilment, etc.)?

Summarizing, the members found – encouraged also by a detailed field study [13] - that a smooth integration of business services into supply networks, combined with an intelligent and context-sensitive information conditioning have significant potentials [11].

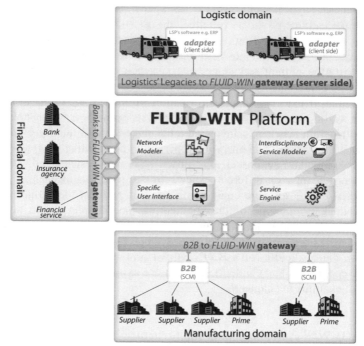

Figure 1 The FLUID-WIN integration platform

This is especially the case when manufacturing networks are geographically distributed across state borders, the duration of transportation is significant (carrying over days or weeks) and in cases where cross-border payment and trade finance is not as good as gold.

Based on these finding, the FLUID-WIN project targets to B2B manufacturing networks and their interactions with the LSP and FSP (Figure 1). This cross-discipline service integration concept is called business-to-(business-to-business) or shorter B2(B2B). Within that context the project has developed the innovative FLUID-WIN platform, which can integrate data from all three domains and distribute them among the relevant partners, in order to improve the competitiveness and to make the business processes of the integrated service network as efficient as possible. Thanks to the platform, the Financial Service Providers (FSP) and their clients in the B2B network can collaborate in factoring and invoice discounting service. And, Logistic Service Providers (LSP) can provide and manage transportation and warehouse services with their B2B network-partners, taking into account current order information that includes announced or expected delays as well as forecast information. Related to each business service, the FLUID-WIN platform provides various functionalities which support or use the cross-domain data exchange, e.g. Logistic: Forecast, Order Management,

Document Management, Performance Assessment, Stock Information and Financial: Electronic Invoice Management, Service Management, Service Status Monitoring, KPI for Financial Service Providers and Service Performance Assessment [14].

The clou is, that the already existing local IT software from the LSP and FSP (back office software, legacy tools etc.) as well as the established B2B platform can be used further on. For that purpose, FLUID-WIN provides three domain-related gateways which simply *couple* the local tools and B2B system via an ASP-based platform to ensure the seamless data exchange (Figure 1). Moreover, the gateways ensure the secure communication. As far as possible, the FLUID-WIN philosophy aims to let manage and store the relevant data by the local IT systems instead of saving data in a big central database. This principle shell ensures the data consistency, privacy and also the availability of important and sensitive data in case of non-influenceable technical problems with the internet.

For example, if the local IT system of the LSP and its B2B partner supports the management of logistic orders, then FLUID-WIN ensures, that the logistic order including all relevant data and status are exchanged from one local tool into the other and vice versa. Moreover, the platform provides additional functionalities, such as the KPI monitoring for the business service quality assessment. Anyway, it is very likely that at least one partner's local IT systems don't support the management of certain information, for example the creation and handling of factoring orders and confirmations. Therefore, all FLUID-WIN platform functionalities can also be entered via an html-based graphical user interface by using a usual web-browser. There is no need to install additional software to utilize the FLUID-WIN platform, and the hardware requirement is reduced to a PC with an internet connection and web-browser. This is, especially, suitable for small and medium-sized enterprises (SME) with their often low IT capabilities and resources.

2. Information System Evaluation Methods

Nowadays, IT engineers and managers are responsible for planning, designing, implementation and ranging software systems and IT environments based on end-users' needs. They are supported by various, already established standards for measuring or guidance of different aspects of software engineering. Partially, the standards focus on the software engineering process e.g. ISO 15504 "Information technology - Process assessment" [8] and CMMI "Capability Maturity Model Integration" [2], partially they concentrate on the software product as outcome of the engineering, e.g. ISO 9126 "Software engineering - Product quality" [7] and ISO 9241 "Ergonomics of human-system interaction" [9]. Also the evaluation process itself is supported by ISO/IEC 14598 "Information technology - Software product evaluation" [6]. Further approaches are the approaches from Ortega, Pérez and Rojas [12], McCall [10], Boehm et al [1], Grady (FURPS) [5] and Dromey [3]. In any case, the evaluation of systems and processes, before its implementation in practice, shall ensure that the end users get a safe and reliable system that matches their requirements.

With respect to the evaluation of a B2(B2B) platform, the most important norm is the ISO 9126 [7]. It defines product quality as a set of product characteristics. The characteristics that govern how the product works in its environment are called external quality characteristics, which include, for instance, Usability and Reliability. The internal quality characteristics is relating to how the product was developed; they include, for example, size, tests and failure rate, exchange rate, structure, etc. taken in the development of the product. Generally, ISO 9126 indicates that the software quality has been described in terms of one or several of the six characteristics listed below.

Each of these six characteristics is defined as a set of attributes that are supported by a relevant aspect of the software. The internal attributes of the software influence the external attributes; thus there are internal aspects and external aspects for the majority of the characteristics. In ISO 9126, the quality characteristics are defined with the associated sub-characteristics:

- Functionality: Suitability, Accuracy, Interoperability, Compliance, Security
- Reliability: Maturity, Fault Tolerance, Recoverability
- Usability: Understandability, Learnability, Operability
- Efficiency: Time behavior, Resource behavior.
- Maintainability: Analyzability, Changeability, Stability, Testability
- Portability: Adaptability, Installability, Conformance, Replaceability

The advantage of this model is that it identifies the internal characteristics and external quality characteristics of a software product. However, at the same time it has the disadvantage that some very important aspects like Process-Maturity, Flexibillity and Reusability are not overall covered [12].

Based on a detailed survey and analysis of quality models, Ortega, Pérez and Rojas have developed the "Systemic Quality model for Software Products" (Figure 2). It combines the advantages of several approaches and tries to close the gaps of the ISO 9126. Especially of interest for the B2(B2B) evaluation is the fact that the approach differentiate between product and process as well as efficiency and effectiveness.

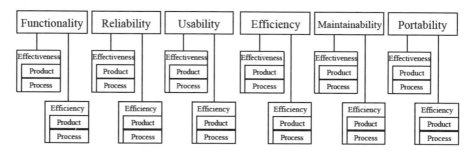

Figure 2 Elements of the Systemic Quality model for Software Products [12]

3. Specific Challenges of a B2(B2B) Platform Evaluation

The B2(B2B) concept is characterized by its purpose to "link". That means it moderates between different enterprises in different domains, between different actors along certain workflows and processes, and between different local and network-bounded IT systems. Thereby information are exchanged but also used to gain and offer added values, such as performance indicators. This, of course, induces a broad variance of scenarios where the B2(B2B) platform can be adopted and therefore have to be evaluated. Moreover, not only the platform but also the business process influenced by it has to be investigated. In this context, the evaluation has especially to tackle following challenges:

1. To use a service, the number of companies which are accessing the platform is at least 2 but more usual 4 and more. This depends on the used kind of business service in combination with the platform functionalities. For example, to utilize and evaluate the "stock information" functionality within the warehouse service, the LSP as stock level provider and a manufacturing company as LSP's client are involved. But, depending on the configuration of the workflow, it is possible that also further clients can access the stock level data. More difficult is the factoring service. Here, a FSP buys outstanding debits of its client which are resulting from a business transaction with the client's customers. The client's customers, of course, have now to pay to the FSP instead of to his supplier. Hence, the client's customers have to confirm the correctness of the factored invoice. In this service at least 4 enterprises are involved: the company which uses the factoring service, its customer(s), the customers' bank and finally the factoring service providing FSP. Last but not least, in each configuration, also the provider of the FLUID-WIN platform itself has to be investigated. All that business partners have to be a) found for the test, b) embedded in the assessment and c) synchronized during the evaluation.
2. The enterprises to be investigate belong to the three different domains manufacturing, logistic and finance. Even if they work within the same cross-domain service and cross-enterprise workflow, each enterprise have domain-related and individual interests that have to be taken into account at the evaluation preparation and during the test, for example saving potentials.
3. Beside the high number of enterprises, also their configuration and constellation within the service workflow may influence the usability and acceptance of the platform. For example, an enterprise which offers transport capabilities to manufacturing clients is a LSP within the transportation services. This LSP usual writes invoices to its client. If the same LSP wishes, it can use these invoices as base for a factoring service. In this context the LSP plays as client of a FSP. Hence, the LSP might be both service provider and service user. Dozens of such potential scenarios are conceivable.
4. Moreover, different persons act in each company within the business service, e.g. IT responsible person, persons who are responsible to set-up the network and workflow configuration, service operators, managers.
5. Each service provider uses their own local IT tool, and the manufacturing companies within the B2B networks are already interlinked by their B2B system. Hence, the IT system interoperability between those software and the B2(B2B) platform is a very crucial aspect.
6. But the IT interoperability is also a critical point, because of high security relevant processes. Especially, it is obviously that the evaluation of the financial service capabilities can't be done in the runtime environment and needs a special test scenario. Moreover, FSP-specific security mechanisms have to be fulfilled.
7. The evaluation of the business processes influenced by the new concept and platform requires the comparison by reliable indicators of the situation before and after the implementation.

4. Approach to Evaluate the FLUID-WIN B2(B2B) Platform

Within FLUID-WIN project the team decided to apply a detailed test to provide evaluation from user's point of view. The project started in 2006 and the final version of the mentioned platform was proposed to the end-users in March 2008. Nowadays the application tests are running. Anyway the application tests are structured in 3 main phases with following main sub-tasks:

1. Application test preparation phase
    *   Selection of platform functionalities to be tested
    *   Environment specification where the functionalities can be tested (enterprise networks, service providers)
    *   Definition of personal roles which have to be taken into account during the evaluation; assign real actors to each role
    *   Development of a questionnaire (role-based, cover all functionalities and aspects)
    *   Set-up a time frame for the evaluation
    *   Ensure that the relevant data required for the test are already available at the companies (e.g. as base to check the KPI generation based on historical data)
    *   Set-up an easy applicable tool to automate the statistical evaluation (KPI, calculation, etc.)
    *   Installation and establishing the FLUID-WIN platform; train the actors
2. Platform users' application test
    *   Use of the platform within various services; malfunctions and problems are send to the R&D partners to be solved immediately,
    *   Evaluation of the selected FLUID-WIN platform functionalities within eleven various scenarios specialized on separate functionality and note the important facts and impressions into the feedback form
3. Application test evaluation
    *   Analysing and evaluation the feedbacks from various users.

The most crucial phase was the preparation. For the application tests four networks are specified. The three production-centred networks are a diesel engine network (represented by Lombardini and TS Motory), a thermostat network (represented by Tecasa, Matalflex) a system provider network (represented by MBAS). And, one logistic service provider-centred distribution network (guides by Hödlmayr) is investigated as an additional platform application spectrum. The networks are established by 19 companies – 5 project partners and 14 "outsider" companies. Additionally, also the future provider of the FLUID-WIN platform is investigated. For each of those companies, 5 actor's roles were specified. Overall the platform is tested by 11 different scenarios (constellation of companies, services and functionalities).

As mentioned, a feedback form was worked out very carefully, which will collect the experiences, founded bugs and opinions of the users. It will be continuously filled during the three month test period and afterwards collected. The feedback form has a very detailed structure due to aim to systematically collect maximum amount of relevant information about the platform usability and functionality for the end users.

The structure of the feedback form can be divided into following parts:

*   **General information**, which is aimed to basic information about end user's company like name, responsible person and her/his role within company, tested platform functionalities, etc.

- **Event protocol/Journal** containing the list of events done and obtained results.
- **(General) Software quality characteristics**, where users evaluate the platform characteristics like general efficiency, usability, user interface, learning effort needed to manage platform and accessible tools, available documentation and last but not least - security aspects.
- **Network model and interdisciplinary service model definition and implementation** concerned on general questions related to the customization of the final version of the platform.
- **Logistic service** part obtains questions related to transportation service, warehouse service and combined logistic service.
- **Financial service** part is about functions used working with invoice discounting and factoring.
- **Free comment** present space for expressing user's opinion, remarks and possible improvements of the platform and its functionality.

This specific structure was necessary to get a domain-oriented feedback and ease the very detailed filling process of the end-user. Anyway the most subchapters contain indicators which follow the ISO 9126 plus the differentiation by product and process indicators. After the collection of the feedback forms from the platform users, an evaluation, especially of the numerical feedback (scaled question), will be done by using different statistical methods. As far as possible this work will be supported by a database. More difficult to evaluate but partially also more substantial are the free commented feedbacks. The evaluation of these questions can only be done manually.

The obtained questionnaires' evaluation will be provided in months August and September, so it can't be predicted the real results of user evaluation process. But the results will be ready until the conference, where they will be shortly presented.

5. Conclusion

The B2(B2B) concept is a new and innovative approach to seamlessly tooth the business service related processes of financial and logistic service providers with its clients in already established manufacturing supply networks. Anyway, the all-embracing evaluation of the concept and the software behind it requires a special procedure and an accurate preparation. For wide areas, well-known standards and approaches can be used to guide the evaluation. However, the B2(B2B) evaluation requires to tackle certain specifics like the broad variance of possible scenarios to be tested, comprehensive interoperability of cross-domain processes and IT system, and the attention on security relevant activities. Based on a practical example from the FLUID-WIN project, it has been shown how it possible to deal with the challenges of the evaluation of a B2(B2B) platform.

Acknowledgement

This work has been kindly funded by the European Commission through the IST Project FLUID-WIN: Finance, logistics and production integration domain by web-based interaction network (No. IST-FP6-27083). The authors wish to acknowledge the

Commission for their support. We also wish to acknowledge our gratitude and appreciation to all the FLUID-WIN project partners for their contribution during the development of research presented in this paper.

References

[1]   Boehm, B. W., Brown, J. R., Kaspar, H., Lipow M., McCleod, G. J., Merritt M. J. (1978) . *Characteristics of Software Quality*, Amsterdam, North Holland.

[2]   CMMI Product Team (2002) *Capability Maturity Model Integration (CMMI)*. Carnegie Mellon University, Pittsburg

[3]   Dromey, G. (1996) *Cornering the Chimera*, IEEE Software, 1996, pp. 33-43.

[4]   FLUID-WIN consortium (2008) *FLUID-WIN: Finance, logistics and production integration domain by web-based interaction network*. FP6 IST STREP 27083 funded by European Commission. Available at: www.fluid-win.de

[5]   Grady, R. and Caswell, D. (1987) *Software Metrics: Establishing a Company-Wide Program*, Prentice Hall.

[6]   ISO/IEC (1999-2001*) ISO/IEC 14598 Information technology –Software product evaluation, Part 1 to 6*. ISO copyright office, Geneva

[7]   ISO/IEC (2001) *ISO/IEC 9126 Software engineering - Product quality, Part 1 to 4*. ISO copyright office, Geneva

[8]   ISO/IEC (2004*) ISO 15504 Information technology - Process assessment, Part 1 to 4*. ISO copyright office, Geneva

[9]   ISO/IEC (2006) *ISO 9241-110 Ergonomics of human-system interaction, Part 110: Dialogue principles*. ISO copyright office, Geneva

[10] McCall, J. A., Richards, P. K., Walters G. F. (1977) *Factors in Software Quality*, Vols I, II, III, AD/A-049-014/ 015/055. Springfield, VA: National Technical Information Service.

[11] Mertins, K.; Rabe, M.; Schallock, B.; Weinaug, H. (2007) *Logistic Performance Improvement and Synchronization of Material and Money Flow*. In: Ivanov D., Müller E., et al (Eds.) Logistics Collaboration, Logistic Collaboration, Publishing House of the St Petersburg State Polytechnic University, 2007 pp. 160-170

[12] Ortega, M.; Pérez, M.; Rojas, T. (2003) *Construction of a Systemic Quality Model for evaluating a Software Product*. In: Software Quality Journal, 11:3, July 2003, pp. 219-242. Kluwer Academic Publishers, 2003

[13] Rabe, M., Weinaug, H. (2007) *Distributed Analysis of Financial and Logistic Services for Manufacturing Supply Chains*. In: Pawar, K. S.; Thoben, K-D.; Pallot, M. (Eds.) ICE2007 - The 13th International Conference on Concurrent Engineering, Proceedings Sophia-Antipolis, France 4.-6. June 2007, pp. 245-252

[14] Rabe, M.; Mussini, B.; Weinaug, H. (2007) *Web-based integrated services for manufacturing networks*. In: Rabe, M.; Mihók, P. (Eds.): New technologies for the intelligent design and operation of manufacturing networks. Stuttgart: Fraunhofer IRB Verlag, 2007, pp.129-147.

Ambient Intelligence Perspectives
P. Mikulecký et al. (Eds.)
IOS Press, 2009
doi:10.3233/978-1-58603-946-2-203

Modelling of e-Services

Libuša RÉVÉSZOVÁ [a], Jozef BUCKO [a], Peter MIHÓK [a]

[a] *Technical University of Košice, Faculty of Economics, Slovakia*
libusa.reveszova@tuke.sk

Abstract: Different electronic services offered in e-banking, e-commerce, e-government, e-manufacturing, e-learning, etc. are becoming to be a part of everyday life for people everywhere. As a basis for decision to use an e-service the trust is one of the most critical factors. In this paper we deal with modelling of e-services related to trust and security aspects of collaborative information sharing systems. Developing the identity management for the next generation of distributed applications digital signature can be used. We use IEM as a possibility to model this e-service.

Key words: modelling, business processes, IEM/MO^{2}GO, digital signature

Introduction

In a short time we should see different manners how to get the information, how to communicate, how to buy and do payments for goods and services. We can use the information and communication technology (ICT) for simplifying the trade and for the direct business from our house, office or another place.

The highly competitive global economy forces companies to:

- fully understand and harness the way they operate;
- align their organisation structure with changing business needs;
- integrate enterprise networks (Extended Enterprises, Virtual/Agile Enterprises, Supply Chains, …);
- implement large interoperable information systems;
- continuously optimise their operations, facilities and management in terms of Quality, Costs and Delays;

Why modelling of e-services? The essential goals of modelling are to understand and explain, to experiment (analyse, compare, test, evaluate/predict performances), to learn and decide (what-if scenarios), to operate/control and govern developments in everyday life. Major advantage e.g. in enterprise modelling is building a common consensus on how the enterprise operations work or should work (see [19]). Parallel to "the Internet of Objects" "the Internet of Services" will be used in Enterprise Networking. Thus e-services will become to be a part of the models. We present a short overview of modeling languages and methodologies and we use IEM to model digital signature in identity management services. Our work is based on the research which is a part of IST Project FLUID-WIN (FLW): "Finance, logistics and production integration domain by web-based interaction network" (No. IST-FP6-27083). More about the FLUID-WIN project can be found at www.fluid-win.de and in the papers [3],[14], [15], [20].

1. Business processes and the importance of modelling and simulation

Manufacturing companies are in need of tools and methods to support the decision-making processes to maintain a competitive advantage in the rapid changing economic environment. Modelling and simulation are the key methods to optimize the total product and system design before production; for optimisation of the design for speed, quality and affordability in production; and the production processes so that they are in place and ready to execute upon production go-ahead. By Osuna and Tuoko [13], maturation of the enabling technologies will enable system developers to slash months and years of development time and reduce costs by 50% or better from current design/build/test/fix practices.

Manufacturing simulation focuses on modelling the behaviour of manufacturing organizations, processes and systems. Today, simulation models are used in all the different system levels and phases of the manufacturing system life cycle. The following steps are found: concept creation, layout planning, production simulation, software development and operator training (see e.g.[5], [6]).

There are many commercial enterprise modelling tools (ARIS Toolset, FirstSTEP, Bonapart, KBSI tools, PrimeObject, Enterprise Modeler, MO2GO, emaGIM, CimTool, etc.) and many workflow management tools (IBM Flow Mark, Oracle Workflow, Ultimus, WorkParty, Ensemble, InConcert, Action Workflow, OPEN/Workflow, Staffware, Lotus Notes, etc.), but by [19] the pattern of enterprise modelling is the same (see Figure 1). Often the related/corresponding e-services have to be modelled (see e.g. [14], [20])

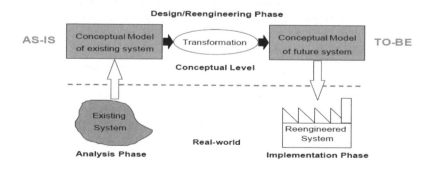

Figure 1 Enterprise modelling pattern [19].

2. Process modelling languages

Let us summarize the known and used process modelling languages.

IDEF0/SADT is procedural process modelling language. It explicitly supports hierarchic definition of processes. Complex processes can be defined in different level of details. Each activity can be detailed as own sub process. [7]

Event-Driven Process Chain (EPC) is a procedural process modelling language supporting different level of details. Compared with IDEF0 it is more powerful to support different integration scenarios and levels and it has more objects in the language. EPC supports events and activities between events. For the process flow EPC allows explicit branching and aggregation of processes. Furthermore there are additional objects, which support the process. These are information and/or resource objects, person and/or organizations.[16],[17]

Process Modelling with the UML - the Unified Modelling Language (UML) offers an all spanning modelling language. Regarding data and information model the language is object oriented. Looking at the process modelling capabilities of UML the processes are still described in a procedural way. Most important process diagrams within UML are the activity, state chart and the sequence diagram. Each of process diagrams shows the process in exactly one instance. For each instantiation the object oriented nature of the data model allows different processes.[4], [12]

Business Process Modelling Notation (BPMN) was developed to provide a notation for process descriptions. The specification includes the visual appearance of the elements and the semantics of the elements. Furthermore it deals with the exchange of process definition either between tools or as scripts. BPMN representation of processes is quite similar to the UML activity diagram. Processes are defined as a sequence of activities in swim lanes. [11]

Integrated Enterprise Modelling (IEM) was developed out of SADT. It capsules activities as objects and adds static information as job, product or resources. Due to this further information it is possible to generate views on the complete enterprise, not only on its processes. [18]

Process Specification Language (PSL) is a neutral language for process specification to serve as an interchange language to integrate multiple process-related applications throughout the manufacturing process life cycle. As it only defines itself in informal manner it has no formal and graphical constructs. Therefore it is not capable for process modelling. [9]

Semantic Object Model methodology is an enterprise architecture, which allows to divide an enterprise model into the model layers enterprise plan, business process model, and resources, each of them describing a business system completely and from specific point of view. Within the process model the activity the activity objects are connected with events. This concept allows flexible and robust process modelling. Out of this diagram the interaction scheme and the task-event scheme are developed. [2]

Within the project FLUID-WIN the modelling tool MO^{2}GO/IEM was chosen and used. MO^{2}GO/IEM was commercialised by PSI Germany, developed by IPK Berlin in 1994. MO^{2}GO is based on SADT model, has strong object orientation and three fundamental types of objects: Order, Product, Resource - see Figure 2. [19]

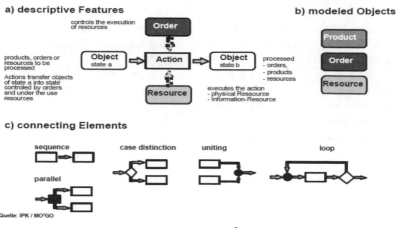

Figure 2 Fundamental of MO^{2}GO/IEM [19]

3. Modelling trust and security mechanism

Organizations and projects are looking for ways to optimize their supply chains in order to create a competitive advantage. Consequently, the same organizations are modifying their business processes to accommodate the demands that information sharing requires. Integrating and sharing information in inter-organizational settings involves a set of complex interactions. The organizations and institutions involved must establish and maintain collaborative relationships in which information and data of sensitive and critical nature are transferred outside of the direct control of the organization. Trust and security mechanisms are often stated in literature as being of critical importance in the creation and maintenance of an information sharing system.

Within the FLUID-WIN there is the high number of actors from different domains as well as their technical connection within the B2(B2B) concept (see [14]). For secure access to the FLUID-WIN Platform it could be convenient to use digital signatures (private keys), which are saved at a secure device (chip card, USB key) and protected by other safety elements (PIN and static password). It is necessary to take the existence of a digital signature couple as granted, the first one for access and cryptography and the second one for designation. The strength of this securing form is the fact that the method of digital signature cannot be breached by "brute" force at the present time. The weakness of this security method is insufficient knowledge of this method and infringement of all safety rules that are related to the physical security of digital signature storage site and safety elements, which allow its operation. Therefore, it is necessary to work out the security policy, in which the method of usage, security principles and risks of improper use of this method will be exactly specified. [10]

The next part gives a description of the Trust and Security mechanism B2(B2B) model of FLUID-WIN (see Figure 3, Figure 4).

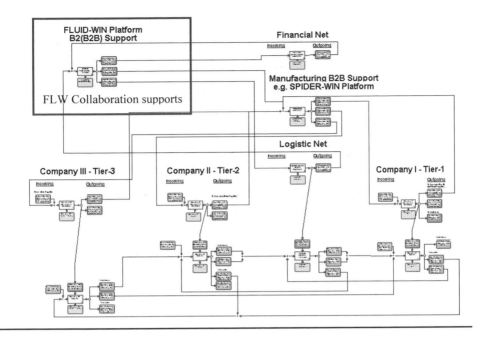

Figure 3 FLUID-WIN B2(B2B) Business Process Model

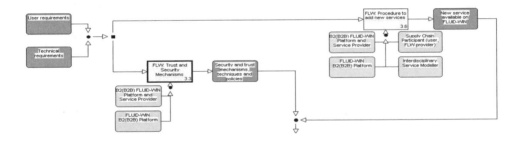

Figure 4 FLW trust and security Mechanisms

The detailed processes are modelled and described as follows in Figures 5-7.

Process of the obtaining of a certificate (Figure 5):

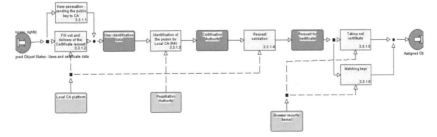

Figure 5 Obtaining certificate

Description of actions:

Fill out the certificate request and enter: On the web site of Local Certification Authority FLW (LCAFLW) the applicant (organisation, partner) fills the form "Application form for certificate" with personal data and confirms it. The applicant also prints the filled-out form for identification requirements. In this moment the key couple is generated in the safety core. The public key is forwarded to the server (LCAFLW) together with the application form. Private Key is saved in the safety core of browser (eventually in the safety equipment – chip card, USB key)

Identification of person by CA (RA): With the printed application form the user is registered and identified in the Registration Authority (RA) (eventually in LCAFLW).

Request validation: Following the identification in RA (LCAFLW), the LCAFLW issues the certificate for the user, what means, that the public key of applicant is signed by LCAFLW private key.

Taking out certificate: Following the confirmation and issue of certificate LCAFLW, the valid certificate is taken out by user on the basis of identifier, on the same computer as the "Application form for certificate" was filled.

Matching keys: In the process of certification withdrawal, in the safety core of browser, the user public key obtained form the web site is coupled with the private key inhere in safety core of browser (in safety equipment).

Sending data to the FLW platform (Figure 6):

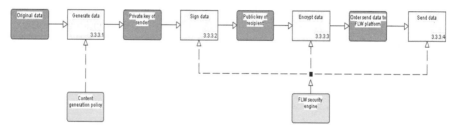

Figure 6 Sending data to FLW platform

Description of actions:

Generate data: Preparation and generation of the data designed for FLW on the basis of original data

Sign data: The electronic signature of inserted data is generated on the basis of senders` (the data owner`) private key.

Encrypt data: On the basis of public keys of users, who are the data designed, the content of inserted data is encrypted.

Send data: Confirmation of data insertion (sending) to the FLW platform.

Receiving data from the FLW platform (Figure 7):

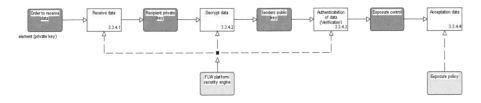

Figure 7 Receiving data from FLW platform

Description of actions:

Receive data: Taking out (delivery) of required data from FLW platform.

Decrypt data: Decryption of the received data content on the basis of private key of data recipient.

Authenticate data (Verification): Verification of the received data authenticity on the basis of sender public key (the author of inserted data).

Accept data: Acceptation of data for further use.

4. Conclusion

Modelling and simulation technologies represent tremendous opportunities for radical improvement of our ability to design, develop, manufacture, operate, and support complex products (see [8]). Modelling of e-services will be a challenge in the near future. We presented how IEM through MO²GO tool can be used to model digital signature.

Acknowledgements

This work has been partly funded by the European Commission through IST Project FLUID-WIN: Finance, logistics and production integration domain by web-based interaction network (No. IST-FP6-27083). We wish to acknowledge our gratitude and appreciation to all the Fluid-Win project partners for their contribution during the development of research presented in this paper.

References

[1]   ANDERL, R. – MALZACHER, J. – RASLER, J.: Proposal for an Object Oriented Process Modelling Language, In Enterprise interoperability III, New Challenges and Industrial Approaches, p. 533, Springer-Verlag, London, 2008, ISBN 978-1-84800-221-0
[2]   BERNIUS, P. – MERTINS, K. – SCHMIDT, G.: Handbook on Architectures of information Systems, 2nd Edition Springer-Verlag, Berlin, Heidelberg, 2006
[3]   DELINA, R. – MIHÓK, P.: Trust building processes on Web-based information-sharing platforms. Proc. of the 13th International Conference on Concurrent Enterprising (ICE), 4.-6. June 2007, Sophia Antipolis (France), pp. 179 - 186.
[4]   ERIKSSON, H. E. – PENKER, M.: Business modelling with UML: business patterns at work. John Wiley & Sons, Inc, New York 2000
[5]   HEILALA, J. – HENTULA, M. – MONTONEN, J. – ALHAINEN, J. VOHO, P. – SALO, J. – KUOKKANEN, K. – LEIVO, K. – ALI-RAATIKAINEN, J.: Simulation aided decision support

for customer driven manufacturing. In 16th International Conference on Production Research, Praha, Czech Republic, 2001.

[6] HEILALA, J.: Modelling and simulation for customer driven manufacturing system design and operations planning, online http://www.informs-sim.org/wsc07papers/231.pdf 2.5.2008

[7] IEEE Std 1320.1 – 1998. IEEE Standard for Functional Modelling Language – Syntax and Semantic for IDEF0, New York: IEEE, 1998

[8] IMTI, Inc., „Modelling & Simulation for Affordable Manufacturing", Technology Roadmapping Initiative, 18th of January, 2003   IMTI 2003. Roadmap modeling and simulation for affordable manufacturing, Available via http://www.imti21.org/resources/roadmaps.html

[9] International Standards Organization (ISO): ISO 18629 series: Process Specification Language www.iso.org

[10] MIHÓK, P. – BUCKO, J. – DELINA, R. – PAĽOVÁ, D.: Trust and Security in Collaborative Environments In Enterprise Interoperability III, Springer – Verlag London Limited, 2008, ISBN 978-1-84800-221-3

[11] OMG: Business Process Modelling Notation Specification www.omg.org 2008

[12] OMG: Unified Modelling Language, Superstructure v 2.1.1, www.omg.org 2008

[13] OSUNA, R., V. – TUOKKO, R.: Modelling and Simulation as a Tool for Decision Making in Adaptive Value Networks, In: Proceedings of the 12th International Conference on Concurrent Enterprising, ICE 2006, 26-28 June 2006 Milan, Italy, ISBN 0 85358 228 9

[14] RABE, M. – MUSINI, B. – WEINAUG, H.: New, Web-based Integrated Services for Manufacturing Networks, Technologies for the Intelligent Design and Operation of Manufacturing Networks, Results and Perspectives from the European AITPL Project Cluster Fraunhofer IRB Verlag, Stuttgart (2007), 129-148.

[15] RABE, M. – WEINAUG, H.: Distributed Analysis of Financial and Logistic Services for Manufacturing Supply Chains. In: Pawar, K.S.; Thoeben, K.-D.; Pallot, M. (eds.): Proc. of the 13th International Conference on Concurrent Enterprising (ICE), 4.–6. June 2007, Sophia Antipolis (France), pp 245 - 252.

[16] SCHEER, A.W.: ARIS – Business Process Frameworks, 2nd Edition, Berlin, 1998

[17] SCHEER, A.W.: ARIS – Business Process Modelling, 2nd Edition, Berlin, 1999

[18] SPUR, G. – MERTINS, K. – JOCHEM, R. – WARNECKE, H. J.: Integrierte Unternehmensmodellierung Beuth Verlag GmbH 1993

[19] VERNADAT, F. B.: Enterprise Modelling: Objectives, constructs & ontologies, LGIPM, University of Metz, France, Eurostat, European Commission, Tutorial held at the EMOI-CAiSE Workshop, Riga, Latvia, June 7, 2004

[20] WEINAUG, H. – RABE, M.: Models and Methods for Web-support of a multi-disciplinary B2(B2B) Network. Enterprise Interoperability III: New Challenges and Industrial Approaches. London: Springer 2008, S. 113-123.

Ambient Intelligence Perspectives
P. Mikulecký et al. (Eds.)
IOS Press, 2009

211

doi:10.3233/978-1-58603-946-2-211

An Approach of Implementing a Virtual Hotel Organization Using Web Services Technology

Cristina-Maria ŞTEFANACHE, Anda-Mina SIMON, Ilona-Mariana NAGY, Dan-Andrei SITAR-TĂUT

Babeş-Bolyai University, Cluj-Napoca, Romania

stefanache.cristina4873@mailbox.ubbcluj.ro

Abstract: In the context of Globalization, the "World Economy" is going through a full scale changing process, while adapting to the newly imposed conditions. The "New Economy" has been developing new standards in the need to overcome the barriers in crossing the line from small business to large organizations, both in management and informational systems. Databases are essential tools for obtaining information, vital in the decision making process. In monolith organizations, managing and retrieving information through queries does not represent a challenge anymore; however larger structures deal with difficulties due to data distribution, autonomy and heterogeneity. The latter need adequate data processing and decision making systems, capable of offering essential information rapidly and cost efficient. By integration in the new structure of preexistent systems, the communication between and within the organization must ensure the premises of economic growth and profit increase. Web services represent the next stage of evolution for e-business – the visualization of systems from the perspective that "everything is a service", manipulation and dynamic discovery by using messaging through a network. To ensure efficient and rapid communication, the present tendency is to provide mobile solutions, available with the latest technology, capable of ensuring similar functionalities as the classic applications. Their main advantages are mobility, remote access, and the growth of the market segment of each organization. The goal of the paper is achievement of interoperability in heterogeneous systems, by taking the necessary steps to get the integration. The basic idea was developing a useful and economically efficient application that comes in support of small companies by offering the possibility of participating in a larger organizational structure and of maximizing their profits by doing so.

The main objectives that were set are: facilitating data integration and communication in a hotel virtual organization, extracting data in the organization, information retrieval at lower costs – premises for economic growth and profit increase – as well as remote access by using mobile devices. Ensuring interactivity with the user through a user friendly interface and facilitating the decision making process by offering several possible solutions were amongst our main goals. The system was built upon the principle of separating the interface from the implementation; the user does not need to know details about the used technologies, location of the data sources or the means of transmitting information, his only task being that of searching for keywords and taking the best decision, according to his needs.

Keywords: web services, mobile applications, federated databases, virtual organization, integration, hotel

1. The Virtual Organization

Organizations are currently put in the position of dealing with a dynamic and turbulent environment that imposes the need for flexibility and fast response in order to adapt to the ever changing conditions. As IT&C overcome the barriers imposed by time and territorial distribution, the development of virtual organizations becomes possible. In general, "virtual" refers an entity without physical existence. A typical definition of what the term of virtual corporation could refer is: "A temporary network of companies that comes together quickly to exploit fast-changing opportunities." [1]

A second one refers an organization without a physical location: "A geographically distributed organization whose members are bound by a long-term common interest or goal, and who communicate and coordinate their work through IT." [2] A virtual organization represents "A network of independent geographically dispersed organizations with different missions overlapped. Within the network, all partners provide their own core competencies and the cooperation is based on semi-stable relations." [3]. The members assume well defined roles and status in the context of the virtual group that ca can be independent from their role and status in the company that is their official employer.

Motivations for choosing the virtual organization are ●Globalization, the tendency to grow in order to include clients at a global level ●The possibility to access rapidly expert resources ●Creating excellence communities ●Continuously changing needs ●Specialized products and services ●The ever growing need of specialized knowledge.

The conceptual model of implementation of a virtual organization:

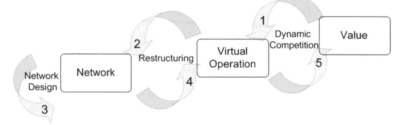

Figure 1. Conceptual model of the Virtual Organization

Value is the engine that ensures the restructuring of the virtual organization and it is represented by the business opportunity within the network as well as future or yet unexplored markets.   Virtual operations are cooperative processes that combine competences and resources in order to achieve value. Success in realizing and implementing a virtual organization is dependent on the network (the preexisting industrial structures that form the network). The development and implementation of virtual operations lead to the evolution of the network and represents the main motivation for its reform.

Among the advantages of this type of virtual organization we consider the following:

- The possibility of permanently renewing the list of participants to the organization
- The agreements are flexible and focused on satisfying precise purpose
- The emphasis on creating new products and services

- The processes involved in the organization can be rapidly changed by achieving an agreement among partners.

The virtual organization presumes a different manner of perceiving the world for the participants. There are four key features of the virtual organization taken as a process: support for developing connections with a wide variety of potential partners, each having particular competences that are complementary; mobility and prompt response in order to face problems related to distance; synchronization – key aspect for relations among members in the case of decision making; the efficiency of the organization is determined by the degree of trust present among the participants.

2. Federated Databases

The principle of federalization has proven to be a successful pattern both for living organisms as well as successful communities.[4] Having as a starting point this analogy with the real world, we have focused on simulating such a structure in the virtual world (digital). As a large variety of systems with different characteristics has invaded the market, the need to develop technology that allows communication and efficient collaboration was imminent. Federated databases provide support for harmonizing the differences in order to achieve an integrated working environment.

"A federated database represents a collection of cooperating component systems which are autonomous and are possibly heterogeneous. The three important components of an FDBS are: autonomy, heterogeneity and distribution. Another dimension which has also been considered is the Networking Environment Computer Network, e.g. many DBSs over a LAN or many DBSs over a WAN update related functions of participating DBSs (e.g. no updates, nonatomic transitions, Atomic updates)."[5][8] The architecture of the federation allows that distinct databases to appear to the end user as a single entity. Federations also allow a unified vision on data from multiple sources. The sources of the federated database can include relational, XML-based or object based databases, text documents, Excel spreadsheets as well as any other form of data structured or non-structured.

The federated database represents a logical unification of distinct databases that run on independent servers, do not share resources and are interconnected. This type of databases hides any differences of interface, data models, optimization details and execution details.[6][7] The user has the option of simultaneously accessing heterogeneous and autonomous databases using an integrated schema and a single querying language (SQL) and is not required to know where the data is stored and how the result is processed.

The difficulty in associating data in the case of these virtual organizations resides in the diversity of data types, data representation, data definition language (DDL), data manipulation language (DML), transaction management and security.

In the attempt of offering coherent access to a wide variety of data and sources of information a series of problems arise that need to be addressed: ●**Query performance** ●**Dependence on autonomous data sources** ●**Scalability** ●**Cost reduction** ●**Data opportunity** ●**Data replication** ●**Evolution of the federated schema.**

By accessing heterogeneous data sources in a federation, the premises of inter-operation and exchange of data between platforms are created as well as improving global data management. Considering these advantages, as well as those linked to cost, the conclusion was reached that the federative systems are preferable to those distributed as they best respond to current requirements that are in a continuous and rapid change.

3. Web Services

A Web service is a software system that can handle interactions between hardware systems through a network, having an interface described in a format that can be processed by the host machine (WSDL). Other systems interact with the Web service using SOAP messages, based on XML, and transmitted using different Internet protocols: HTTP, SMTP, or FTP. The foundation of Web services is represented by the XML technology.

"XML (Extensible Markup Language) represents a set of rules used to create text formats that allow data structuring."[8] XML is extensible because it allows users to define their own elements; it is platform independent and sustains localization and internationalization. Its main goal is to facilitate sharing of structured data between different informational systems, mainly over the Internet and is used both to encrypt document as well as serialize data. XML offers solutions for heterogeneity problems, the main barrier in data integration. [9] XML is the fundament of what Web services stands for, the different levels that define such a service. Among these levels we need to mention due to their relevance: SOAP, WSDL and UDDI (Universal Discovery Description and Integration).

"SOAP represents a protocol used to exchange XML-based messages throughout a computer network". [10] If SOAP specifies the means of communication between a service requester and the service provider, WSDL is used in order to describe the offered service.

"WSDL is an XML-based language that permits the description of Web services."[11] This description is made using XML and practically offers the necessary documentation so that applications can automatically communicate amongst themselves.

"UDDI is a register that allows a Web services provider to publish and describe the services it offers to potential users so the latter may know the availability of these services."[12]

In order to ensure the functioning of a Web service a series of requirements must be met:

A Web service must be created and the interfaces and methods must be defined

A Web service must be published in a location on the Internet or Intranet in order to be easily located by the potential users

A Web service must be located in order to be queried by potential users

A Web service must be invoked in order to resolve the requests of the users

A Web service can be erased when the moment comes when it is no longer necessary.

The architecture of the Web service is dependent on three fundamental operations: publishing of the service, finding and binding the service, according to Figure 2. **Service Requester** is the client of the Web service, as for **Service Provider** that is the host of the service. A client may address a SOAP request to the service provider, the latter responding accordingly. **Service Registry** may be considered the database of Web services, containing URI (Uniform Resources Identifier) definitions for each service. The Web service is published in a Service Registry that can be later on queried in order to obtain information about the published services using the UDDI (Universal Description, Discovery and Integration) mechanism. A client can query the Service Registry using UDDI so it can obtain the information in the WSDL. The client can then establish connections with the Web service and send SOAP requests, receiving messages in the same format as a response. SOAP, being platform and language independent, based on XML, is used to ensure communication between applications over the Internet.

WSDL is an XML document used to describe the Web service and locate it.

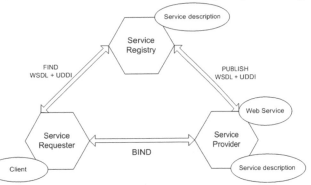

Figure 2. The architecture of the Web services

Elements included in the WDSL are ●Type (data type definition) ●Messages (abstract, definition of interchanged data – request/response) ●Operations (abstract description of an action) ●Type of port (collection of operations, abstract definition of a service) ●Bindings (the actual protocol) ●The port (defines a single end point of the communication for the binding) ●The service (set of interconnected ports).

The Web services architecture brings about several benefits:

It promotes interoperability, minimizing the requirements for collaboration between service requester and service provider, the only requirements being: an interface definition language based on XML (NASSL(*Network Accessible Service Specification Language*) document – that provides operational information, the interface of the service, implementation details and access protocols), a WDS(*Well-Defined Service*) document – it provides the description of the service, description based on XML, and a collaboration protocol. In this manner the services can be truly platform and language independent.

It ensures Just-In-Time integration. The collaboration in Web services is dynamically bound at Runtime. The user describes the characteristics of the requested service and using Service Registry locates the adequate Web service. Once found, the information in the NASSL document of the service is used to realize the connection.

It reduces the complexity by encapsulation: all the components of the Web services are also services. The behavior ensured by the service is most important and not the manner in which it is implemented. The WDS document is the mechanism by which the behavior encapsulated by a service is described.

Web services technology represents the next stage of evolution for e-business – visualizing the systems from the perspective that "everything is a service", manipulation and dynamic discovery by using messages through the network. Each component is assimilated to a service that encapsulates behavior and ensures this behavior through an API available for request through a network.

The fundamental roles in Web services are attributed to service providers, service requesters and service brokers. These roles include operations of publishing, finding and binding. The intermediation of the operations introduces several aspects like: security, flow of activities, transactions, quality of service, etc.

The mechanisms of the service description language are fundamental in operating with Web services. A full description of the latter can be found in two separate documents: a NASSL document and a WDS document.

4. Presenting the application

The application is set to simulate the behavior of a hotel virtual organization. The goal of the organization is offering a supplementary method of promoting the services provided by the partners, designed for the users of mobile technologies. The functionality provided by the application allows these potential clients to directly access information from the data sources supplied by the participants. The main beneficiaries of this application are those members of the virtual organization that do not possess classical means of promoting their services and those that are pursuing newly developed market segments characterized by mobility and dynamism and supported by the new technologies.

Essential elements in initiating the development process of the application are the different data sources, as in real life situations. We have started from the hypothesis that the participants in such a hotel virtual organization do not own the same technologies and the change is not justifiable. The data sources were built in different environments. We have chosen for one of the data sources to be in BCNF (Boyce-Codd Normal Form) to serve as an example as to what a database should be like while the other data sources did not represent a topic from this point of view, the emphasis being set on integrating data whatever the degree of normalization, otherwise we should have developed a complete design. BCNF was considered to be most adequate so that this data source will act as a model of canonic schema for integrating other data sources. We have accomplished the integration of the data sources by developing a hierarchy of Web services (a central node dedicated to reunite data and several specific Web services each involving a single source).

As for the user interface we have chosen to pursue a mobile device approach, justifying this choice with the fact that it implies new and innovative technologies as well as the degree of mobility it confers to dynamic users, but the application is also available for those users familiarized with desktop applications.

The architecture of the federated database. The members supply the federation with the necessary information needed for the customization of each of the participants involved in the federation as well as sufficient to create a panoramic view for the potential clients (information about identification data, contact data, services provided, lodging facilities, images, prices, etc.).

Creating the federation is justifiable because of the heterogeneity of the data sources provided by the participants. In the simulated virtual organization we assume the existence of three participants, each having the data source developed in a different DBMS. The general architecture of the federation is made of three databases developed in Microsoft SQL Server 2005, Oracle Database 10G Express Edition and MySQL Server 5.0. In order to ensure integration each database was associated with a dedicated Web service, adapted to the particular structure of the data source and intended to allow retrieval of interest data and presenting it in a format common to the federation.

The current application is based on the **three tier application model**: the **presentation layer** that ensures the interface with the user, second layer is the **logic** of the application that coordinates the processing of received requests from the clients and the return of the results and the **data layer** that ensures the storage and locating the date supplied by the members of the federation.

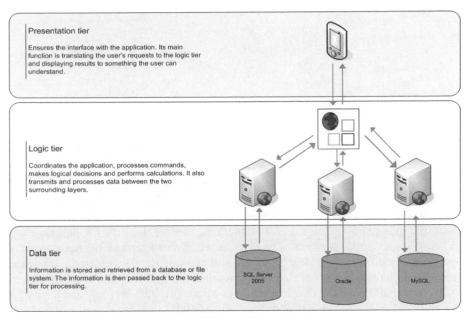

Figure 3. The architecture of the application

The schema represents a panoramic view of the application's architecture: ● The mobile device that provides the interface with the user ●The hierarchy of Web services ●Database management systems that provide support for storing and locating data.

We considered that this architecture accomplishes the requirements of this system, it makes possible the rapid retrieval of data and the results are displayed in a format that can be easily understood by the user.

The central Web service. It is responsible for centralizing data returns by the dedicated Web services as result to the queries transmitted by the user through the interface of the mobile application. It implements an interface that contains class and method definitions that will ensure the communication and return data from all the actual data sources. The declared attributes of the classes follow the filters (parameters requested by the user) and the structure of the data relevant for the client. The data is stored in a list of objects, instances of the classes specially defined for this purpose.

The user interface. The set goal is visualizing the data supplied by the system using a mobile device.

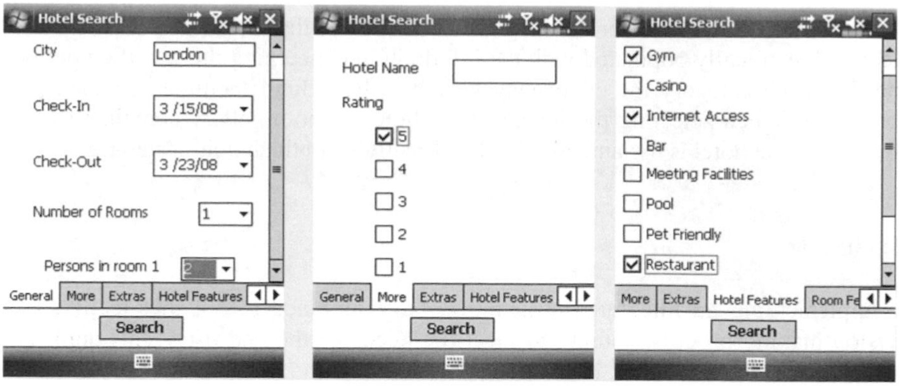

Figure 4. Main Search criteria page

Technologies used for the implementation. In the development process of the application we used specific tools and technologies for ensuring the proposed functionality. Web Services technology is widely used and it can be implemented in multiple programming languages. For the logic tier we used the C# language and the Visual Studio 2005 platform. The data sources characterized by heterogeneity are managed by different DBMSs based on international standards: Oracle Database 10g Express Edition and the development environment Oracle SQLDeveloper; Microsoft SQL Server 2005 and the development tool Microsoft SQL Server Management Studio Express; MySQL Server 5.0 and Toad for MySQL with its specific dialects of the query language: PL/SQL, Transact SQL and MySQL Dialect.

How to use the application. At the first contact with the application the user seems to be in the position to select multiple search criteria: •The availability in between two selected dates •The number of needed rooms with the facility of selecting the number of occupants in each room (there is an extra option to be taken into consideration at every return of results for rooms of any category and the option is "extra bed") •Choice of hotel category(rating) •Choice of desired services to be provided by the hotel •Extra options available for the rooms (chargeable) •Room features. All these filtering criteria are optional. If the client does not select any criterion, the list of returned results will include all of the hotels in the federation. When running the application a list of hotels that meet the selected criteria will de provided. For each result (hotel) there are details available for viewing, details concerning: contact, a link to the official Web site of the hotel if any, details about room categories and facilities

Figure 5. Results - View 1

According to the number of categories or facilities that meet the criteria, a list of prices is dynamically populated with the information concerning the specified period of time. For each category the client may visualize the default facilities included in the room price. When selecting the image of the hotel a photo gallery containing images provided by the hotel is dynamically loaded directly from the hotels' database.

Conclusions

By implementing an integrated system, we have obtained a tool that facilitates the decision making process, coming to meet the needs of the end user. This application proves itself very useful in the context of globalization, facilitating the organization into clusters of hotel associations (economic aggregates).

Many of the small companies become aware of the advantages of participating in a virtual corporation that they may benefit from resources equivalent to those of a large organization at the same time maintaining their agility and independence.

The Web services technology, used in order to obtain this virtual organization represents the next stage of evolution for e-business - visualizing the systems from the perspective that "everything is a service", manipulation and dynamic discovery by using messaging through the network. The modular development of the system does not affect its functioning. We have already made several steps towards the automation of the process of including new data sources into the federation.

Once the integration of the system's participants to the federation was achieved by implementing the presented technologies, as a future development we plan to extend the federation by integrating new data sources. Another important aspect will be to secure the access and the connection to the database as well as data transmission in the virtual organization. In order to provide further assistance to the end user we plan to extend the list of functionalities of the application by integrating the Live Maps module in order provide access to a digital map of the location of the hotels in different cities and also a classification of the results returned in descending order according to customer benefits (price-category and features selected).

Acknowledgment

This work was supported by Romanian National Authority for Scientific Research under the grants no. 91-049/2007 (NP2) and IDEI 573/2007

References

[1] J. Lee, Mike (Tae-In) Eo, Bonn-Oh Kim, Pairin Katerattanakul, Virtual Organization: Resource-Based View, International Journal of E-Business Research, Volume 3, Issue 1
[2] M. Ripeanu, M.P. Singh, S. S. Vazhkuda, Virtual Organizations, IEEE Internet Computing, March/April, 2008
[3] G. Starmack, From Virtual to Reality, Adweek; Jul 9-Jul 16, 2007; 48, 27; ABI/INFORM Global, pg. 14
[4] D. A. Sitar-Taut, Distributed Databases, Risoprint, Cluj-Napoca, 2005, pp. 220-233
[5] Sheth and Larson, 1990. Federated Database Systems for Managing Distributed, Heterogeneous, and Autonomous Databases. ACM Computing Surveys Vol 22, No.3: 183-236
[6] M. T. Ozsu, P. Valduriez, Principles of Distributed Database Systems, Prentice – Hall, 1991

[7]   Date, C.J., An introduction to database systems, Edison – Wesley, 1995
[8]   Wikipedia Encyclopedia http://en.wikipedia.org
[9]   Web Services. http://www.w3.org/2002/ws
[10] SOAP, XML Protocol. http://www.w3.org/2000/xp/Group/
[11] Web Services Description Languages, WSDL. http://www.w3.org/TR/wsdl
[12] UDDI Technical Committee Specification. http://uddi.org/pubs/uddi_v3.htm, 2003

Ambient Intelligence Perspectives
P. Mikulecký et al. (Eds.)
IOS Press, 2009
doi:10.3233/978-1-58603-946-2-221

A wearable system for Tele-monitoring and Tele-assistance of patients with integration of solutions from chronobiology for prediction of illness

Antonio J. Jara VALERA [a], Miguel A. Zamora IZQUIERDO [a],
Antonio F. Gómez SKARMETA [a]

[a] *Department of Information and Communications Engineering*
Computer Science Faculty, University of Murcia, Spain
jara@dif.um.es

Abstract. The aged population and life expectancy has been increasing worldwide in the last years and this continues to increase. This poses a series of challenges to satisfy the care of elder people, to assure their quality of life and treatment of illness. Unfortunately, the current infrastructure is not sufficient to meet the emerging demand, so many of these people continue living in their homes. In this context, we propose a tele-assistance solution to satisfy that demand.

In order to take into account this new needs, we propose to extend the basic functions from a tele-assistance system (i.e. the patient is able to launch an alarm explicitly pushing a button if he needs attention from specialized staff) the use of algorithms from chronobiology to predict changes in vital signs or biological rhythm. Additionally we propose to prevent and predict illness via complex functions from advanced tele-assistance (such as detection of abnormal situations and falls from inference of the data from a set of sensors that the patient has over his body).

Keywords. health, chronobiology, ambient intelligence, homecare systems, tele-monitoring, tele-assistance, ZigBee, Bluetooth, illness prediction, WBAN.

Introduction

The world is ageing. With people living longer and fewer children being born, the absolute number of older people is increasing. Today there are around 600 million persons aged 60 and over worldwide. The number will double by 2025 and will reach almost two billion by 2050 when there will be more people aged 60 and over than children under the age of 15 [2].

Because of ageing, the demand of healthcare services will increase in Europe and also the possibilities to react to the demand of healthcare services has decreased because of increased costs and lack of personnel.

It is well known, that the information and communication technology could provide an answer to problems arisen in the field of healthcare. All these possibilities have traditionally been attached to support health care's re-organisation. With the help of ICT, it is possible to connect to up-to date patient information which is neither depending on time nor place. By this reason, we are going to define a system so that this people can live alone in home with a correct assistance condition.

About this kind of solutions based on ambient intelligence for homecare, tele-assistance etcetera…, let's make a difference between solutions that are based in a extern monitoring to the user with environment sensors and cameras at the home and a montoring directly in the user with a wearable sensors network as we can find in [8].

We are going to work over the second kind of systems because the main objective of our solution is to obtain vital constants as beat rate, peripheral temperature, central temperature…, to define a solution of medical monitoring like [14] but furthermore extends services for diagnosis of anomalies and prediction of illness with chronobiology.

We are going to analyze the system architecture in section 1, we will continue in section 2 with an analysis of chronobiology where we will show two solutions from it which include our system, and finally, in section 3, we will expose our next goals and conclusions.

1. System architecture

We have three elements: a belt and a bracelet over the patient and a unit of processing and store of data from sensors, we can see this architecture in the following picture.

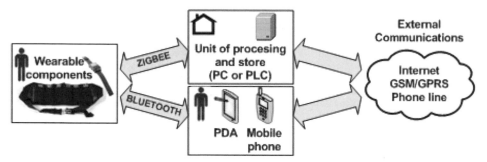

Figure 1. System architecture and communications.

The components in the belt are the next:

a) Electrodes to capture heart beat and make EKG (electrocardiogram), we are going to use two, one on each side of the thorax, this component already has been used in other projects as show [5].

b) EKG is a very important source of information; we can detect a lot of anomalies, in this paper we are going to analyse the prediction of myocardial infarction. Furthermore we are going to store the EKG signals in the PC or PLC (Programmable Logic Controllers) so that in case the patient suffers a cardiovascular sickness, those data may be able to be accessed by a web service, providing a continue monitoring of those patients for a better diagnosis.

c) Transceiver 802.15.4 (ZigBee) with MCU for processing and send of information from the sensors to a unit of processing as PLC or PC central. This component also can be a transceiver Bluetooth if the unit of processing is a PDA or mobile device, this kind of communications for wearable systems has been already used in [1][8].

d) The most important part of this element is to get connectivity with PLC, PC, mobile or PDA. We are going to use in the prototype ZigBee by his coverage and low consume and because we are going to use a PLC as a processing unit and storage system, but we can use Bluetooth for any other type of installations or even other technologies like Wibree, Wifi or proprietary.

e) A button so that the patient can throw an alarm if he feels bad or in need of help, this component also can appear in a necklace, in the bracelet and strategic points of the home (e.g. together the bed).

f) Strain gages for detection of corporal position, for example if he is sleeping or sitting the strain gages detect a weight and if he is standing up the weight is zero.

g) With this element, we can detect long periods sitting or in the bed, that is one of the most usual consequences when old person starts feeling ill.

h) Temperature sensor for central temperature, these elements are going to be used for detection of fever and in applications of chronobiology that we will study afterwards.

i) Chip that together with the electrodes obtains the beats per minute (bpm) and EKG. To detect tachycardia and in applications of chronobiology [5].

j) Vibration sensor and accelerometer for detection of falls and long periods of inactivity together strain gages.

BELT COMPONENTS

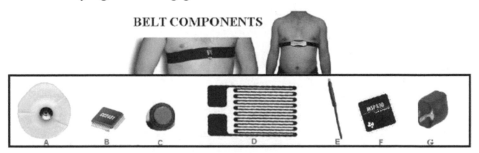

Figure 2. Belt components.

The component in the bracelet is a chip to measure the peripheral temperature (thermography) for chronobiology applications and a button to throw alarms.

2. Chronobiology

Chronobiology is a field science that studies the temporal structure (periodic (cyclic) phenomena) of living beings, the mechanism which control them and their alterations. These cycles are known as biological rhythms. The variations of the timing and duration of biological activity in living organisms occur for many essential biological processes. These occur in animals (eating, sleeping, mating, etc), and also in plants.

The most important rhythm in chronobiology is the circadian rhythm, a period of time between 20 and 28 hours [4].

We are going to focus the use of chronobiology in the topics that are working with the estimation of blooding pressure and prediction of myocardial infarction.

On the next two points we are going to show the information we have obtained from the inference of the data from the system described on section 1. The first inference has been obtained from [6] and the second one is the result of our own investigations.

2.1 How we detect myocardial infarction eight days before.

This detection based on the beat rate of a patient that is very variable from a moment to other, is chaotic in a normal patient. This is very usual because a person can make an effort, move, go up stairs and even without conscious activity as digestion or heat the body the heart is working.

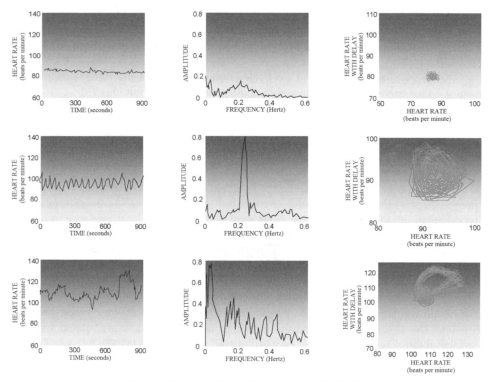

Figure 3. Heart rate days before a myocardial infarction.

In figure 3 we can see the variability of the heart beat rate in a normal situation and days before to a myocardial infarction.

On the left column we can see some graphs which show the cardiac frequency (i.e. the variation of the cardiac rhythm over time). On the second column we see the spectral analysis (i.e. the variation of pulses' amplitude over time) and on the third one wee see the trajectories in a space of phases (the cardiac rhythm at a given moment over the cardiac rhythm at a time immediately preceding). These phase diagrams show the presence of an attractor (An attractor is the pattern we see if we observe the behaviour of a system for a while and found something like a magnet that "attracts" the system towards such behaviour [12]).

The individual represented in the top row shows an almost constant heartbeat, suffered a heart attack three hours later. We can observe that the variability is less of 10 beats.

The central register of the row, showing a rhythm with periodic variations, was obtained eight days before sudden death.. We can observe that 8 days before the variability it is between 10 and 20 beats

The bottom row corresponds with a heartbeat of a healthy individual. We can observe that in a normal situation the variability is between 30 and 40 beats

So we can analyze this variability in heart beat rates in circadian periods to detect the risk of myocardial infarction [6].

2.2 We blood pressure from peripheral temperature

It is interesting for this type of systems to be able to infer blood pressure without using a sphygmomanometer which would be invasive for the patient as it has to press the arm or wrist.

We propose to infer it form peripheral temperature, because it is related with central temperature, blood pressure and muscular strength

This relationship between peripheral resistances and blood pressure can be established by Ohm's law:

Pressure = Flow x Resistances

Just as the peripheral resistance, as it increase, flow on the periphery decreases, thus reducing their temperature (peripheral temperature). So we suggest the hypothetical relationship between peripheral temperature, blood pressure and oral temperature , and check the pattern of these relationships.

This hypothesis was tested in December 2005 on a group of 30 persons from the University of Murcia by Ángel Aledo Serrano, one of our advisors, obtaining the findings detailed below:

On the next picture we have the graphic with the data from the study, where we can obtain a relationship between peripheral temperature and average blood pressure R =-0.65. So it can be concluded that although the pressure data are related with the peripheral temperature, will not get a high level of precision.

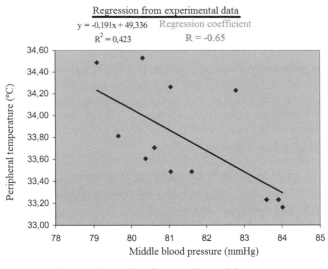

Figure 4. Regression from experimental data

On the next graph we see how to obtain the average blood pressure from peripheral temperature with this equation:

MBP = (-PT + 49.336) / 0.191

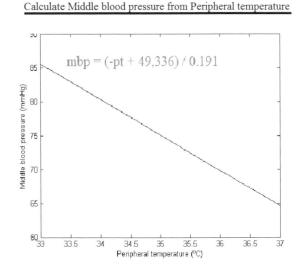

Figure 5. Relation between middle blood pressure (MBP) and peripheral temperature (PT)

Finally, once obtained an estimated average blood pressure [14], we can obtain systolic and diastolic pressures from the next relationships, and when we know them, we can check if they are normal [13].

Relations:

Systolic = 0.55 * MBP   —— Diastolic = 0.85 * MBP

Normal blood pressure (below these values, it is hypotension, an above, hypertension):

Systolic: 110–140 mmHg   Diastolic: 70–90 mmHg

3. Future work and conclusions

The main objective of our work has been to apply the studies and results we obtain from chronobiology to a domestic environment, thus, extending the systems' services that exist in tele-assistence. So with the system defined we will have services that were already in the referenced solutions, such as detecting anomalies, falls, launch alarms, remote medical monitoring and now we also predict diseases and obtain estimates of biological rhythms from other of non-invasive or annoying ways to the user.

We consider the interest of this solution to assist population having more risk to catch illness and it's more difficult for them to recover as age rises. Hence, if we can predict and prevent illness before it happens or in its early stage, then we are going to increase our chances of success and give better quality of life to them.

About chronobiology conclude that all algorithms from it must always be seen as a source of interesting information but not deterministic, e.g. it may help us predict some kind of pathology happening when a series of patterns have been found to trigger it, as we have seen in the myocardial infarction, but there is no absolute security that this pattern always triggers a heart attack, thus these forecasts should be evaluated with caution, as we know to determine some biological rhythms from other, there is always a degree of correlation so it also leads us to a certain margin of error. You can find more information on chronobiology in [6].

Currently, we are developing the prototype, and trying to reduce the weight and consume of the belt. At the same time we are analyzing more chronobiology solutions for the most typical illness in the aged population.

We are working also in the possibility of integrating ipv6 (6LowPAN) in these elements to improve the connectivity and avoid the use of a local unit of processing and store, so that this is only need in the monitoring center [7].

Acknowledgements

This work has been partially supported by the students of medicine Ángel Aledo Serrano and José Javier Campuzano Jara as biomedicine advisories in the chronobiology field. This work has been carried out in frames of the Spanish Programa de Ayuda a los Grupos de Excelencia de la Fundación Séneca 04552/GERM/06.

References

[1]   Smart Homecare System for Health Tele-monitoring First International Conference on the Digital Society (ICDS'07) By Peter Leijdekkers , Valerie Gay , Elaine Lawrence - Date:January 2007

[2]   Actitudes hacia el envejecimiento de la población en Europa By Alan Walker, Teacher of socialpolitcs, University de Sheffiel, United Kingdom
www.imsersomayores.csic.es/documentos/documentos/walker-actitudes-01.pdf, accessed 23 May 2008.

[3]   Sensor Network Design and Implementation for Health Telecare and Diagnosis Assistance Applications 11th International Conference on Parallel and Distributed Systems - Workshops (ICPADS'05)   pp. 407-411 By Ming-Hui Jin, Ren-Guey Lee, Cheng-Yan Kao, You-Rui Wu, Wu4,D. Frank Hsu, Tse-Ping Dong, Kuan-Tsae Huang

[4]   Definition of Chronobiology http://en.wikipedia.org/wiki/Chronobiology, accessed 23 May 2008.

[5]   Development of Telemedicine and Telecare over Wireless Sensor Network 2008 International Conference on Multimedia and Ubiquitous Engineering (mue 2008) pp. 597-604 By Shuo-Jen Hsu, Hsin-Hsien Wu, Shih-Wei Chen, Tsang-Chi Liu, Wen-Tzeng Huang,   Yuan-Jen Chang, Chin-Hsing Chen, You-Yin Chen

[6]   Cronobiología básica y clínica By Juan Antonio Madrid and Mª Ángeles Rol de Lama – Editorial: EDITEC RED

[7]   Ipv6 over low power WPAN (6LowPAN), www.ietf.org/proceedings/04nov/6lowpan.html, accessed 20 June 2008.

[8]   An Assisted Living Oriented Information System Based on Residential Wireless Sensor Network Processing of the 1st Distributed Diagnosis and Home Healthcare Conference – Arlington, Virginia, USA, April 2.4 2006 By G. Virone, A. Wood, L. Selavo, Q. Cao, L.Fang, T. Doan, Z. He, R. Stoleru, S. Lin and J.A. Stankovic – Departament of Computer Science, University of Virginia

[9]   Combining wireless with weareable technology for the development of on-body networks. By Sarah Brady, Brian Carson, Donal O'Gorman, Niall Moyna and Dermot Diamond. – Adaptive Sensors Group and School for Human Health and Performance from Dublin City University.

[10]   Wearable Multisensor Heart Rate Monitor By Liliana Grajales, Motorola, Schaumburg, Illinois.

[11]   Living Assistance Systems – An Ambient Intelligent Approach – By Jürgen Nehmer, Arthur Karshmer, Martin Becker and Rosemarie Lamm.

[12]   The attractor definitions, http://www.atractor.es/, accessed 6 July 2008.

[13]   The blood pressure descriptions, http://en.wikipedia.org/wiki/Blood_pressure, accessed 10 July 2008.

[14]   The   blood   pressure   studies,   http://www.depeca.uah.es/docencia/BIOING/ib/Trabajos/02-03/PresionSanguinea.htm, accessed 10 July 2008.

[15]   Remote Medical Monitoring By Andrew D. Jurik and Alfred C. Weaver from University of Virginia

Ambient Intelligence Perspectives
P. Mikulecký et al. (Eds.)
IOS Press, 2009
© 2009 The authors and IOS Press. All rights reserved.
doi:10.3233/978-1-58603-946-2-229

Credit Risk Decreasing By Usage Of Electronic Platforms

Martin VEJAČKA, Kristína VINCOVÁ
Technical University Košice, Faculty of Economics, Slovakia
martin.vejacka@tuke.sk

Abstract. Banks (financial services providers in general) are taking risk with process of lending funds to small and medium sized enterprises. It is necessary for them to decrease risk resulting from issuing loans in any possible way. This article deals with options of decreasing risk by gaining and analyzing information from electronic platforms and environment. Electronic systems supporting enterprises and banks and integrating supply and demand of products and money on its platform can contain valuable information which can be used by banks to classify client's ability to repay a loan. It is even more necessary to have real time information when loans are short-termed and financial service provider needs to rate clients quickly and more flexibly.

Keywords. Bank, Financial Services Provider, Credit Risk, Electronic Platform, FLUID-WIN

Introduction

Banks (financial services providers in general) are taking risk with process of lending funds to small and medium sized enterprises (SMEs). Key problem areas that can lead to losses from loans are:

- Poor or insufficient loan documentation,
- No formal loan policy,
- No formal loan pricing procedure,
- Concentration of loan in one area of business,
- Violations of maximum loan amount to single borrower,
- Poor loan review,
- Focus on loan fees rather than creditworthiness.

For financial services providers it is necessary to minimize credit resulting from issuing loans in any possible way. Therefore the banks use the credit risk management system [2]. Credit analysis is one part of this system. The main aim of credit analysis is to consider the client's ability to pay back the credit in future and to perform agreed engagement with bank. In literature [1] we can find one of many approaches, so called "The 5 Cs of Credit". The approach includes the key areas, which are important in decision about granting of credit. The name of this approach consists of five English words:

- *Character* is determined by reviewing the business' and owner's credit reports or contacting their creditors and vendors. The credit report contains a financial picture of how past and current credit obligations are being met. The aim is to consider the will of client to pay back his obligation and his credibility as an adverse party in credit relation.
- *Capacity* determines the business' ability to pay back the credit from current or projected cash flow.
- *Collateral* refers to assets used to secure credit, such as real estate, receivables, inventory or equipment, whereby the forms of collateral depend on the type or structure of a loan.
- *Capital* is the equity or assets an owner possesses. A determination is made of how much, if any, leverage is currently on the equity and leads to a debt-to-worth ratio calculation.
- *Conditions* refer to any unique market forces that may be affecting the business. The objects of examination are especially economic conditions and their changes (for example changing rates of interest, the impact of business cycle, market fluctuations and so on).

Credit analysis

We can see that for this credit analysis there is necessary to have much information about prospective clients, for example about SMEs. This information has to be submitted by SMEs every time when they want to drawdown the bank loan. The process of gathering this information on one hand and the process of evaluation of this information by banks on other hand is very time-consuming .

Many of the big business have credit rating assigned by rating agencies such as Standard & Poor's or Moody's, which identifies the credit quality of a firm, but the most small and medium sized enterprises are not rated. The financial services providers also have internal rating systems to identify credit risk of all client enterprises even the SMEs. These internal systems depend on quality information contained in them. This information has vital role in the processes of providing financial services. Making right decisions always requires reliable and up-to-date information. Real time information is the key for financial services providers. This imposes demanding requirements on information systems used by financial services providers [6]. The internal information systems must support FSP during following credit process:

1. gathering basic necessary information,
2. credit approval/ sanction – guidelines for parties and individuals involved in a decision,
3. credit documentation,
4. credit administration,
5. disbursement,
6. monitoring and control of individual credits – early identification of possible problem facilities,
7. monitoring the overall credit portfolio,
8. classification of credit,
9. managing problem credits.

Electronic platforms

Information useful during credit process can be gathered by bank also from external information systems. Among the most sophisticated information systems are counted electronic platforms where manufacturing enterprises, financial services providers and logistics services providers can share valuable information with each other. By the medium of these platforms are also agreed deals, contracts and orders between the subjects with access to these platforms.

The e-platforms can help to improve also key financial functions of banks such as:

- Design appropriate credit processes, operating policies and procedures,
- Monitoring and review of credit origination,
- Portfolio monitoring,
- Monitoring of credit policies,
- Attention to structure of financing deals.

The example of such platform, which integrates SME sector, financial services providers and logistic services providers in one place, is FLUID-WIN.

"The European IST project FLUID-WIN is oriented to business-to-business (B2B) manufacturing networks and their interactions with the logistics and financial service providers. The main aim of the project is to develop a platform, which can seamlessly integrate and transfer data among all the various partners in order to enhance the competitiveness of the whole business sector in Europe and to make the business processes as efficient as possible. The platform will enable the European manufacturing companies to keep their ability of quick response, achieving competitive prices by integrating the suppliers from other parts of the world. This platform will be supported through easy-to-adopt e-commerce applications and will integrate the commonly used logistics and financial services without installing thousands of peer-to-peer relationships (see: www.fluid-win.de)" [2].

As stated before, insufficient loan documentation and loan review are key problem areas in loan process. The FLUID-WIN platform contains pre-loan and loan documentation and also decreases necessity of paper-form documents by using following documents in electronic forms:

1. Purchase Order Requests,
2. Quotations for Products / Services,
3. Sales Order Confirmations,
4. Pro-forma Invoices,
5. Delivery Notes,
6. Goods Received Notes,
7. Invoices,
8. Receipts,
9. Statements.

From the variety of documents, that can be interchanged in electronic form, results great amount of information contained in the platform. Banks (financial services providers) can access this information as they are engaged on the platform. It helps them to gain data on client enterprises such as:

- Amount of orders,
- Financial volume of orders,
- Status of orders,
- Satisfied orders.

Those are operational information that justify about client's ability to repay provided loan and can help them to gain credit from banks. On the other hand it can decrease possibility of a fraud, as long as platform contains information from both parties concerned in a contract [3].

It is intended that FLUID-WIN platform should support following forms of lending funds to small and medium enterprises:

Documentary Credit

This is the most common form of the commercial letter of credit. The issuing bank will make a payment, either immediately or at a prescribed date, upon the presentation of stipulated documents. These documents will include shipping and insurance documents, and commercial invoices. The documentary credit arrangement offers an internationally used method of attaining a commercially acceptable undertaking by providing for payment to be made against presentation of documentation representing the goods, making possible the transfer of title to those goods. A letter of credit is a precise document whereby the importer's bank extends credit to the importer and assumes responsibility in paying the exporter. A common problem faced in emerging economies is that many banks have inadequate capital and foreign exchange, making their ability to back the documentary credits questionable. Exporters may require guarantees from their own local banks as an additional source of security, but this may generate significant additional costs as the banks may be reluctant to take the risks. Allowing internationally reputable banks to operate in the country and offer documentary credit is one way to effectively solve this problem.

Factoring

This involves the sale at a discount of accounts receivable or other debt assets on a daily, weekly or monthly basis in exchange for immediate cash. The debt assets are sold by the exporter at a discount to a factoring house, which will assume all commercial and political risks of the account receivable. In the absence of private sector players, governments can facilitate the establishment of a state-owned factor; or a joint venture set-up with several banks and trading enterprises.

Pre-Shipping Financing

This is financing for the period prior to the shipment of goods, to support pre-export activities like wages and overhead costs. It is especially needed when inputs for production must be imported. It also provides additional working capital for the exporter. Pre-shipment financing is especially important to smaller enterprises because the international sales cycle is usually longer than the domestic sales cycle. Pre-shipment financing can take the form of short-term loans, overdrafts and cash credits.

Post-Shipping Financing

Financing for the period following shipment. The ability to be competitive often depends on the trader's credit term offered to buyers. Post-shipment financing ensures adequate liquidity until the purchaser receives the products and the exporter receives payment. Post-shipment financing is usually short-term.

Buyer's Credit

A financial arrangement whereby a financial institution in the exporting country extends a loan directly or indirectly to a foreign buyer to finance the purchase of goods and services from the exporting country. This arrangement enables the buyer to make due payments to the supplier under the contract.

Supplier's Credit

A financing arrangement under which an exporter extends credit to the buyer in the importing country to finance the buyer's purchases.

The FLUID-WIN platform, as example of an electronic platform, has many other functionalities, that support activities of all subjects engaged. Financial services providers, for example, provide also export credit insurance, investment and exchange rate insurance, export credit guarantees, payment services and accountancy e-documents interchange[4].

SMEs financing status in Slovak banking sector

As stated above, using electronic platforms brings many opportunities and benefits for banks. Decreasing credit risk is one of the biggest of them. The usage of electronic platforms is not spread in Slovakia yet. To keep in touch with progress, Slovak banks should adapt this new trend and start to use electronic platforms for financing SMEs. To know which ways of SME financing can be provided in electronic form in Slovakia, we need to take an overview of traditionally provided financing (in paper form).The Slovak banks offer in their portfolio many products for financing of SMEs. Every bank has in its portfolio the financing through documentary instruments, e.g. letter of credit; provision of banking guarantees and factoring or forfeiting services. These three types of banking services belong between basic banking products offered by Slovak banks. On the other hand we can find in some Slovak banks special banking product for trade financing.

For example Slovenská sporiteľňa in cooperation with EXIMBANKA SR provides special product for trade financing "Export loans in cooperation with EXIMBANKA SR". This loan is provides for supporting the export of products and services prevailingly of Slovak origin. The credit is provided by Slovenská sporiteľňa on the basis of a Refinancing Loan Contract, which the bank has signed with Eximbanka SR, or in the case of bill trades, on the basis of a Contract on Bill Trades. The maturity of the loan is at maximum 1 year from the date of drawing the loan and the loan is provided in Slovak currency.

The second bank, VUB BANKA offers three special products for trade financing - Export buyer's credit, Pre-export financing and Invoice discounting.

Export buyer's credit means a prompt pay out of the exporter by the foreign importer to which the exporter's bank provided necessary funds in form of a trade-related bank loan. Through this loan can be financed the export of goods, services and investment units. VUB provides the loan to a bank of the importer's country or directly to the importer with a foreign bank's guarantee or the given country government's guarantee.

The purpose of Pre-export financing is to make financial resources available to producer (exporter) prior to the beginning of the production related to the concluded export contracts. Through this loan can be financed mainly the goods and services of Slovak origin. VUB bank (creditor) provides a loan to the producer/exporter (debtor) for financing the production for export on the basis of an insurance with the EXIMBANKA SR and on the assumption that a contract on goods and services delivery (export trade contract) was made between the Slovak exporter (debtor) and the foreign buyer, and the receivable thereby was insured by the EXIMBANKA SR prior to insuring the loan for production financing.

Invoice discounting is the purchase of receivable based on contract denominated in a foreign currency with a deferred maturity, concluded between the exporter and importer. The receivables are unsecured; usually the revolving receivables are repurchased. After the delivery of goods, and presentation and acceptance of the export documents by the bank, the bank pays the equivalent value reduced by the discount and management fee to the exporter's account. The advantage of this bank product is the prompt payment to the Slovak exporter immediately upon the presentation of the contract.

Citibank (Slovakia) a.s. provides for its clients the ability to finance the sale of their goods. Financing of distribution channels allows through the supplier's guarantee provide the loan to firm's customers. From these resources the customer can remit the liabilities towards supplier.

Istrobanka offers special product for trade financing - Pre-shipment financing of exporter's receivables before the delivery, with export documentary credit. The product represents a form of short-term financing of existing contracts/agreements to overcome the time period between the receipt of the export documentary credit until completion of production and actual delivery. Financing is provided with the rights of recourse against the exporter, i.e. if documents are not presented or the documentary credit is not used because the presented export documents were not accepted by the foreign bank, the Client's account will be charged with the amount provided as pre-financing. The main advantages of these products are: operative solution to liquidity problems caused for example by purchase of raw materials or manufacturing process until the delivery of the contracted goods/investment assets; payment risk eliminated by documentary credit, which serves as payment and security instrument.

As we can see, the list of services for SMEs provided by Slovak banks is similar with services that can be provided through electronic platforms. By adapting these electronic platforms Slovak banks could decrease their credit risk related to SMEs' financing and also gain all other benefits resulting from it.

References

[1] WILSON, T. 1987. Portfolio credit risk I. Risk 10 (9)
[2] FLUID-WIN Proposal. 2005, Available on: www.fluid-win.de
[3] FLUID-WIN. Deliverable D07. Company Networks Requirements and Potentials. 2006, Available on: www.fluid-win.de
[4] FLUID-WIN. Deliverable D04. Field Study Definition. 2006, Available on: www.fluid-win.de
[5] SANTOMERO, A. M. Commercial Bank Risk Management, University of Pennsylvania, 1997
[6] RAMKE CH., Credit Risk Management in Banking Institutions – Information, Processes and Procedures, Economics and Management 4/2006, p.112 – 118, ISSN 1212-3609
[7] www.slsp.sk
[8] www.vub.sk
[9] www.citibank.sk
[10] www.istrobanka.sk

Ambient Intelligence Perspectives
P. Mikulecký et al. (Eds.)
IOS Press, 2009
© *2009 The authors and IOS Press. All rights reserved.*
doi:10.3233/978-1-58603-946-2-236

Ontology access patterns for pervasive computing environments

F.J. VILLANUEVA, D. VILLA, J. BARBA, F. RINCÓN, F. MOYA, J.C. LÓPEZ
Department of Information Technologies and Systems
University of Castilla-La Mancha, Spain
felix.villanueva@uclm.es

Abstract. Lately, the use of ontologies for semantic description in pervasive systems has been researched and applied in numerous projects. The characteristic of this type of representation for data, services, interfaces, etc. allows the interaction between entities in a pervasive environment and then the development of advanced services. However, pervasive systems include a high number of mobile devices that have to access to several ontology-based information repositories with different representations, interfaces, etc. This fact limits the interaction capacity of mobile devices which have not been designed taking this interaction into account. In this paper we define an access extension for ontology-based pervasive systems that can be automatically generated. Based on the general structure of such systems and on the characteristics of the applications specifically developed to interact with them, we have derived several patterns in order to ease the information lookup and to allow a basic interaction with the system. In this way, we define a set of access patterns based in common structures and interactions. These patterns work in a similar way that design patterns do in software engineering. They are designed independently of the specific ontology implementation and representation. Finally, we present a tool that automatically generates a specific implementation of the defined patterns and we describe a prototype that uses this extension by means of Web Services.

Keywords: Patterns, Pervasive Computing, Ontology, Web Services.

1. Introduction

Since the definition of pervasive computing, the research community has been looking for methodologies and structures for the semantic description of the information that resides in pervasive computing scenarios. In fact, this has been one of the key problems in the implantation of pervasive environments. Lately, the use of ontologies seems to be a good approach to solve this problem as we can see in [1], [2], [3], [4] and [5].

Additionally, if we take into account that a pervasive environment must provide its services and information to mobile clients that appear and disappear it seems clear that the model of use supposes a key issue to improve the usability of any pervasive environment.

From the user's point of view, the installation of client applications for each one of the candidate scenarios to which it is possible to interact (home, office, airports, railway stations, restaurants, etc.) is, at least, disturbing.

The use of different languages for ontology specification (e.g. RDF, DAML+OIL and OWL which is lately coming dominant) and the development of interfaces to access the information stored in the ontologies, show a set of combinations where only the clients applications developed for those systems can interoperate with them, excluding the rest of devices and restricting the use of them for third party applications.

In this article we propose an extension to these ontology-based pervasive systems by means of access patterns. The definition of these patterns has been extracted from the observation and abstraction of how the information is accessed and used by users in a pervasive ontology-based environment, in conjunction with a study of the corresponding existent APIs.

However, if we assume that it is not realistic that all the systems implement a standard API, neither is it to suggest, that they all should adopt our proposed extension. Different opinions and different business strategies usually avoid to reach an agreement. To mitigate this problem, a tool which makes it possible to generate a candidate implementation of the defined patterns has been developed.

Project/Arquitecture	Ontology Language	Ref.	Project/Arquitecture	Ontology Language	Ref.
Amigo	OWL	[5]	User Policies	DL	[7]
MoGATU	DAML+OIL	[6]	TAP	RDF	[9]
GAS Ontology	DAML+OIL	[13]	SOUPA	OWL	[4]

Table 1. Ontology-based pervasive environments examples

2. State of the Art

Currently, many information systems have been designed using ontologies as supporting technology. They range from systems that classify general information like TAP [9], where different types of information are represented (e.g. music, geographical information, etc.) to specific ones that gather the particular knowledge of a specific application field (e.g. software patterns design [11]). Some examples of these systems are presented in Table 1.

Ontology engineering has acquired importance in last years due to the increasing complexity of building general ontology-based systems. The abstraction pattern is a powerful tool in software engineering that has been also proposed in some areas of ontology engineering as explained in [10].

If we look carefully at ontology-based systems, we can find in general the structure represented in Figure 1. Actually, the most considerable effort has to be done for knowledge representation in a set of ontologies and the storage of these ontologies in a repository.

Generally this database is called *Ontology Repository* and is able to keep the knowledge structure and its relationships. Directly associated with this ontology repository we can find the knowledge base or KB which, using the ontology repository, stores all the different knowledge entities..

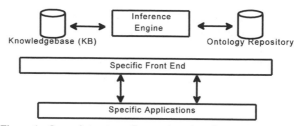

Figure 1.- General structure of an ontology-based pervasive system.

Additionally, systems add to this structure an inference engine which is aimed at generating conclusions from the KB and their relationships (as they are expressed in the repository).

Finally, to use the structure described in Figure 1, *front-ends* for specific applications are developed. Their role have been considered in works like Jena [12], XQUERY [14] or RDFQ [15]. The different approaches have in some way aggravated the problem of the interoperability and heterogeneity.

3. Motivation

The main target of this project is to provide the software clients (that resides for example in mobile hand-held devices) with a basic access to the information of a pervasive system.

In this way, from the initial architecture developed in SENDA [17], where services are described by means of ontologies, we propose a pervasive system for travelers assistance which it is oriented to be implanted in airports, ports, railway stations, etc. The goal is to help people with traveling information (timetables, tickets, renting, transfers, information about cities, hotel reservation, etc.) as it is required, using their mobile devices and in an integrated way.

The structure of the SENDA project is out of the scope of this paper, however two main problems were faced by means of the definition of patterns (as they are described in this paper). Regarding the mobile device, a minimal software component, to interact with the system, has to be developed. The first problem arises when this software component has to interact with a pervasive system different from which it was developed for. On the other hand, ontology-based systems favor the reutilization of the knowledge and its structure as it is stored in the ontology. So, when a client wants to obtain some information, besides to be compatible with the different systems, it needs to find which ontology has the right information and then, to retrieve that information from that specific system.

There are several approaches to solve the interoperability problem:

- To define all the information with the same structure and to utilize the same API to access the information. This approach is taken in SOQA[16]. However, it is not likely that all the environments share the same architecture. Additionally, to develop a standard API for all the applications is unrealistic.
- To implement and to install in every mobile device all the necessary applications for each possible environment. This option is again unrealistic due to the resource constrains of the mobile devices.

We think that an important work has to be done to make it homogeneous, at least, a basic access to ontology-based systems and extending their use to applications resident in mobile devices.

4. Access patterns

As we mentioned before, to propose a common API for all the different types of ontology-based systems becomes an unrealistic assumption. Nevertheless, the definition of some extensions for specific APIs (originally developed for each system), so clients can get some information about the ontology-based systems by means of a basic interaction, turns out to be more reasonable. Additionally, the possibility of obtaining an automatically generated service for such basic information will definitively favor the use of this approach.

If we take a look at the different types of ontology representation languages we can derive a set of concepts (classes, relations, attributes, etc.) and their implementations in each language (Table 2).

DAML	OWL	OIL

```
<daml:Class rdf:ID="T">          <owl:Class rdf:ID="T" />      Class-def T
<rdfs:label>T</rdfs:label>         <owl:Class rdf:ID="A">       Class-def A
</daml:Class>                         <rdfs:subClassof            Subclass-of T
 <daml:Class rdf:ID="A">          rdf:resource="#T" />
 <rdfs:subClassOf rdf:resource="#T"/>   </owl:Class>
</daml:Class>
```

Table 2.- Ontology structure in DAML, OWL and OIL language.

We can see how, in all the different approaches, T and A are classes and their relationship (A is a specialization of T) is of type subclass-of. If we look at some of the APIs developed for ontology-based systems (e.g JENA, XQUERY or SOQA) we can see how most of the APIs work with these general concepts. We have studied these common practices in existent APIs to define a set of patterns in order to provide an starting point to develop automatically generated services which make it possible that generic applications interact with an ontology-based system.

Traditionally, a software pattern has been defined like a probed solution for a recurrent problem. Lately, patterns have been broadly (and successfully) used in software engineering to solve recurrent problems. So extending the concept of pattern to the problem described in this article we get to abstract the access to a pervasive ontology-based system from implementation and platform details.

5. Patterns definition

In a general way, when a client interact with an unknown ontology-based system we identify three different steps: first, the client needs to know which ontology (out of several ones) is the best candidate for its purposes (e.g. searching some type of information); then, after selecting the most appropriate, it need to get some information about the general structure of the system; and finally, it needs to access to the knowledge stored in the system. So, we can define three sets of patterns:

- *Suitable contents patterns:* this set of patterns provides with metrics that allow the client to choose the best candidate, that is, the system that better fits its needs.
- *Description patterns*: this set solves the problem of getting information about the knowledge represented in an ontology-based system. So, it allows the client to know the concepts and relationships represented in the ontology, so it can conveniently explore the ontology structure.
- *Use patterns:* after selecting the appropriate ontology and being able to navigate through its structure, the client is ready to get the information it needs from the KB. So, these patterns allow to access to the information itself.

Regarding the set of *suitable contents patterns*, it includes some of them that implement the metrics defined in [8] for quality of ontology-based systems. We use such metrics for getting an ordered list of systems related with the client concept target. They are the following:

- *Class importance:* This pattern gives an estimation of a concept importance. For example, and according to [8], our implementation relates the importance of a specific concept with the total number of instances associated to such a concept or class in the KB.
- *Class connectivity:* This pattern gives information on which classes an ontology is centered on. This is accomplished studying the relationships of every class with the others. The more relationships a class has, the more central role it plays in the ontology.
- *Attribute richness:* This pattern offers a measure of the richness of a class or concept by getting the number of its attributes.

With the three simple patterns defined before, we can get a quick idea about the description of a concept in an ontology-based system so we can choose the most appropriate system for the client purposes. Once the most appropriate system is selected, we need to ascertain the internal structure of the knowledge stored in it. For such proposes we define *the descriptions patterns*:

- *Domain*: This pattern allows to get all the concepts a system contains. Generally a simple list of classes can give this information.
- *Family:* This pattern allows to know how all the concepts are related. For example, it offers all the relationships (e.g "parent of", "subclass of", "equivalentClass", "disjointWith") for a given class.
- *Description:* this pattern allows to access to all the attributes of a given class.

Finally, the *use patterns* grant the access to the real information in the KB:

- *Population*: this pattern allows to obtain all the instances of a class in the KB.
- *Value-of:* For a class, instance and attribute, with this pattern is possible to get the associated value.

The patterns defined in this paper represent the minimum set needed to get a basic interaction by means of lightweight clients resident in mobile devices. All this patterns can be implemented in different ways, using either specific APIs like Jena, or query languages like XQUERY or RDFQ.

Even though all these patterns have some limitations to access to any kind of knowledge an ontology can represent, they have demonstrated to be powerful enough for our purposes.

6. Prototype

A prototype has been designed that uses the proposed set of patterns to get pervasive information from an ontology-based system. Our target device is a PDA which has to be able to access the information stored in a traveler assistance system.

We chose Web Services as the implementation technology due to its special orientation to develop Internet applications. As we said in the introduction our main target is extending the number of systems that can be accessed by a generic application resident in the PDA. Although our actual prototype has been specifically designed using the proposed approach, we are developing tools for third party systems so our generic PDA application can access to a higher number of systems, at the same time, it could be easily integrated in applications such as those described in [9].

Web Services also allow to make available to other Internet applications the generic information that can be accessed by means of the proposed patterns.

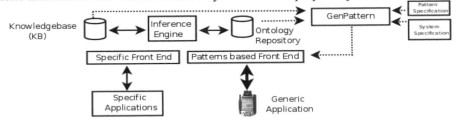

Figure 2.- GenPatterns infraestructure

We have also developed a plugin-based application called *GenPattern* which takes the pattern specification in MOF/XMI (from OMG) and a system specification as inputs, and generates, in an automatic way, a Web Service which represents a pattern-based front-end (Figure 2).

The *Pattern Specification* represents a metamodel which describes the concepts associated to the patterns and their representation in different ontology languages. It also represents the way in which different KBs can be accessed (so far only MySQL based KBs are supported).

The *System Specification* includes two types of information: first, the ontology language used in the system, and second, the method used to access to the KB. Additionally, some other type of information, like the operating system, may be necessary, .

The use of patterns is independent of the final generated front-end. However the use of Web Services adds some benefits: first, the generated UDDI can be exported and then used for service discovery of our system; and second, the WSDL description can help third parties developers to develop other applications to interact with our system.

Finally, the client application is also automatically generated by *GenPattern*. It will reside in the mobile device and will be able to interact with any ontology-based pervasive system which has a Web Service front-end generated as described before.

A basic dialog of the client application with a Web Service is showed in Figure 3. The application interacts with the sub-set of patterns defined in this paper in order to get some specific information.

In the current implementation, the web service returns in each invocation an XML structure which can be interpreted by the library libglade generating a GUI for such answer. This GUI is specific for the mobile device (in our case a PDA) and simplifies the application itself building dynamically the GUI in function of the XML returned by the Web Service.

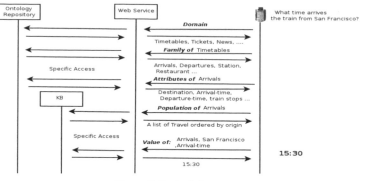

Figure 3: Basic dialog

The client application is able to navigate through the ontology structure and to access the KB in a basic way. Currently the application is running on a PDA with GNU/Linux Familiar OS and interacts with the Web Service by means of `pywebsvcs` (Web Services for Python).

7. Conclusions

Interacting with pervasive ontology-based systems from mobile devices has to do with unifying both, the access methodology to the KB as well as the way the knowledge is represented in the ontology. Assuming both, the impossibility of getting a unique access methodology and the difficulties in installing in a mobile device a set of different applications to access every potential information system, we have proposed a set of patterns that allows an easy and homogeneous interaction with ontology-based pervasive systems.

This set of patterns has been defined taking into account the way client applications are developed currently, as well as how a user interacts with a pervasive environment. Those patterns have been grouped into a metamodel.

From well-known practices in accessing and using ontology-based systems we have identified three set patterns grouped in *accurate contents*, *description* and *use* patterns that allow a basic interaction with any ontology-based pervasive system. An implementation example of these patterns has been developed using Web Services. The implementation export the system knowledge to general (mobile) applications.

The use of patterns has demonstrated to have similar benefits than its use in software engineering, facilitating the development and maintenance of access software for ontology-based systems.

Additionally the *GenPattern* tool has been developed with the aim of automating the generation of the pattern-based front-end from a specification of the system (that includes the language used for the ontology, the KB access method, etc.). This tool expects to extend the use of automatically generated front-ends to make it possible the interaction of a general application without any manual modification of the application itself nor the system front-end.

Finally, we have developed an application for a PDA which interacts with the Web Service generated by *GenPattern* and creates, in a dynamically way, a GUI from the XML returned by the Web Service.

Our efforts are currently centered on improving the *GenPattern* tool and extending its possibilities to enlarge the set of possible inputs of the system specification and to extend the outputs to other possible interfaces like, for example, Jena. We also are working in testing our tools in third party systems in order to allow the interaction with the same PDA application developed for our project.

Lately, other important efforts include, first, the study of different inference engines in order to get their patterns of use, and second, the development of some methods to allow machine to machine interactions, that is, the access to an ontology-based system can be done without the user guidance.. This second approach could make it possible to enrich a system with the information from third party systems.

In general we believe that an important work has to be done to homogenize the access to ontology-based systems. Our work is a first step in such a way by means of patterns. The goal must be to allow the designer to get rid of the accessing layer implementation details while focusing in the specific knowledge needed by any pervasive system.

Acknowledgement

This work has been funded by the Spanish Ministry of Science and Innovation under project SODA (TIN2005-08719) and by the Spanish Ministry of Industry under project CENIT Hesperia.

References

[1] E. Jung, H. Jik, J. Woo. *Ontology-Based Context Modeling and Reasoning for U-HealthCare*. IEICE Transactions on information and Systems, Vol. E90-D, No. 8, 2007.
[2] X. Wang, J. Song, D., C. Chin, S. Hettiarachchi, D. Zhang. *Semantic Space: An Infraestructure for Smart Spaces*. Pervasive Computing. Vol. 3 No. 3, 2004.
[3] R. Masuoka, Y. Labrou, B. Parsia, E. Sirin. *Ontology-Enabled Pervasive Computing Applications*. IEEE Intelligent Systems, Vol. 18, No. 5, 2003.
[4] H. Chen, T. Finin, A. Joshi. *The SOUPA Ontology for Pervasive Computing*. Ontologies for Agents: Theory and Experiences. Springer, 2005.
[5] B. da Silva, P. Wijnen, P. Vink. *A Service-Oriented middleware for context-aware applications*. In Proc. of the 5th international workshop on middleware for pervasive and ad-hoc computing. ACM international conference proceedings series, 2007.
[6] F. Perich, A. Joshi, Y. Yesha, T. Finin. *Collaborative Joins in a Pervasive Computing Environment*. The international journal of very large databases, Vol. 14 No. 2, Springer Verlag, 2005.
[7] J. Weeds, B. Keller, D. Weir, T. Owen, I. Wakemna. *Natural Language Expression of User Policies in Pervasive Computing Environments*. In Proc. of OntoLex, 2005..
[8] S. Tartir, I. Budak, M. Moore, A. P. Sheth, B. Aleman-Meza. *OntoQA: Metric-Based Ontology Quality Analysis*. IEEE Conf. on Data Mining, 2005.
[9] R. Guha, R. McCool, E. Miller. *TAP: A Semantic Web Text-based*. J. of Web Semantics, 2003.
[10] A. Rector, G. Schereiber, N. F. Noy, H. Knublauch. *Ontology design patterns and problems: Practical Ontology Engineering using Protege-OWL*. 3th. International Semantic Web Conference, 2004.
[11] J. Rosengard , M. F. Ursu. *Ontological Representations of Software Patterns* . In Proc. of KES'04. LNCS. Vol. 3215. Springer-Verlag, 2004.
[12] HP Development Company. *Jena 2 Ontology API, http://jena.sourceforge.net/*, 2006.
[13] E. Chirstopopulou and A. Kameas. *GAS: an ontology for collaboration among ubiquitous computing devices*. I. J. of Human-Computer Studies. Vol. 62, 2005.

[14] W3C. *XQuery 1.0: An XML Query Language.* W3C *http://www.w3.org/TR/xquery/*

[15] A. Malhotra, N. Sundaresan. *RDF Query Specification.* W3C Query Languages Workshop, 1998.

[16] P. Ziegler, C. Sturm, K. R. Dittrich. *Unified Querying of Ontology Languages with the SIRUP Ontology Query API.* In 11st GI-Fachtagung für Datenbanksysteme in Business, Technologie und Web, 2005.

[17] F. Moya, J. C. López. SENDA: An Alternative to OSGi for Large Scale Domotics Networks. World Scientific Publishing, 2002.

Author Index